MEDIA
ECONOMICS

MEDIA
ECONOMICS

Understanding Markets,
Industries and Concepts

Second Edition

Alan B. Albarran

Iowa State Press
A Blackwell Publishing Company

TO BEVERLY, BETH AND MANDY

ALAN B. ALBARRAN received his B.A. and M.A. degrees from Marshall University in Huntington, West Virginia, and his Ph.D. degree from The Ohio State University in Columbus. Dr. Albarran is Professor and Chair of the Department of Radio, Television and Film at the University of North Texas in Denton and Editor of the *Journal of Media Economics.*

© 2002 Iowa State Press
A Blackwell Publishing Company
All rights reserved

Iowa State Press
2121 State Avenue, Ames, Iowa 50014

Orders: 1-800-862-6657
Office: 1-515-292-0140
Fax: 1-515-292-3348
Website: www.iowastatepress.com

(∞) Printed on acid-free paper in the United States of America

First edition, 1996
Second edition, 2002

Library of Congress Cataloging-in-Publication Data
Albarran, Alan B.
Media economics: understanding markets, industries and concepts
    Alan B. Albarran — 2nd ed.
    p. cm.
    Includes bibliographical references and index.
    ISBN 0-8138-2124-X
    1. Mass media—Economic aspects. I. Title.
P96.E25 A48 2002
338.4'730223 — dc20   2001005802

CONTENTS

VI. MEDIA ECONOMICS RESEARCH

VII. SUPPLEMENTS

PREFACE

Media economics is the application of economic principles to the study of media industries. The contemporary media industries dominate our culture, and the daily news is filled with the latest innovations and news of mergers, divestitures and competition. The impact of technology, government regulation and globalization has focused attention on the importance of the media not only as information and entertainment resources but also as economic entities. Students, professors and media practitioners and policy-makers need an understanding of how economics and economic concepts affect media firms and industries. By understanding the economic activities of media industries, one can better understand the role, function and purpose of media in society.

Media economics is a relatively young discipline, having gained recognition and stature since the 1980s. As a subfield of mass communication scholarship, media economics research is regularly reported in publications such as the *Journal of Media Economics* and other scholarly journals.

This second edition of *Media Economics: Understanding Markets, Industries and Concepts* examines the activities of the mass media from an economic perspective. The book centers on the domestic (U.S.) activities of media companies and industries and is aimed primarily at undergraduate and graduate students as well as professors and professional practitioners. For more of a global perspective on the topic of media economics, readers can consult a companion text, *Global Media Economics* (1998), also published by Iowa State Press.

Topics discussed in the chapters devoted to specific media industries include the following questions: What is the market? Who are the major players in the market? What is the type of market structure? Is the market concentrated? Are there barriers to entry for new competitors? What types of government regulation (if any) are found in the market? What is the impact of technological forces on the market? What is the future for the market?

An understanding of media economics is useful in analyzing the functions and activities of companies involved in the media. It is important to recognize that although the media industries serve as agents of culture and vital sources of information and entertainment, the media also operate as a business with the goal of producing profits. This text examines the media industries as economic institutions operating in a capitalist environment.

Chapter 1 offers a rationale for the study of media economics. This introductory chapter explains the focus of the book and introduces the other chapters and their purposes. Chapters 2 through 4 cover principles of media economics; Chapter 2 discusses economic concepts, and Chapter 3 centers on understanding media markets. Chapter 4 presents tools and approaches used in analyzing media markets.

Chapters 5 through 7 cover the broadcast and multichannel television industries. Chapter 5 is devoted to the radio industry, and Chapter 6 examines the broadcast television industry. Chapter 7 covers the cable and satellite television industries, integrating information on premium and pay-per-view channels.

Chapter 8 is a new chapter devoted to the Internet. The chapter looks at the various segments that make up the Internet industry.

Chapter 9 covers the motion picture industry. Chapter 10 introduces the reader to the economics of the recording industry.

Chapters 11 through 13 examine the print industries. These three chapters cover newspapers, magazines and books, respectively. The book concludes with Chapter 14, devoted to issues in media economics research.

Features in this book include:

- objectives at the beginning of each chapter to guide reading
- review and discussion questions at the end of each chapter
- exercises and projects at the end of each chapter
- a list of references at the end of each chapter
- tables, figures and graphs as warranted
- an appendix of materials useful in conducting media economics research, including key websites on media industries
- an appendix of commonly used financial ratios
- a glossary of key terms mentioned in the text

The second edition of this book includes one new chapter and many other chapters that have been completely revised and updated. Like any author, I feel this second edition is a much stronger work than the original edition, largely due to my tenure as editor of the *Journal of Media Economics*, a position I have held since 1997.

Serving as editor of a scholarly journal has not only improved my own research and writing skills but also given me the firsthand opportunity to review the latest research in the field. Serving has a journal editor has also allowed me to gain insight and wisdom from the outstanding group of scholars who make up the editorial board for *JME*, many of whom I consider my mentors and peers.

I'm grateful to the many students enrolled in my courses in media management and economics over the years who were also helpful in formulating the ideas for this book. I've had the good fortune to conduct several seminars and workshops in Europe since the first edition was published, and members of those audiences also helped contribute new perspectives to this edition.

I'm grateful for the support of my faculty and staff colleagues at the University of North Texas, where I have the opportunity to teach and research while also serving as Chair of the Department of Radio, Television and Film. Christine Paswan, my administrative assistant, keeps the department running so well that it allowed me the time to write. Dean Warren Burggren of the College of Arts and Sciences supported my writing with a summer research grant to finish the book in the summer of 2001. Terry Moellinger, a graduate student at UNT, also was a tremendous help as a research assistant. Ellen Truax, one of the fine reference librarians at UNT, was very helpful in gathering research sources related to the media industries for Appendix A.

This work represents my fourth book published by Iowa State Press. I've enjoyed a long and positive relationship with the Press. I appreciate the assistance of my current editor, Mark Barrett, along with Linda Ross. I will always be grateful to Judi Brown and Gretchen Van Houten for their encouragement and support over the years.

I've been blessed with a loving family that is the source of much of my motivation toward my work. My wife, Beverly, and daughters, Beth and Mandy, have always supported my research and writing, as has my mother, Jean. To them I owe my love, gratitude and deep appreciation.

Alan B. Albarran
University of North Texas

I

Introduction

1

WHY STUDY MEDIA ECONOMICS?

After reading this chapter, you should:

- Understand the terms *economics, media economics, macroeconomics*, and *microeconomics*

- Recognize the advantages of studying media economics

- Understand the focus and scope of the text

What is media economics? Why should we be concerned with the study of media economics? How can an understanding of media economics help in evaluating and analyzing the activities of different media companies? This book attempts to answer these and other questions by examining the mass media as economic institutions.

There are many ways to analyze the activities of the mass media. For example, there is much interest in understanding the impact of the media on individuals and society. This area of study seeks to find answers to why and how people are affected by media content and its implications for society. Ratings for television and radio programming help determine which programs are the most popular among audiences, and box-office receipts and rentals of videotapes and digital videodiscs (DVDs) indicate which movies are the most popular. Critical evaluations of media content enable us to understand the underlying themes behind the programming we see and hear and the messages they try to convey.

Most important, we must recognize that the mass media are economic institutions, engaged in the production and dissemination of content targeted toward consumers (Picard 1989). Because media firms are economic entities, their behavior is governed by economics. Likewise, consumers are an important part of the economic system. Consumers indicate preference for media content through the exchange of money (as in the case of a magazine subscription or video rentals) and time (as in the case of broadcast radio and television). In many media markets, the content is designed to attract not only consumers but also advertisers who want access to consumers. Consumers and advertisers influence media firms and the content they produce. Thus, media content is clearly linked to economics.

The study of media economics provides a context within which one can better understand the behavior of media firms, media markets and consumers. As both a consumer and student of the mass media, no doubt you have had questions about specific media industries. For example, why did the WB television network emerge at a time when the other broadcast networks were losing audiences? Why are daily newspapers declining nationally while suburban newspapers are on the rise? Why has there been so much merger activity in different media markets, involving large corporations such as AOL Time Warner, Viacom and Bertelsmann? An understanding of the various concepts and principles used in media economics helps answer these questions.

What is Media Economics?

Economics is defined in many ways. According to Samuelson and Nordhaus (1992, 3), economics is "the study of how societies use scarce resources to produce valuable commodities and distribute them among different groups." Several key concepts in this definition need clarification. *Resources* are defined in economic terms as items used to produce goods and services. Resources consist of both tangible and intangible items. Think of production of a situation comedy for network television—many tangible resources are used in producing the program, including personnel, scripts, cameras, sets, costumes and film or tape. The actual time used to produce the program is an example of an intangible resource. Resources are considered scarce because they are *finite*—that is, the amount of resources available is limited. Further, the individual *wants* and *needs* of consumers, producers and distributors are infinite, further increasing scarcity among resources.

Production is the actual creation of different goods for consumption. In the media industries, different types of production exist; most can be classified into broad categories of print (books, magazines, newspapers), electronic (radio, television, recordings, Internet), and photographic (film). Producers make numerous decisions in the production process, ranging from how much of a product to produce to the different types of products targeted toward specific markets.

Consumption is the utilization of goods and resources to satisfy different wants and needs. In the media industries, consumption of entertainment and informational content occurs primarily on the consumer level. As members of the audience, we use the media to satisfy different motivations and preferences. At certain times, we demand news and other informational products; at other times, we use the media to pass time and as a form of relaxation. Another interesting trait of media consumption is that it differs from regular consumption. After we use a newspaper, television program or magazine, it can be still be used by others. Consumption directly influences the production process, and the behaviors of consumers are an important variable in understanding the economic system.

Using this information, it is possible to define media economics using the Samuelson and Nordhaus definition as a guide. ***Media economics* is the study of how media industries use scarce resources to produce content that is distributed among consumers in a society to satisfy various wants and needs.** In this sense, media economics helps us understand the economic relationships of media producers to audiences, advertisers and society.

Macroeconomics and Microeconomics

Economists make a distinction between the study of *macroeconomics* and that of *microeconomics* (see Fig. 1.1). Macroeconomics examines the whole economic system and is primarily studied at a national level. Macroeconomics includes topics such as economic growth indexes, political economy (defined as public policies toward the economy) and national production and consumption. Microeconomics centers on the activities of specific components of the economic system, such as individual markets, firms or consumers. Microeconomics tends to focus on market structure, conduct and behavior.

Macroeconomics deals with:
Political economy
Aggregate production and consumption
Economic growth, employment and inflation

Microeconomics deals with:
Specific markets
Market structure, conduct and behavior
Activities of producers and consumers

FIGURE 1.1. *Differences between macroeconomics and microeconomics.*

It is important to recognize that macroeconomics and microeconomics are interrelated and influence each other. The study of media economics involves both macroeconomic and microeconomic issues. For example, the decision by the Federal Communications Commission (FCC) to require all existing television stations to convert to digital transmission illustrates the interplay between these two areas of study. The decision to require all station owners to convert to digital (a macroeconomic-based decision) affects local cable television operators and consumers in specific markets (a microeconomic outcome).

In addition to government policies, technological change can affect the relationship between macroeconomics and microeconomics. For example, the decision to adopt the DVD as a new format reflects a macroeconomic decision made by the motion picture industry. In turn, consumers (operating at the microeconomic level) had to decide whether to adapt to the new format by purchasing new hardware and software to accommodate DVDs or to be content with their existing videotape collections.

In later chapters in this text, the study of media economics shifts to specific media industries. As such, most of the material reflects a microeconomic orientation; however, where appropriate, macroeconomic issues will be introduced and examined as well.

The Importance of Studying Media Economics

Having defined and clarified exactly what media economics is, it is perhaps useful to discuss why the study of media economics is important to you. There are three main reasons. First, an understanding of media economics is as useful as the study of other traditional subjects connected with the mass media. It is just as important that you understand the economic activities of individual media markets as it is that you understand writing, production, management, advertising and promotion. In fact, one could argue rather strongly that the study of media economics is the most important, in that the ability to attract revenues (and ultimately profits) enables producers to continue to operate in media markets.

A vivid example of the relationships among producers, advertisers and consumers is in the newspaper industry. Most major cities in the United States are now served by only one newspaper. In markets that have seen one or two competing papers fail, the reason given for their demise is usually the same—the inability to maintain subscribers and advertisers. Network television represents another example of these interrelationships. The broadcast networks continually introduce new programming to attract audiences and advertisers in order to maintain revenues. If programs fail to attract enough of an audience to cover the network's investment, they eventually will be removed from the schedule in hopes of finding a more profitable replacement. Hence, the economic relationships among content producers and consumers determine much of the media content available for consumption.

Second, the study of media economics is important to your career. If you are reading this text, you may be planning—or at least considering—a career in some area of the mass media. Major corporations dominate the media industries (see Fig. 1.2). In fact, if you pursue a career in the media, it is likely that you may someday work for one of these corporations. By studying media economics, you not only learn how to research and analyze different companies but also can understand and predict firm and market behaviors. You will be able to determine which companies operate most efficiently, and you can learn which companies are the leaders in their respective markets. Not only will this process make you better informed, but it can also help you achieve your career goals.

Third, a study of media economics will give you the knowledge to analyze different media industries. Through the use of both descriptive and analytical methodologies, you will be introduced to different tools to help analyze the activities of media firms and markets. You will be able to understand how market structure affects the activities of different media companies, how concentrated certain media markets are and how external forces like government regulation and advances in technology may affect future market performance.

The Plan of the Book

Chapter 1 offers a rationale for the study of media economics. This introductory chapter explains the focus of the book and introduces the other chapters and their purposes. Chapters 2 through 4 represent a unit called *Principles of Media Economics*. Chapter 2 introduces key economic concepts and their

Television:
Viacom, News Corporation (Fox) , General Electric, Disney

Motion Pictures:
Disney, Viacom, AOL Time Warner, Sony, Vivendi Universal

Book Publishing:
AOL Time Warner, Bertelsmann, News Corporation

Newspaper Publishing:
Gannett, Knight-Ridder, Tribune

Recording Industry:
Sony, Bertelsmann, AOL Time Warner

FIGURE 1.2. *Examples of corporations in the mass media.*

application to the study of media economics. You will be introduced to many different terms and their application to media industries. Chapter 3 focuses on the concepts of market and market structure. You will learn to identify the common types of market structure and understand how market structure affects the behavior of individual firms. In Chapter 4, tools used in evaluating media markets are presented. Ways to measure concentration and diversification are introduced, along with a discussion of how regulation and technology impact the activities of media markets.

Chapters 5 through 13 center on specific media industries. You can follow the chapters in their order of presentation or jump to specific chapters of interest. Each chapter is unique in its presentation of content, and each builds on the concepts introduced in Chapters 2 through 4.

Chapters 5 through 8 form a unit called *The Broadcast, Cable and Satellite Television and Internet Industries.* Chapter 5 discusses radio, Chapter 6 broadcast television and Chapter 7 cable and satellite television. Chapter 8 looks at the Internet and the submarkets that make up the Internet.

Chapters 9 and 10 compose a unit called *The Film and Recording Industries.* Chapter 9 covers the motion picture industry and Chapter 10 the recording industry.

Chapters 11 through 13 make up a unit called *The Print Industries.* Chapter 11 looks at the newspaper industry, Chapter 12 the magazine industry and Chapter 13 the book industry.

Last but not least, Chapter 14 is the sole chapter in the unit called *Issues in Media Economics Research.* This final chapter examines current issues confronting media economics research.

Following the final chapter is a *Supplement* unit featuring two appendixes and a glossary. Appendix A contains a list of resources available for conducting media economics research, including industry and corporate information as well as various electronic databases and websites. Appendix B includes commonly used financial ratios. The Glossary of Key Terms consolidates important terms used throughout the text (terms listed in the glossary are printed in italics in the text).

What the Book Does Not Do

It is helpful to clarify several limitations of this book. First, this text centers on media economics in the United States, a Western country established as a democracy built on capitalism. Although the principles and concepts introduced have broad application, they may not be as useful in studying media economics in other countries with different economic systems and philosophies. Readers interested in the subject of international media economics should consult the companion book *Global Media Economics* (1998), also published by Iowa State Press.

Second, the mass media are not stagnant industries. Change is inevitable due to mergers and acquisitions, and some of the material in the text will become dated prior to publication, particularly with respect to data on current industries. At the time of writing, the most current information available was used in each chapter.

Finally, this text is not designed to replace a course in economics. Although the student will be introduced to many key economic concepts, at times the presentation will be cursory. Readers desiring more detailed information, particularly on theoretical aspects of economics, should supplement their learning experiences through other texts and specific courses in the field of economics.

Despite these limitations, it is hoped that this text will provide a useful framework for the study of media economics, not only to students and professors of the mass media but also to industry practitioners and decision makers.

Discussion Questions

1. How does the study of media economics differ from more traditional ways of studying the mass media?
2. What is the difference between macroeconomics and microeconomics? Give an example of each.
3. What do we mean by *scarce resources*? Why are resources scarce?
4. What can be learned from a study of media economics? How might the material be useful to you?

Exercises

1. Look through a newspaper like the *New York Times* or a magazine like the *Economist* for stories that discuss economic activities of the country (for example, gross national product, employment statistics or housing starts). Then look for any articles relating to specific industries such as the mass media, the auto industry or some other industry. How many articles reflect the area of macroeconomics? How many articles reflect microeconomics?
2. Review a recent issue of the *Wall Street Journal*. How many articles did you locate about companies involved in the mass media? Prepare a brief report on one of the articles.
3. Examine the annual index to one of the following scholarly journals and determine how many articles are related to the study of media economics.
   a. *Journal of Broadcasting and Electronic Media*
   b. *Journalism and Mass Communication Quarterly*
   c. *Journal of Media Economics*
   d. *Journal of Communication*

References

Picard, R. G. (1989). *Media Economics*. Beverly Hills, Calif.: Sage.
Samuelson, P. A., and W. D. Nordhaus. (1992). *Economics*. 14th ed. New York: McGraw-Hill.

II

Principles of Media Economics

2

ECONOMIC CONCEPTS

After reading this chapter, you should understand:

- How an economic system is organized

- The differences between command, market and mixed economies

- The concepts of supply and demand and how they guide the economic system

- How price affects supply and demand in the media industries

The economic structure of any society is affected by the political, legal and social characteristics that influence and shape business practices among firms. The nature of a society's political system determines the environment in which media firms operate. Many types of political systems are possible, ranging from a totalitarian-based authoritarian system emphasizing strict government control to one of laissez-faire, denoting the absence of any sort of regulatory or governmental control.

In the United States, media companies operate primarily in a capitalistic, free enterprise system. Economists refer to this type of system as a *mixed capitalist society*, with rights primarily in the hands of the citizenry, but where regulatory and other types of constraints affect business practices (Owers, Carveth and Alexander 1993). In a mixed capitalist society, both public and private institutions produce and distribute products and goods. In the United States, most of the production of media content is handled by *private companies* (also referred to as the *private sector*) rather than by government companies and entities (also called the *public sector*).

Media companies produce and distribute products to consumers in order to generate revenues and ultimately profits in a mixed capitalist society. This system encourages the interaction and interplay among media producers and consumers and, in the case of advertisers, media buyers. Consumers influence media companies by the types of media content they use or demand. In terms of television, local broadcast channels, cable networks and superstations compete for consumer attention (and advertising dollars), along with other forms of video entertainment such as premium cable channels, pay-per-view and consumer rentals and purchases. Have you ever wondered how all of these entertainment options can effectively coexist?

As for the print industries, there are numerous choices in regard to selecting a book or magazine to purchase. Depending on the subject matter, the options may seem unlimited. There are fewer choices, however, when it comes to reading a daily newspaper. Most cities are now served by only one major newspaper. Why is it that magazines and books have multiplied while local newspapers have suffered a decline?

These questions can be answered in part by understanding the basic concepts of how the economic system is organized. In Chapter 1 you learned that the resources used to produce media content and other goods are considered scarce because there are not enough resources to satisfy all the needs and wants of consumers. Therefore, allocative decisions must be made regarding how best to utilize existing resources in a society. Economists refer to this decision-making process as the *economic problem* of a society.

The Economic Problem

The economic problem involves a process of dealing with the important issues of production and consumption. These include the following questions: (1) How much of which goods will be produced? (2) How will the goods be produced? (3) Who will consume the goods? The answers to these questions determine the underlying organization of the economic system.

In addition to determining what goods will be produced, the producers must also consider the quantity of the goods that will be produced and the method of production. Differences exist between the public sector and the private sector in determining the amount of goods to produce. For example, in the public sector, the government makes decisions on how much money to spend for the nation's defense while at the same time determining how much to allocate for domestic programs such as Medicare. In the public sector, decisions are often based on social and politically sensitive choices (i.e., Social Security and other entitlement programs) rather than as a response to specific economic considerations.

In the private sector, production decisions are influenced by the interaction between buyers and sellers or, in the case of the media, content providers and consumers. For example, in the book industry, not only must the selection of which titles to print be considered but also how many copies of each book to print. Further, publishers must decide the format of the book—whether it will be available as a hardcover or softcover edition or in an audio format. In considering the first edition of this book for publication, the publisher had to consider a number of different variables including the demand for the book, the likely users of the book and the value of the work.

With respect to determining *who* will produce the goods, individual media outlets determine *how many* people to use in the production of the content. *Labor* is an important concept in any decisions involving production of goods and services. In the media industries, labor represents one of the most expensive resources (Dunnett 1990). In the radio industry, the issue of labor may involve the decision to use a live, on-air staff or to select an automated, satellite-delivered service. Film producers and directors determine the location for their movies—whether to shoot in a Hollywood studio or to travel to a specific site that captures the essence of the picture, perhaps an exotic tropical island or a bustling European city. The more elaborate the locale, the greater the labor needed to create the film.

In determining who will consume the goods, certain policies established by the individual media outlets or some form of government may determine who will be able to consume the content. For example, cable television rates vary from city to city, but broadcast signals are available for free. Early in broadcast history, regulators claimed the airwaves were public property, so broadcast radio and television were provided to the public at a very low cost (the cost of buying a receiver and possibly an antenna). Governmental policies led to the establishment of separate classes of broadcast service (AM, FM, VHF, UHF) and ultimately created a three-network system that dominated broadcasting for several decades. In answering the three economic questions posed earlier, the government, through the Federal Communications Commission (FCC), decided (1) how many channels each community would receive; (2) who would be allowed a license to those channels through the licensing process; and (3) that the public would only have to pay for a receiver in order to use or consume the content.

As for cable television, the situation is different. Local municipalities determine how many cable companies will be awarded a franchise (how much will be produced) and also specify basic requirements of the system (how the good will be produced). It is left up to individual households to determine whether or not they subscribe (who will consume).

These two examples illustrate how a society may provide different answers to the three questions that form the economic problem. The type of economic structure in a society influences production, distribution and consumption.

Types of Economies

When a government regulates answers to the economic problems facing a society, a *command economy* exists. In this type of economy, the government makes all decisions regarding production and distribution. The government decides what will be produced and the quantity; it establishes wages and prices and also plans the rate of economic growth. Choice of available consumer goods is limited to what the government produces. Clearly, countries utilizing command economies are on the wane with the collapse of communism in many parts of the world. However, countries such as China and Cuba still maintain command economies.

In a *market economy*, a complex system of buyers, sellers, prices, profits and losses determines the answers to questions regarding production and distribution, with no government intervention. The market economy is more or less an idealized economic system and is not truly represented in any major countries in the world today.

In a *mixed economy*, combinations of the market and command economies are found. In the United States, as well as in most of the developed countries of the world, the mass media operate under a mixed economic structure. Typically, these mixed economic systems involve some governmental policies and regulations while allowing the media to be privately owned. In the United States, the individual media industries establish their own policies in pricing their products through either advertising or direct payments by consumers (Vogel 2000).

Perhaps what is most interesting in studying the U.S. mass media as economic institutions is the amount of order that exists due to the elements of the market economy. Adam Smith first theorized the economic system function in an orderly fashion in a book published in 1776, titled *The Wealth of Nations*. Smith introduced the *invisible hand doctrine*, which suggests that the economy is directed by an unseen force to the benefit of all producers and consumers. Smith advocated the idea of noninterference by the government (*laissez-faire*) in letting market forces prevail.

Other philosophies recognized that not everyone would benefit from a system of laissez-faire, leading to some segments of society being impoverished and enslaved by the market system. As a result, government involvement led to the creation of mixed economies. Economists have long since argued and refined the concept of the invisible hand as other economic philosophies have emerged, but the idea of unseen order leading the economic system still has merit. Consider that every day of the year, the mass media are involved in producing and distributing media content, which is in turn consumed in different quantities by various audiences. Yet much more is involved on a daily basis than just production, distribution and consumption.

Take, for example, the daily newspaper. Many scarce resources, such as newsprint, ink, water, electricity and equipment, are used to produce the paper. These raw materials must be obtained from suppliers and then converted into the finished product during the production process. Concomitantly, advertisers purchase space in the newspaper in different forms and formats in order to reach the people who read the newspaper. The space must be sold in advance to make sure the advertisements meet the objectives of the client. Thus, a system of buying and selling of future advertising space continues on a daily basis. The finished paper reaches consumers in various ways. Some customers purchase subscriptions, though others may purchase only a single paper, such as the Sunday paper, at a supermarket or convenience store. Other consumers may access an online version or simply read someone else's paper. Some avoid reading the newspaper altogether.

Supply and Demand

At work driving the market economy (the notion of an invisible force) are a number of buyers and sellers working on behalf of their own self-interests. The newspaper example illustrates in a rather simplistic fashion how the market economy functions, starting with the raw materials needed to print the paper and ending with the creation of the finished product purchased by the consumer. Underlying this example are two fundamental concepts of the market system: *supply* and *demand*. In a market economy, supply and demand mechanisms work together to solve the economic problems of a society (see Fig. 2.1).

Supply refers to the amount of a product a producer will offer at a certain price. Producers determine the quantity but make most of their production decisions based on the anticipated needs of those who will consume the product. The newspaper publisher purchases enough ink, paper and equipment to produce the daily paper but will be hesitant to print more copies than consumers normally purchase. In other words, the producer attempts to produce enough of the product to meet the anticipated demand of the consumer. This not only ensures proper allocation of scarce resources but also enables the publisher to anticipate profits (or losses) based on revenues and expenses.

The available supply of a product is directly affected by the demand for the product placed by consumers. *Demand* is defined as the measure of the quantity of a particular product or service that consumers will purchase at a

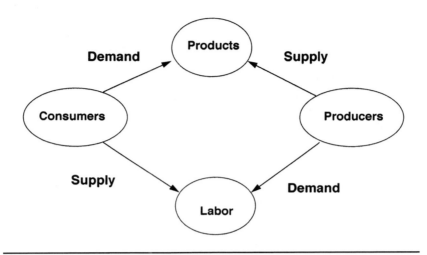

FIGURE 2.1. *The market system.*

given price. The interplay of product, price and market characteristics influences consumer demand. In general economics, production decisions in competitive markets are based on supply, rather than demand, characteristics. In media economics, demand characteristics are somewhat problematic given the unique nature of media products (content) and the fact the product can be reused.

The Demand Curve

Economists use a tool called a *demand curve* to chart the changes that supply and price cause on consumer demand. Demand curves are normally downward sloping, meaning that as the price for a particular good or service decreases, the quantity (or supply) demanded by the consumers increases. On the other hand, if prices increase, the quantity demanded will decrease. There are occasions in media economics where the demand curves may not follow normal patterns through the range of possible price values; in most cases, though, the demand curve is usually thought of as downward sloping.

Figure 2.2 illustrates a typical demand curve. In this example, the demand curve reflects the price of a video recording (such as the movie *Star Wars Episode 1: The Phantom Menace*). Note that the higher the price, the lower the quantity demanded for the product. As the price for the video drops, the quantity demanded for the product increases. The demand curve normally holds true for both consumers and markets as a whole, in that market demand is simply an aggregate of a number of individual consumer demand curves.

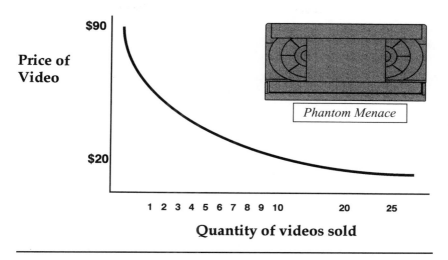

FIGURE 2.2. *Demand curve for differently priced products.*

Elasticity of Demand

Change in price resulting in a change in the quantity demanded by consumers is referred to as *elasticity of demand* or more commonly called *price elasticity of demand*. Economists have identified three types of price elasticity of demand: (1) elastic, (2) unit-elastic and (3) inelastic. The types of price elasticity of demand are presented graphically in Figure 2.3. In elastic demand, a change in price results in a greater change in the quantity demanded. We often see this happen as new technologies are introduced. Initially, prices for certain technologies were highly priced when first introduced to consumers (e.g., computers, cellular phones, DVD players), but as prices dropped, many more households adopted the technology. In unit-elastic demand, a change in the price results in an equivalent change in quantity. Lowering the price not only increases the quantity demanded but does so on a directly proportional basis. Inelastic demand occurs when a change in price results in no significant change in the quantity demanded. Lowering the price does not always mean that consumers will demand more of the good; if it is not wanted or needed or has little value, then the quantity demanded will not change. Perhaps this explains why eight-track tapes are no longer for sale!

Price elasticity of demand can be calculated by dividing the percentage change in the quantity of a product by the percentage change in price:

$$\text{Price elasticity of demand} = \frac{\text{Percent change in quantity}}{\text{Percent change in price}}$$

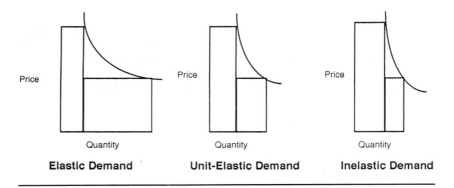

FIGURE 2.3. *Price elasticity of demand.*

A positive or negative sign preceding the statistic indicates the direction of the demand. In most cases, price elasticity of demand is a negative number. Economists use the following criteria to determine elasticity. If the statistic is greater than or equal to 1.0, demand is said to be elastic. If it is less than or equal to 1.0, demand is inelastic, whereas a statistic of ±1.0 represents unit elasticity. Table 2.1 illustrates the price elasticity of demand formulas, how they are defined and their impact on revenues.

Price elasticity of demand is an important concept to grasp in the study of media economics because it helps show how consumer demand is affected by the value of particular products to consumers and the price at which goods

Table 2.1. Summary of price elasticities of demand

Value of Demand Statistic	Type of Demand	Definition	Impact on Revenues
Greater than one $(E_d > 1)$	Elastic	Percentage change in quantity demanded *greater* than percentage change in price	Revenues *increase* when price decreases.
Equal to one $(E_d = 1)$	Unit-elastic	Percentage change in quantity demanded *equal* to percentage change in price	Revenues *unchanged* when price decreases.
Less than one $(E_d < 1)$	Inelastic	Percentage change in quantity demanded *less* than percentage change in price	Revenues *decrease* when price decreases.

Source: Adapted from Samuelson and Nordhaus (1992).

are made available by producers (suppliers). Price elasticity of demand provides producers with information regarding production and consumption for particular goods and aids the producer in understanding how demand for products varies at different price levels.

Cross-Elasticity of Demand

Although price is a very important factor in analyzing consumer demand, it is important to recognize that demand is also affected by the availability of other products (and their respective prices) that can be substituted for one another. Changes in tastes and preferences, demographic characteristics, individual household income and technology all encourage the substitution of different media products or services. In the media industries, a number of competitors produce similar media content, and consumers often sample and substitute other media products regularly. In the study of economics, this process is called *cross-elasticity of demand.*

In a very broad sense, the media industries are engaged in the production and dissemination of information and entertainment content, yet this does not necessarily mean that any of the media are interchangeable. For example, to access news, a consumer can choose a newspaper, radio, television or the Internet. Each differs in the amount of time and space devoted to the presentation of the news. These media serve more as *complements* to one another than as pure substitutes. On the other hand, the same movie shown on a premium cable television channel can usually be accessed in other ways, such as through a video rental store or through direct purchase at a store or via the Internet. These methods serve as substitutes for the cable movie.

Cross-elasticity is a useful tool in economic analysis, in that it can be used to determine "the extent to which different media compete for different portions of media product and service markets" (Picard 1989, 47). Cross-elasticity has been used in the public policy arena, particularly in analyzing antitrust cases that examine competitive practices in certain markets (such as the Microsoft case).

In the media industries, cross-elasticity of demand usually increases when there are many potential substitutes, as in industries such as magazines or cable television. In general, studies examining cross-elasticity in the mass media among consumers have shown that as the percentage of income required for consuming a good increases, so does cross-elasticity.

Types of Demand for Media Products

It is important to note there are different types of demand present at different levels of analysis in the mass media. Clearly, there is a demand for the media content by the audiences. Here, demand can be measured on the individual level by consumer usage of the product, which can be derived by examining direct consumer purchases (such as a newspaper, book or movie ticket) or, in the case of content offered for free (such as television) by the *utility* (satisfaction) offered by the product. Typically, utility is a subjective measure, and individuals assign *value* (Fig. 2.4) to the content based on the satisfaction derived from the product. Studies of audience uses and gratifications routinely measure the satisfaction, or utilities, desired from media content.

Representative studies by Dimmick (1993) and Albarran and Dimmick (1993) relate the concept of gratifications to economic utility in a series of studies involving the ecological theory of the niche. In calculating measures of utility, the authors found cable television to be superior to broadcast television and other forms of video entertainment in serving audience needs.

There is also demand for access to audiences by advertisers trying to market their products and services to consumers. The advertising industry operates in an interdependent relationship with much of the mass media in our country. Without cooperation, neither industry would flourish. The demand for advertising can thus be studied on an organizational, or macro, level. Most studies of advertising demand have observed little cross-elasticity in the advertising industry. For example, Busterna (1987) found no cross-elasticity of demand for national advertising among several different advertising media, and Picard (1982) found that newspapers are more concerned with industry trends than with consumer demand in setting advertising prices.

Another type of demand is the demand for media outlets, as evidenced by the large number of mergers and acquisitions that occur annually in the media

What is value? Economists think of value as the worth of a particular product or service. It is a subjective process that is linked to individual satisfaction.

Consumers assign value based on individual wants and needs for a particular product. In terms of media use, this process helps consumers decide what type of media content to utilize in order to meet their needs.

FIGURE 2.4. *Value.*

industries. Most of these studies attempt to determine what variables influence the price of a particular media property—such as a television or radio station or a cable television system. In most cases, this type of analysis occurs on the market level, which is the focus of Chapter 3.

In addition to the studies mentioned in the preceding paragraphs, a limited number of academic studies have been conducted to determine the demand for media content, advertising and media outlets. Studies are limited because so much of the data needed by researchers are proprietary in nature and are held confidentially by media companies and independent firms. A sample of these studies, the industries examined and their findings regarding demand are shown in Table 2.2.

Summary

The economic system determines who will produce goods, how goods will be produced and who will consume the goods based on the type of economic structure found in a society. In most developed countries, a mixed economy is in operation regarding the mass media, which establish a market economy with limited governmental regulation.

The market economy is guided by supply and demand interacting throughout the market to maintain *equilibrium* (the balance point at which supply equals demand). In a market-based economy, supply and demand interact to make the economy function. In the United States, the mass media are continually engaged in supply and demand, obtaining resources on a daily basis in order to supply consumers with the media content or products they desire.

Table 2.2. Examples of demand studies

Author(s) and Date	Industry Examined	Findings
Lacy (1990)	Newspaper	Competition increases higher quality news operations
Childers and Krugman (1987)	Cable, VCR, PPV	There is significant cross-elasticity of demand in these industries
Mayo and Otsuka (1991)		Demand for basic cable ranges from inelastic in rural areas to elastic in urban markets; demand for pay services is also elastic
Lindstrom (1997)	Internet	Internet usage affects demand for traditional media like television

Source: Information compiled by the author from published works.

Demand can be measured at different levels and is affected by many variables including price, value, income and changing tastes and preferences. When different forms of media content can be substituted for each other, cross-elasticity of demand exists. Cross-elasticity of demand is a useful tool in economic analysis and is often used in public policy decisions.

This chapter has presented the basic concepts of an economic system and their application to the mass media industries. In Chapter 3, the focus shifts to the individual market level rather than the economic system as a whole. Markets are discussed in terms of their structure, conduct and behavior in an economic system.

Discussion Questions

1. What three questions must a society address in solving the economic problem? How can they be applied to the mass media?
2. What are the differences between the command, market and mixed economies?
3. What are supply and demand? How do they work together to maintain the economic system?
4. What is a demand curve? What are the three types of demand? What do we mean by the terms *elasticity of demand* and *cross-elasticity of demand*?
5. Give examples of demand in the media industries from the standpoint of individual consumers, advertisers and media outlets.

Exercises

1. Investigate the concept of *supply* based on the market in which you now live and prepare a brief report. For example, how many television stations are there in your market? How many people subscribe to cable television? How many cable channels are available, including premium and pay services? How many people subscribe to satellite services? How many video rental outlets exist in the market?
2. Examine the concept of *demand* based on one type of media in the market in which you live and prepare a brief report. Describe the demand for the audience. What do audience ratings and other local indicators tell you about the demand for media from the consumer level? Next, analyze demand for advertisers. Are most channels sold out of their advertising inventory, or does there appear to be a lot of advertising time or space available? Finally, investigate the demand for media outlets in your market. When was the last time a media property was sold? How much was paid for the property? Was it considered a good investment at the time? Why or why not?
3. As a consumer, chart your media activities for a day by keeping track of the following information: (a) type of medium used (i.e., book, radio, newspaper, Internet); (b) amount of time used; (c) reason you used the medium (e.g., to study for an exam, for entertainment, to pass time); (d) other media that could have been substituted for the one you selected (if no substitute available, so indicate); and (e) how satisfied

you were from using that particular medium for a specific time period. This summary helps illustrate how you make decisions regarding media usage and also illustrates the concepts of supply, demand, cross-elasticity, utility and value.

References

Albarran, A. B., and J. Dimmick. (1993). Measuring utility in the video entertainment industries: An assessment of competitive superiority. *Journal of Media Economics* 6 (2):45–51.

Busterna, J. (1987). The cross elasticity of demand for national newspaper advertising. *Journalism Quarterly* 64:346–51.

Childers, T. L., and D. M. Krugman. (1987). The competitive environment of pay per view. *Journal of Broadcasting and Electronic Media* 31:335–42.

Dimmick, J. (1993). Ecology, economics, and gratification utilities. In *Media Economics: Theory and Practice*, edited by A. Alexander, J. Owers, and R. Carveth. New York: Lawrence Erlbaum Associates, pp. 135–156.

Dunnett, P. (1990). *The World Television Industry: An Economic Analysis*. London: Routledge.

Lacy, S. (1990). A model of demand for news: Impact of competition on newspaper content. *Journalism Quarterly* 67:40–48, 128.

Lindstrom, P. B. (1997). The Internet: Nielsen's longitudinal research on behavioral changes in usage of this counter intuitive medium. *Journal of Media Economics* 10 (2): 35–40.

Mayo, J. W., and Y. Otsuka. (1991). Demand, pricing and regulation: Evidence from the cable TV industry. *Rand Journal of Economics* 22 (3): 396–410.

Owers, J., R. Carveth, and A. Alexander. (1993). An introduction to media economic theory and practice. In *Media Economics: Theory and Practice*, edited by A. Alexander, J. Owers, and R. Carveth. New York: Lawrence Erlbaum Associates, pp. 3–46.

Picard, R. G. (1982). Rate setting and competition in newspaper advertising. *Newspaper Research Journal* 3 (April): 2–13.

———. (1989). *Media Economics*. Beverly Hills: Sage.

Samuelson, P. A., and W. D. Nordhaus. (1992). *Economics*. 14th ed. New York: McGraw-Hill.

Vogel, H. L. (2000). *Entertainment Industry Economics: A Guide for Financial Analysis*. 4th ed. Cambridge: Cambridge University Press.

3

UNDERSTANDING THE MARKET

After reading this chapter, you should understand:

- How a market is defined in media economics

- Different types of market structures found in the mass media

- How individual firms are affected by market structure

- How market structure impacts market conduct and market performance

The market economy introduced in Chapter 2 is actually composed of many individual markets; but what exactly is a market? A *market* is where consumers and sellers interact with one another to determine the price and quantity of the goods produced. A market consists of a number of sellers that provide a similar product or service to the same group of buyers or consumers. Market activity varies across different locations because individual products differ and there are different groups of buyers and sellers. The market for fast food is much different than the market for life insurance. Likewise, the market for magazines is different from the pharmaceutical market. Yet any market can be analyzed using similar concepts. In this chapter, the focus is on analyzing a market in terms of its structure, behavior and performance.

A market is sometimes referred to as an industry. In reality, a market and an industry are not the same. A *market* is an interrelated group of buyers and sellers, whereas an *industry* is only the sellers in a particular market (such as the film industry) or across several markets (as in the newspaper industry, which is engaged in selling the paper itself as well as retail, classified and perhaps online advertising to put in the paper).

Today, many media companies participate simultaneously in several markets. For example, Sony manufactures electronic hardware such as DVD players and other electronic equipment. Sony also participates in the manufacture and sale of software and in the sale of blank audio and videotape through its ownership of CBS Records. Sony also owns a film studio, Columbia Pictures, which produces programming (another form of software) for film and television. Hence, Sony is a major "player" in three separate, yet related, media markets. And Sony encounters different competitors, as well as different buyers, in each market.

The Sony example illustrates one of the important aspects of studying media economics: that media firms operate across a range of product and geographic markets. This distinction is clarified later in this chapter in a discussion of product and geographic markets.

Markets Defined: Product and Geographic Dimensions

Picard (1989) explains that media industries are unique in that they function in a *dual product market*. That is, although media companies produce one product, they participate in two separate good and service markets.

In the first market, the good may be in the form of a newspaper, radio or television program, magazine, book or film production. The good is marketed to consumers, and performance is evaluated in different ways. Newspaper and magazine performance is measured through circulation data from subscribers and purchases of individual issues. Radio and television programs use audience ratings, and film performance is measured by ticket sales. Some products require a purchase to be made by the consumer, such as a cable television subscription or a video rental. In the case of broadcast radio and television, you can access programming by simply acquiring a receiver (a radio or TV set). However, all media products require the use of individual time (a scarce resource) in order to be consumed.

The second market in which many media companies are engaged involves the selling of advertising. Advertisers seek access to the audiences using media content. These two areas strongly influence each other (see Fig. 3.1). Greater demand for media content enables companies to charge higher prices for their advertising. Likewise, a drop in audience ratings, reader circulation or other media usage will trigger a decline in advertising revenues.

This dual product market is a unique characteristic for many of the mass media. Most companies that produce consumable products only participate in a single market, that of providing the good to the consumer. Take McDonald's as an example. As a leader in the fast-food industry, McDonald's offers a vari-

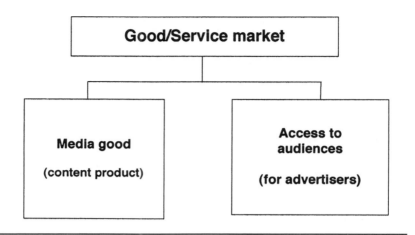

FIGURE 3.1. *The dual product market.*

ety of food products to its customers. However, when we consume food from McDonald's, the product is used up. In contrast, media products represent entertainment and informational goods that can be used over and over again. As such, media firms do not produce typical products, as information goods are not consumable in the purest sense of the term.

In addition to operating in a dual product market, many media companies operate in specific areas, or *geographic regions*. Some firms, such as radio, television, and cable networks, compete on a national basis, whereas other companies, such as local radio and television stations and newspapers, compete in a regional geographic area.

In a few media industries, government may regulate the geographic region. For example, the Federal Communications Commission (FCC) grants broadcast licenses to specific areas, while local municipalities award franchises to cable television system operators. Media industries that are not subject to governmental regulation simply pick and choose the geographic markets in which to operate. With the Internet, geographical markets do not exist; you can access websites from any place in the world provided you have a computer and a network connection.

Defining a media market consists of combining both the product and geographic dimensions (Fig. 3.2). This process delineates a specific market for the firm in which it offers some of or its entire media products to potential buyers. The number of suppliers in a particular market—and the extent of the competition among suppliers for buyers—is affected by the characteristics of the market, or what economists refer to as *market structure*. In turn, the type of

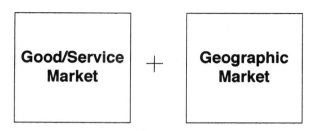

FIGURE 3.2. *Defining the market.*

market structure affects the conduct and performance of the market. A theoretical tool used to understand the relationship of market structure, conduct and performance is the industrial organization model.

The Industrial Organization Model

The industrial organization model is commonly used to understand the relationships among market structure, conduct and performance. The industrial organization model (see Fig. 3.3) explicated by Scherer (1980) offers a systematic approach to analyzing the many abstract concepts encountered in studying a market. Busterna (1988) adds that the model helps in understanding the interaction of market forces and their impact on market activities. Further, the industrial organization model explains why market performance is linked to market structure and conduct.

In the following sections, the components of the industrial organization model are briefly examined, with an explanation of key terms and principles. Readers desiring more detailed treatment should consult Scherer (1980) or Bain (1968), two widely cited sources on industrial organization.

Market Structure

A market is better understood through an examination of its economic characteristics. The structure of a market is dependent on several factors, but several important criteria clarify the type of market structure. These criteria are the concentration of buyers and sellers (producers) in the market, the differentiation among the various products offered, barriers to entry for new competitors, cost structures and vertical integration.

CONCENTRATION OF BUYERS AND SELLERS   The number of producers or sellers in a given market explains a great deal about the *concentration* in

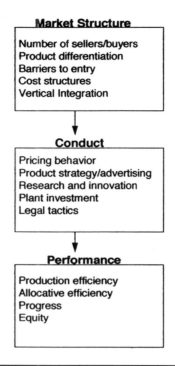

Market Structure

Number of sellers/buyers
Product differentiation
Barriers to entry
Cost structures
Vertical Integration

Conduct

Pricing behavior
Product strategy/advertising
Research and innovation
Plant investment
Legal tactics

Performance

Production efficiency
Allocative efficiency
Progress
Equity

FIGURE 3.3. *Industrial organization model.* (Modified from Sherer, 1980)

a given market. A market is concentrated if it is dominated by a limited number of large companies. The lower the number of producers, the larger the degree of power each individual firm will wield. For many years, three broadcast networks (ABC, CBS and NBC) dominated the network television market, particularly with respect to advertising. But as cable television, other video technologies and the Fox Broadcasting Company emerged as competitors, competition for viewers and advertisers intensified.

Concentration can be measured in various ways, but in media economics two approaches prevail. One method measures the percentage of the market (using circulation or ratings data) reached by competitors through the product. Another method involves calculating the percentage of revenues (sales) controlled by the top four (or eight) firms. Concentration measures are discussed more fully in Chapter 4.

PRODUCT DIFFERENTIATION *Product differentiation* refers to the subtle differences (either real or imagined) perceived by buyers as existing among products offered by sellers. A number of magazines are geared to specific markets. For example, there are several publications targeted toward the business world. Yet *Forbes, Business Week*, and *Money* all present different editors, columnists and other features geared toward their readers. Radio stations offer a variety of music formats, and their call letters, personalities, marketing campaigns and technical facilities create perceived differences from one station to the next.

BARRIERS TO ENTRY   *Barriers to entry* are obstacles new sellers must overcome before entering a particular market. Barriers may be limited to capital (money) or other factors. Wirth (1986) studied barriers to entry for the newspaper and broadcast industries and found that entry into the newspaper business involved far more economic barriers than did entry into broadcast radio or television. Before Rupert Murdoch could purchase a set of television stations in order to establish the Fox network, he first had to meet a number of federally mandated ownership criteria (including obtaining U.S. citizenship) in order for the transaction to be approved by the FCC.

COST STRUCTURES   *Cost structures* consider the costs for production in a particular market. Total costs consist of both *fixed costs*—the costs to produce a single unit of a product, regardless of the total number produced—and *variable costs*—costs that change depending on the quantity produced (e.g., labor and raw materials). Industries that have high fixed costs, such as newspapers and cable television, often lead to highly concentrated markets. *Economies of scale* usually exist in these situations for the producer (seller). By economies of scale, we refer to the decline in average cost that occurs as additional units of a product are created.

VERTICAL INTEGRATION   *Vertical integration* occurs when a firm controls different aspects of production, distribution and exhibition of its products (Fig. 3.4). Viacom is an example of a company engaged in vertical integration. A movie produced by the Viacom-owned Paramount film studio eventually will appear on pay-per-view or premium services such as Showtime. Finally, the movie may be offered as a package of feature films for sale to cable networks or network television, which might be part of the CBS family of stations. Viacom maximizes its revenue for the film through the different stages of distribution and exhibition. Further, the film will be marketed through Viacom's cable networks, websites and other ancillary modes.

The Theory of the Firm

Analyzing the number of producers and sellers in a market, the difference between products, barriers to entry, cost structures and vertical integration gives insight into the structure of a market. Four types of market structure

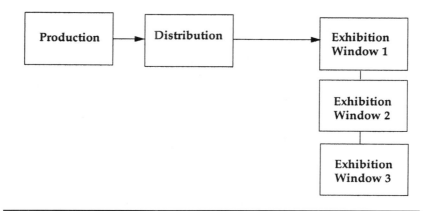

FIGURE 3.4. *Vertical integration.*

serve as theoretical models. These four types of market structure are recognized popularly in much of the literature as the "theory of the firm" (Litman 1988).

The four types of market structure are monopoly, oligopoly, monopolistic competition and perfect competition. The four market structures represent a continuum, with monopoly and perfect competition found at opposite ends and oligopoly and monopolistic competition occupying interior positions (Fig. 3.5). These types of market structure are represented in different industries, including the mass media.

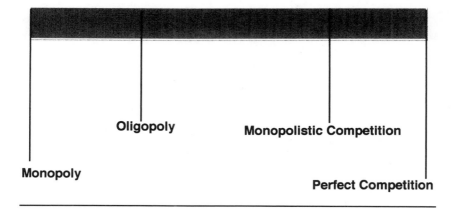

FIGURE 3.5. *Market structure.*

MONOPOLY   A *monopoly* is a type of structure in which only a single seller of a product exists and thus dominates the market. Generally, a monopolistic structure assumes there is no clear substitute for the product; a buyer must purchase the good from the monopolist or avoid consumption of the good altogether. Economists refer to monopolists as *price makers* or *price setters* because they can set the price in order to maximize profits. As expected, barriers to entry are very high in a monopoly.

The monopolist can also exhibit power in the market by restricting production output (if desired). In a monopolistic structure, the demand curve for the product is the same as the industry demand curve (Fig. 3.6). If no close substitute exists, demand is generally perceived as inelastic. It is important to recognize that not all consumers (buyers) demand the seller's product. If demand is weak and substitutes emerge, the monopolist will have little market power.

OLIGOPOLY   An *oligopoly* differs from a monopoly in that this type of structure features more than one seller of a product. Products offered by the sellers may be either homogeneous (alike) or heterogeneous (differentiated). Typically, a market dominated by a few firms is considered an oligopoly, and each firm commands a similar share. Firms in an oligopoly are mutually interdependent, with the actions of the leading firm(s) affecting the other firms in the market. These firms consider their actions in light of the impact on the market and their competitors. Depending on the reaction of other competitors, changes made by the leader(s) may move firms in an oligopoly toward more cooperation or competition.

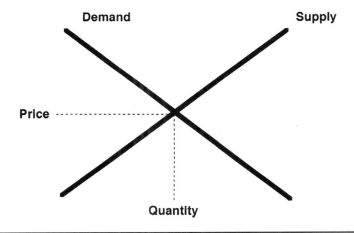

FIGURE 3.6. *Monopoly demand curve.*

In an oligopoly, the leader normally sets price, and others follow suit. The small number of sellers and the lack of substitutes create an inelastic demand curve for the oligopoly market structure (see Fig. 3.7). Barriers to entry may take several forms in an oligopoly, but they are not as significant as those found in a monopoly. For example, the Fox network was able to enter the television network market successfully despite the fact that ABC, CBS and NBC held dominance with audiences, advertisers and affiliates. Later, the UPN and WB networks entered the network market, along with PaxNet.

MONOPOLISTIC COMPETITION A third type of market structure, *monopolistic competition*, exists when there are many sellers offering products that are similar, but not perfect, substitutes for one another. Barriers to entry are lower than those found in an oligopoly. Each firm attempts to differentiate its products in the minds of the consumer through various methods including advertising, promotion, location, service and quality.

Unlike in the oligopoly, price varies in this type of market structure, with price decisions set by both the market and the individual firms. Monopolistic competitive firms, believing they operate independently in the market, will often lower prices to increase revenue. However, other competitors facing similar conditions may also lower their prices, which results in a downward-sloping demand curve (see Fig. 3.8) for the market.

PERFECT COMPETITION In *perfect competition*, many sellers offer the same product, and no single firm or group of firms dominates the market. With

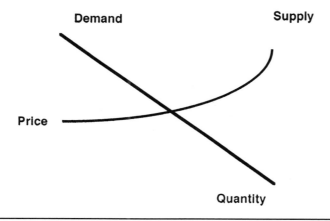

FIGURE 3.7. *Monopolistic competition demand curve.*

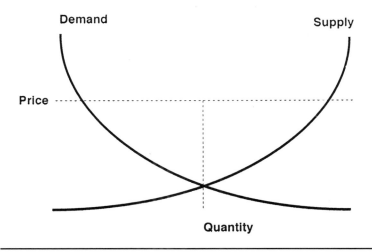

FIGURE 3.8. *Oligopoly demand curve.*

no barriers to entry, the characteristics of the market economy dominate in a perfectly competitive market structure.

Individual firms operate as *price takers*, in that the market sets the price for the product, and prices are naturally constrained downward (Picard 1989). The only production decision the firm makes in this type of market structure is how much of the good to produce, as it has no control over price. The demand and supply curves are straight under perfect competition (see Fig. 3-9).

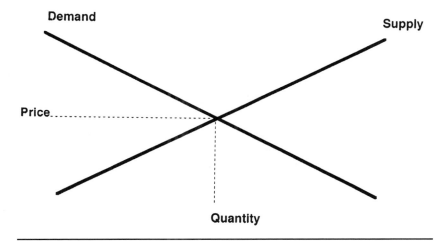

FIGURE 3.9. *Demand curves in perfect competition.*

MEDIA INDUSTRIES AND MARKET STRUCTURE   To apply the theory of the firm to the media industries, one must first understand the specific market and the number of firms operating in the market and then determine the amount of control the firm has over its competitors. Media industries occupy different positions across three of the four types of market structure, as shown in Figure 3.10. (Note that a true market structure of perfect competition does not exist in the mass media.)

An example of a monopoly market structure in the mass media is cable television. Cable systems are locally regulated according to franchise agreements established between the cable operator and the local form of government and are specified for a set period of time. The cable industry has experienced competition from direct-broadcast satellite systems and local telephone companies, but it still maintains a dominant position.

Daily newspapers tend to fall in a monopolistic structure depending on the number of newspapers published in a particular geographic area. The number of cities served by more than one daily newspaper has declined rapidly since the 1970s, indicating a move toward a monopolistic structure.

For the most part, broadcast television stations operate in an oligopoly, as do the broadcast networks, the motion picture studios, and the recording industry. For example, the TV industry utilizes the same types of programming—situation comedies, dramas, movies, sports, news, reality, and so forth. The product is relatively homogeneous—that is, the kinds of programs are about the same no matter which network is producing them—although competition for audiences is intense.

The monopolistic competition market structure is best represented by the magazine industry. Prior to the passage of the Telecommunications Act of 1996, the radio industry fit under a monopolistic competition structure, but increasing consolidation is moving radio more towards an oligopoly.

- **Monopoly**
  - **Newspapers (in most markets)**
  - **Cable television (in most markets)**
- **Oligopoly**
  - **Television networks**
  - **Motion picture studios**
  - **Recording industry**
- **Monopolistc Competition**
  - **Magazines**

FIGURE 3.10. *Key media industries by market structure.*

Type of Product	Number of Firms		
	One	A Few	Many
Homogeneous product	Pure monopoly	Homogeneous oligopoly	Pure competition
Differentiated product	Pure monopoly	Differentiated oligopoly	Monopolistic competition

FIGURE 3.11. *Scherer's two dimensions of market structure.* (Scherer, 1980)

SCHERER'S TWO-DIMENSIONAL MODEL   The theory of the firm helps clarify the distinctions found across the four types of market structure. In addition to the theory of the firm, Scherer (1980) offers a two-dimensional approach to understanding market structure (Fig. 3.11). The first dimension considers the number of sellers in a market (one, a few, many), and the second dimension separates homogeneous products from heterogeneous products.

This two-dimensional approach is helpful in clarifying some aspects of market structure left unanswered by the theory of the firm. This is evident in Scherer's distinction between homogeneous oligopolies and heterogeneous oligopolies. An example of a homogeneous oligopoly would be the broadcast TV networks and their relationships with advertisers. In this sense, the networks are similar; from an advertiser's point of view, they each offer access to audiences in the same way. An example of a heterogeneous oligopoly would be the case of a city served by more than one newspaper. The *New York Times* is a different product than the *New York Post*, just as the *Chicago Tribune* is a different paper from the *Chicago Sun-Times.*

Both the theory of the firm and Scherer's seller-product dimensions are helpful in understanding market structure. The following sections focus on how market structure influences market conduct and market performance, the other components of the industrial organizational paradigm.

Market Conduct

Market conduct refers to the policies and behaviors exhibited by sellers and buyers in a market. Market conduct centers around five specific areas: (1) pricing policies or behaviors, (2) product strategy and advertising, (3) research and innovation, (4) plant investment and (5) legal tactics. Of special interest is how these different types of behaviors appear to be coordinated among firms in certain types of market structure.

PRICING POLICIES OR BEHAVIORS   Pricing policies or behaviors are the most observable type of market conduct. Picard (1989) explains that pricing policies involve a series of decisions regarding how products are packaged, discounted and set. Picard identifies four common price orientations:

1. **Demand-oriented pricing**—prices are set via market forces.
2. **Target return pricing**—prices are based on a desired amount of profit.
3. **Competition-oriented pricing**—prices are based on those offered by competitors.
4. **Industry norm pricing**—prices are set by the industry at large, rather than via market forces.

PRODUCT STRATEGY AND ADVERTISING   Product strategy and advertising refer to decisions based on the actual products offered by a firm, including how a product is packaged or designed. In the media industries, it may involve what type of programming to secure for an afternoon time period, the type of music format selected for an FM radio station or the quality of paper on which to print a magazine. As discussed previously, firms must also consider which market to enter from a geographic perspective, by targeting a national audience or concentrating on specific areas.

Advertising entails a range of activities designed to create awareness of media products and services. Promotional and marketing activities aimed at consumers are ultimately designed to increase market share at the expense of other competitors. Clearly, in more competitive types of market structure, advertising is vital in order for media products to maintain an image and position in a market.

RESEARCH AND INNOVATION   Research and innovation refer to the effort of firms to differentiate or improve their products over time. Because of the insatiable appetite American consumers have for media content, continuing emphasis is placed on research in order to better understand the behaviors and characteristics of media consumers. Further, technological innovations have enabled media content to be delivered to consumers faster, more accurately and with more options. This forces other firms to respond in order to remain competitive in their individual markets.

PLANT INVESTMENT   Plant investment refers to the various resources needed to create or purchase the physical plant in which goods will be produced. Some of the mass media industries involve a significant investment in capital and physical plant. In particular, newspapers, motion pictures and cable television require a sizable investment on the part of participants.

LEGAL TACTICS   Legal tactics encompass the entire range of legal actions utilized by a firm in a particular market. The most visible use of legal tactics occurs through the use of patents and copyrights for particular goods. The history of the electronic media in the United States is replete with examples of patent disputes, particularly in the development of the radio industry. Copyright is still very important today, as video and audio piracy (illegal copying and distribution of copyrighted material) leads to millions of dollars of lost revenue for the film and recording industries.

Market Performance

Market performance involves analyzing the ability of individual firms in a market to achieve goals based on different performance criteria. Market performance is usually evaluated from a societal perspective, rather than from the level of the firm. Policy-makers can examine the economic efficiency of a particular industry through performance criteria and, if necessary, initiate structural or conduct solutions to remedy problems. In this sense, performance is examined from a macroeconomic orientation. A number of variables are considered in evaluating market performance. They include efficiency, equity and progress.

EFFICIENCY   *Efficiency* refers to the ability of a firm to maximize its wealth. Normally, two types of efficiency are reviewed: technical efficiency and allocative efficiency. *Technical efficiency* involves using the firm's resources in the most effective way to maximize output. Much of the conglomeration that has occurred in the media industries is designed to increase technical efficiency through mergers and acquisitions, which create economies of scale. *Allocative efficiency* occurs when an individual market functions at an optimal capacity, spreading its benefits among producers and consumers. Conversely, excess profits are often seen as allocative inefficiency, as they suggest that market resources are being used improperly. Normally, the solution is to encourage more competitors in the market in order to lower profits to more optimal levels. Decisions to limit ownership for television stations encourage allocative efficiency as well as diversity of expression.

EQUITY   *Equity* is concerned with the way in which wealth is distributed among producers and consumers. Ideally, a market economy system will provide a fair distribution of equity so that no single firm receives excessive rewards. Naturally, equity is more problematic in monopolistic and oligopolistic market structures, where wealth is more concentrated among fewer firms.

PROGRESS   *Progress* refers to the ability of firms in a market to increase output over time. Each firm sets goals, and evaluations for a market are determined by the aggregate sum of market output. Various trade associations and governmental agencies to monitor progress in different markets compile statistical data.

As the industrial organizational model implies, the structure of the market affects the conduct of different firms in a market, which in turn affects the performance of the market. This framework is valuable in the study of media economics because it provides both theoretical and practical utility in the analysis of different types of media industries, as well as giving substance to abstract concepts.

Summary

This chapter has focused on understanding an individual market in media economics by introducing one of the unique aspects of media economics: the dual dimensions of product and geography used in defining a market. The industrial organization model is used to recognize how market structure, market conduct and market performance are linked.

Market structure can be identified using several different criteria, including the concentration of buyers and sellers in the market, the differentiation among products, the barriers to entry for new competitors, cost structures and vertical integration. Media industries operate along a continuum involving four models of market structure: monopoly, oligopoly, monopolistic competition and perfect competition.

Market structure affects the market conduct of individual firms and is concerned with pricing behaviors, product strategy and advertising, research and innovation, plant investment and legal tactics. The conduct of firms in a market likewise affects the performance of the market. Market performance is evaluated most often from a macro perspective with respect to different performance variables, including efficiency, equity and progress.

In Chapter 4, emphasis is placed on evaluating individual media markets. Methods used to compare different markets are discussed and tools for analysis are introduced, along with a discussion on how regulation and technology may affect market behavior.

Discussion Questions

1. What does it mean to say the mass media operate in a *dual product market*? Give examples based on your local media.
2. What are the basic differences between the four types of market structure introduced in the chapter?

3. Identify the following terms in regard to analyzing a media market: *product differentiation, barriers to entry* and *concentration.*
4. What is the difference between *market conduct* and *market performance?* How does market structure influence market conduct? How does market structure influence market performance?

Exercises

1. Examine the local media in your market, and categorize them in terms of the types of market structure discussed in the chapter. Is there any type of structure not represented in your market? Are there any indications that one of the media markets may be moving toward a different type of structure? Explain.
2. Compare the news operations among the local television, radio and newspaper outlets. Each outlet is engaged in the distribution of news, but it presents its product differently. How do they differ?
3. Imagine that you are a media consultant in your local market. A group of investors desires your expertise, as the group is interested in starting a new media outlet in your market. Determine the barriers to entry that exist for starting the following types of new media facilities in your local market: (a) a daily newspaper; (b) an FM radio station; (c) a broadcast television station; and (d) a new Internet service provider. What would you advise your client to do?

References

Bain, J. S. (1968). *Industrial Organization.* New York: John Wiley and Sons.

Busterna, J. C. (1988). Concentration and the industrial organizational model. In *Press Concentration and Monopoly: New Perspectives on Newspaper Ownership and Operation*, edited by R. G. Picard, M. McCombs, J. P. Winter and S. Lacy. Norwood, N.J.: Ablex, pp. 35–53.

Litman, B. R. (1988). Microeconomic foundations. In *Press Concentration and Monopoly: New Perspectives on Newspaper Ownership and Operation*, edited by R. G. Picard, M. McCombs, J. P. Winter and S. Lacy. Norwood, N.J.: Ablex, pp. 3–34.

Picard, R. G. (1989). *Media Economics.* Beverly Hills, Calif.: Sage.

Scherer, F. M. (1980). *Industrial Market Structure and Economic Performance.* 2d ed. Chicago: Rand McNally.

Wirth, M. O. (1986). Economic barriers to entering media industries in the United States. In *Communication Yearbook*, 9th ed., edited by M. McLaughlin. Beverly Hills, Calif.: Sage, pp. 423–442.

4

EVALUATING MEDIA MARKETS

After reading this chapter, you should understand:

- How to locate resources for information on media industries and individual firms

- Methods used to measure market concentration

- How to measure diversification within a firm

- How regulation affects media markets and individual firms

- How technology affects media markets and individual firms

An understanding of market structure, conduct and performance is vital in order to properly analyze media markets. Theoretical models of market structure, such as oligopoly and monopolistic competition, provide descriptive information that clarifies the nature and extent of supply, demand, competition and barriers to entry.

Although this information is useful, it is helpful to have more precise analytical information with which to evaluate media markets carefully. In this chapter, you will be introduced to a variety of resources and methodologies to enable you to evaluate media firms and markets.

There are several reasons why an evaluation of media markets is important. First and perhaps most important to this text, an evaluation of media markets enables you to understand the various processes at work that cause media companies to operate the way they do. Business publications bring news of mergers, acquisition or divestiture involving media companies. By understanding the economic characteristics of individual firms and markets and by having the tools with which to analyze their activities, you can better comprehend the role and function of the media in society.

Second, evaluating media markets is important for group and individual investment purposes. Many companies engaged in the mass media are *public companies*, meaning they are publicly owned by individual and institutional stockholders who invest in a firm in hopes of obtaining profits through stock appreciation and corporate dividends. Brokerage firms and other analysts constantly monitor media market performance in order to pass along recommendations to buy, sell or hold shares in publicly traded companies. Prudent investing is thus contingent on the use of accurate information in making these important decisions.

Third, if you are considering employment in some aspect of the media, it is essential that you understand the economic characteristics of the individual market in which you wish to work. This will help you identify potential employers, understand the lines of business in which they are engaged and determine their position in the market—all factors that can affect your potential for salary, advancement and job stability. Surprisingly, many college graduates send résumés to potential employers without any understanding or investigation of the individual company, its ownership or its financial condition.

In the following sections of the chapter, you are introduced to different resources used in evaluating media markets. Many of these resources are available in public and university libraries, through websites and from individual companies. Later, methodological tools are introduced to provide measurements of market concentration. Finally, a discussion of exterior forces in the form of regulation and technology completes this examination of evaluating media markets.

What Is the Media Market?

In Chapter 3, we learned that a *market* is where consumers and sellers interact with one another to determine the price and quantity of the goods produced. Further, in defining a market, one must consider the geographic boundaries in which the market is engaged. Defining media markets, however, can be a difficult process. As Bates (1993, 4) has observed, "media markets are no longer neatly defined" due to increasing competition, close substitutes and geographic boundaries, which overlap on several levels.

For example, consider two markets in which the radio industry is engaged. Nationally, there are more than 20 radio networks, which form a market that serves national advertisers and individual radio stations. National advertisers, working primarily through advertising agencies in media planning, use radio networks to help target specific audiences. Local radio stations may affiliate with a radio network to obtain specific news and features delivered by the network to supplement their local format.

On the local level, there are more than 10,000 radio stations operating in the United States. But the majority of these stations tend to be clustered in different geographic locations (or "markets," as the radio industry uses the term). In Top-10 markets, as many as 40 to 50 different radio stations may be scattered along the AM/FM band, with a variety of different formats. Clearly, not all stations compete for the same listeners and advertisers in the local economy, as different formats attract different groups of buyers and sellers.

Precise definitions of media markets are problematic without specific criteria. In defining a media market, researchers normally consider specific geographic boundaries, such as the international, national, regional or local market. Next, consideration is given to distinct areas, such as the market for advertisers or the market for audiences, both of which serve as indications of demand. Other areas can be used in defining the market, such as the number of sellers (suppliers) or the share of the market (e.g., advertising revenue, audience ratings or circulation data) held by each firm. Clearly, defining a market is not a cursory task but a process involving careful analysis and decision making.

Who Are the Major Players in the Market?

Once the market is defined, attention can be turned to learning who are the major companies, or "players," in the market or industry. There are many different resources to consult to obtain this information, and Appendix A to this text lists a number of resources normally available at most libraries. The following sections describe some of the most useful sources.

Industry Sources

Libraries contain numerous directories and reference volumes for many individual industries. The *Standard Industrial Classification* (SIC) *Manual* provides a complete listing of different industries using the SIC code and is a good starting point if you know little about a particular industry. It categorizes the U.S. economy by numbered segments or codes.

Researchers and analysts use the SIC codes in tabulating economic and financial data for the economy. The SIC system covers economic activity in nine major categories: (1) agriculture, forestry and fishing; (2) mining; (3) construction; (4) manufacturing; (5) transportation, communications and public utilities; (6) wholesale trade; (7) retail trade; (8) finance, insurance and real estate and (9) services. These categories are further divided into major groups, identified by two-digit codes; then into industry groups, with three-digit codes; and finally into industries, using four-digit codes.

Industries are arranged in alphabetical order, and each industry has a unique four-digit numeric code. For example, all companies involved in broadcast television are assigned a code of 4833, cable television services are 4841 and newspaper publishers are 2711. Once you know the SIC code for a particular industry, you can use the code to identify individual companies engaged in that industry. Several different directories show SIC code listings.

Standard and Poor's Industry Surveys, published since 1973, provides analyses of different industries and comparative financial statistics for key companies in each featured industry. The listing of companies in each industry is not exhaustive, but it does offer a quick review of the major players. The material is published quarterly.

Another useful source is the *U.S. Industry and Trade Outlook*, a government publication. This source provides an overview of recent trends and the financial outlook for many industries, including many media-related industries.

One other source for industry data is the *Value Line Investment Survey*. This particular resource provides reports on more than 75 industry groups and also analyzes some 1,500 companies. Brokerage analysts and individual investors seeking more information on a particular company or industry use the *Value Line* service heavily.

Finally, industry-specific directories such as the *Broadcasting and Cable Yearbook*, the *Television and Cable Factbook* and the *Editor and Publisher International Yearbook* are helpful sources. These directories are usually annual publications and contain some economic data.

Company Directories

A number of directories are useful for obtaining more information on specific corporations. Dun and Bradstreet publishes a number of different directories, including the *Million Dollar Directory, America's Corporate Families, America's Corporate Families and International Affiliates*, and *Dun and Bradstreet's Business Rankings*. Each of these publications differs in terms of its specific coverage of different companies, but most contain standard information such as SIC code indexes, parent or subsidiary cross-references, company profiles, employment statistics and annual sales or revenues.

Additionally, *Ward's Business Directory of U.S. Private and Public Companies* is a very useful source for locating information on *private companies*— those not owned by the public and thus not available on any stock market. *Standard and Poor's Register of Corporations, Directors and Executives* is an excellent source for information on corporate officers and directors.

Electronic Resources

A clear advantage to researching media industries and companies today is found in the number of available electronic resources provided for users. Appendix A offers a listing of the major electronic resources. The use of electronic resources has grown immensely with the development of CD-ROM products and Internet access. Check with your local libraries to determine which electronic resources are available. Lots of free information is also available through the Internet, so spend some time surfing as well. Just be careful, however, that you pay close attention to the sources of the information you find online; not all websites are created by reliable sources.

Market Concentration

Identifying the number of players in a given market will help you determine the type of market structure in which the firms are engaged. But remember that market structure does not necessarily explain how concentrated individual markets may be. Market concentration is an important variable in evaluating media markets. Highly concentrated markets usually lead to strong barriers to entry for new competitors. Historically, regulators have frowned on heavily concentrated markets, especially when the threat of anti-competitive behavior is a concern.

There are several tools to measure different aspects of concentration in a market. To determine buyer concentration from the perspective of the audience, you can review the latest audience ratings or circulation data. Economists evaluating market media are usually interested in two other forms of concentration: concentration of ownership and concentration of market share (measured by revenue or some other variable).

Concentration of Ownership

Concentration of ownership refers to the degree to which an industry is controlled by individual firms. Again, careful definition of the market under study is needed. Bagdikian (2000) documents a continuing decline in the number of firms involved in the media industries, based on a variety of different factors. This trend becomes more evident as you review later chapters that examine individual media industries. Concentration of ownership is considered problematic for a democratic society in that it could lead to a decline in diversity of expression.

The mass media are a critical force in helping to promote an informed electorate. Critics (e.g., Schiller 1981) contend that as the media become more concentrated and less competitive, they have not only economic power but political power as well, through the control and dissemination of information. As such, regulators attempt to limit concentration of control in order to maintain a diverse presentation of different views.

Concentration of Market Share

Several tools are used to measure the concentration of market share—that is, the proportion of a particular industry controlled by the top players. These tools include concentration ratios, the Lorenz Curve and the Herfindahl-Hirschman Index (HHI).

CONCENTRATION RATIOS   *Concentration ratios* were mentioned briefly in Chapter 3. This measure of concentration compares the ratio of total revenues of the major players with the revenues of the entire industry, using the top four firms (CR4) or the top eight firms (CR8). If the four-firm ratio is equal to or greater than 50 percent, or if the eight-firm ratio is equal to or greater than 75 percent, then the market is considered highly concentrated (see Fig. 4.1).

Concentration ratios are best used to analyze trends over time. If the concentration ratio increases, this suggests a move toward monopolistic power. One problem with concentration ratios should be noted: the ratios themselves are not sensitive to the individual power held by single firms (Picard 1989). For example, two different television markets may have identical concentration ratios, but the shares within the individual markets for each of the firms are very different. As Figure 4.2 illustrates, the distribution of market share is equal among the top four firms in Market A, but in Market B, the top firm clearly dominates the other three competitors.

The top-four and top-eight ratios have been frequently used to measure concentration in the media industries. An early study by Owen, Beebe and Manning (1974) found the market for television programs to be concentrated.

	Top Four Firms	Top Eight Firms
High concentration	≥ 50%	≥ 75%
Moderate concentration	33% ≤ to < 50%	50% ≤ to < 75%
Low concentration	≤ 33%	≤ 50%

FIGURE 4.1. *Concentration ratios.*

Market A			Market B	
Firm 1	10		Firm 1	25
Firm 2	10		Firm 2	5
Firm 3	10		Firm 3	5
Firm 4	10		Firm 4	5

FIGURE 4.2. *Inequality in concentration ratios.*

Picard (1988) examined the newspaper industry using daily papers in local markets and found high concentration. Albarran and Dimmick (1996) found most media industries to be highly concentrated.

LORENZ CURVE   Concentration can also be assessed graphically through the use of the *Lorenz Curve*. The Lorenz Curve illustrates the inequality of market share among different firms. Suppose one wants to illustrate the fact that FM radio stations are the preferred choice over AM stations among listeners. An examination of a recent ratings book for a radio market finds 10 stations—five AM and five FM—competing for the audience in a particular time period. The five FM stations account for 82 percent of the radio audience, whereas the AM stations together capture the remaining 18 percent. If audience shares were equally divided, then each station should have 10 percent of the audience. Thus, the FM stations should have only captured 50 percent of the market; however, because the FM stations reached far more than that, inequality exists.

The Lorenz Curve for the data in this example is illustrated in Figure 4.3. The 45° line represents equality in the market; the curve represents the actual distribution of shares among the radio stations. The more the Lorenz Curve departs from the 45° line, the greater the inequality. The utility of the Lorenz Curve lies in its graphical presentation, but it can be difficult to interpret (Litman 1985). It is best used when the number of firms in a market is greater than four.

HERFINDAHL-HIRSCHMAN INDEX (HHI)   A final measure of concentration, and probably the most sophisticated, is the *Herfindahl-Hirschman Index* (HHI). The HHI is calculated by summing the squared market shares of all

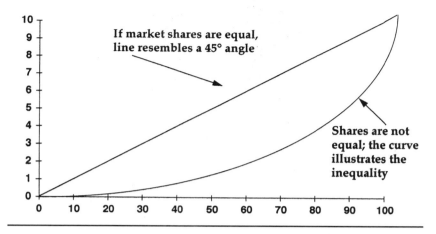

FIGURE 4.3. *Lorenz Curve.*

firms in a given market. The index is considered more accurate than either concentration ratios or the Lorenz Curve in that the index increases as the number
of firms declines and as inequality among individual firms rises. If the HHI is
equal to or higher than 1,800, then a market is highly concentrated. If the index
is less than 1,000, then the market is not considered concentrated (see Fig.
4.4). Calculating the HHI may be tedious if there are many firms operating in
a particular market.

The HHI has been used in several studies to measure media concentration, particularly in regard to network program categories. An early study by
Litman (1979) used the HHI and found high concentration among program
categories for the broadcast networks. Litman theorized that the data supported the proposition that the networks operate interdependently in an oligopoly structure rather than attempt to present a balanced program schedule.

The advantage of these three methods of measuring concentration is that
they offer different ways to measure and analyze concentration in a given market. Although a particular market structure may seem obvious with some

High concentration	HHI > 1,800
Moderate concentration	$1,000 \leq$ HHI $\leq 1,800$
Unconcentrated	HHI $\leq 1,000$

FIGURE 4.4. *Herfindahl–Hirschmann Index (HHI).*

media industries, the concentration measures can clarify the extent to which one or more companies dominate a particular market.

Corporate Diversification

On a related note, it may be of interest to determine how heavily an individual media firm is involved in a particular market. Analyzing the diversification strategy of individual companies accomplishes this goal. *Diversification* is the extent to which a company draws revenues across different markets or business segments. Companies that draw profits from more than one segment or division are thought to be better equipped to handle fluctuations in a normal business cycle. Further, by drawing resources across different markets, the diversified company is also thought to be able to adapt more easily to changing environmental conditions.

In a case study of the broadcast television networks, Dimmick and Wallschlaeger (1986) developed an index to measure corporate diversification. The index is calculated by summing the squared revenues of each segment and then dividing that sum into 1 (see Fig. 4.5). The diversification (D) index ranges from a low of 1 (meaning profits are concentrated in one division) to a high equal to the number of divisions the firm operates. Thus, a firm with seven divisions would have a D range from 1 to 7, whereas a firm with three divisions would have a D range from 1 to 3.

The D measure has been used to study diversification practices in the premium cable industry (Albarran and Porco 1990). The D index is best used when studying a company over a particular time span, as opposed to a single-year measurement, to reflect more accurately the changes companies encounter over time in the normal business cycle.

The D measure can be calculated using financial data from a corporate annual report or from an electronic service such as *Compact Disclosure*. A disadvantage to the D measure is that many corporations lump some of their activities together, and thus the financial information does not reflect the actual

$$D = \frac{1}{\sum_{i=1}^{n} pi^2}$$

FIGURE 4.5. *Diversification index.* (Dimmick and Wallschlaeger, 1986)

differences that may exist within a business segment. Nevertheless, the *D* measure can provide another means to analyze individual firms with respect to how deeply they are involved in certain markets.

Financial Ratios and Market Performance

It is also useful to have a basic knowledge of financial ratios in order to evaluate the financial condition and performance of individual firms and industries involved in the media (see Fig. 4.6). Data used to calculate financial ratios can be found in several sources such as corporate annual reports and financial web sites. Additionally, some resources such as *Compact Disclosure* and *Standard and Poor's Industry Surveys* include a number of financial ratios as part of their overview of individual firms and industries. Appendix B lists formulas for the financial ratios most commonly used by analysts to evaluate media firms and industries.

Different types of ratios are used to gauge different types of performance. For example, *growth ratios,* or *growth measures*, calculate the growth of revenue and assets over time, and also document historical trends. Financial growth is important to any business, and the stronger these measures, the better for the firm or industry examined. These include growth of revenue, operating income, assets and net worth. For each growth measure, the previous time period (month, quarter or year) is subtracted from the current time period (month, quarter or year), and this number is divided by the previous time period.

Performance ratios, or *profitability measures*, are designed to measure the financial strength of a company or industry. Low performance ratios are indicators of high liabilities, low revenues or excessive expenses. Included in this set of measures are return on sales, return on assets, return on equity, price-earnings ratio and profit margins.

Growth Ratios	measure growth over time
Performance Ratios	measure financial strength
Liquidity Ratios	convert assets into cash
Debt Ratios	measure debt and leverage
Capitalization	used in stock valuation

FIGURE 4.6. *Types of financial ratios.*

Other ratios are used to measure liquidity, debt and capitalization. *Liquidity* refers to a firm's ability to convert assets into cash. *Liquidity ratios* include the quick ratio, the current ratio and the acid-test ratio. Ideally, liquidity measures produce at least a 1.5-to-1 ratio of assets to liabilities.

Debt ratios measure the debt of a firm or industry. Two common debt ratios are the leverage ratio and the debt-to-equity ratio. The *leverage ratio* is calculated by dividing total debt by total assets. The *debt-to-equity ratio* divides total debt by total equity. Ideally, the debt-to-equity ratio will be no larger than 1.

Capitalization ratios are concerned with the capital represented by both preferred and common stock. Two ratios are common: dividing preferred stock by common stock and dividing long-term liabilities by common stock.

Impact of Regulation

All media firms and industries are to some degree affected by governmental regulation. The most obvious form of economic regulation concerns taxation. Governments levy various taxes on corporations but may also enact policies either to influence a particular market or to promote social goals. Some media industries are greatly influenced by regulation, though others face little regulation. For example, the FCC currently limits ownership of broadcast television stations. On the other hand, local governments specify the franchise area for a cable system but place no restrictions on newspaper distribution.

Media industries attempt to limit the impact of governmental regulation by forming industry associations, such as the National Association of Broadcasters (NAB) or the Newspaper Association of America (NAA). One way to circumvent potential governmental regulation is to provide self-regulation; industry associations often take the lead in this effort. Trade associations are also involved with professional lobbyists in an attempt to sway regulators to their point of view.

As you investigate later chapters that focus on individual industries, you will discover that some industries face more regulatory challenges than others do. Regulation may have both positive and negative outcomes in regard to media economics. As such, it is important to understand the desired goals regulators hope to achieve through regulation and how those goals affect supply and demand curves, market structure, conduct and performance.

For example, a goal of the Telecommunications Act of 1996 was to promote competition between cable systems, local phone companies and long-distance carriers. Regulators hoped that the legislation would lead to expanded choices and lower costs for consumers. Some time has passed since the legislation was enacted, and competition in the telecommunications sector is just beginning to emerge, and only in the nation's largest markets. Competition to cable is limited primarily to direct broadcast satellite (DBS) operators. Despite good intentions, the 1996 act did more to promote consolidation in the broadcast and cable industries than promote competition.

It is important to understand the impact of regulation on media industries, and an analysis of the regulatory environment and the potential for future regulation is an important consideration in the evaluation of any particular media market. Monitoring the regulatory climate is an ongoing task in many media industries.

Impact of Technology

The media industries are heavily dependent on technology. In the analysis of media markets, an effort should be made to understand the role technology plays in a particular industry. Technological change occurs rapidly in the communication industries. Like regulatory change, advances in technology can have both positive and negative outcomes. For example, high-tech, automated, robotically controlled television cameras can operate flawlessly, but they also displace human camera operators. Satellite-delivered radio formats provide professional-quality radio in many smaller markets but at the same time reduce a station's work force to a handful of employees.

From an economic standpoint, changes in technology will likely mean increases in equipment expenditures. When the newspaper industry moved from the old Linotype typesetting machine to computerized layout and design, it resulted in massive purchases of new equipment. In covering television news, a continuing transition from film to videotape to instant coverage of events via satellite and microwave transmission has taken place since the 1970s. In short, media industries must maintain efficient and modern methods to produce and distribute their content products with the highest possible quality.

The impact of technology must also be considered from the standpoint of the consumer. The decision by recording companies to invest heavily in the compact disc (CD) as the latest format for sound recordings was based in part on the belief that consumers would want the higher-quality sound delivered by a digital audio system. However, this change also drove up consumers' cost for individual recordings and conversion to CD-based systems. Fiber optics and digital compression techniques can provide a television world of more than 500 channels of content, yet many users may prefer only a handful of channels.

The mass media are technologically driven industries and are heavily influenced by technological revolution. From an economic perspective, media industries should be examined in terms of their technical efficiency as well as their ability to produce media content of consistently high technical quality.

Technology should also be evaluated based on its ability to enhance a particular market, as well as the cost of implementing new technologies. Later chapters examine industries where technological change is most likely and how it may affect market performance.

Summary

This chapter summarizes various approaches used in evaluating media markets. This information enables you to understand the intricate processes at work in media economics among buyers and sellers. The ability to evaluate media markets is also important if you desire to invest in some part of the mass media or if your professional goal is to gain employment in the mass media. Overall, a better understanding of the relationship between media and society and how economic factors impact that relationship is gained.

Evaluating a media industry first involves defining a particular market, which can be a difficult task. Careful examination and precise definitions are needed to clarify a particular market. A second step involves a process of determining what major companies are engaged in a particular market. Several reference resources are available to help in this process. Third, media markets should be evaluated in terms of the level of concentration that exists in the market. Several means of measuring concentration were introduced in this chapter, including concentration ratios, the Lorenz Curve, and the Herfindahl-Hirschman Index.

The chapter also introduced tools to examine individual companies, including an index of corporate diversification and a discussion of relevant financial ratios. The indexes and ratios presented in the chapter offer different ways to interpret the economic viability of individual firms and industries.

All media industries are affected by regulation to some degree. Regulators use different goals for different industries, and regulations have an impact on market structure, conduct and performance. Many industries attempt to minimize the impact of regulation by the presence of trade associations and lobbying efforts.

Technology drives much of the mass media, and the impacts of technology must be examined in regard to how technology can affect market economics and performance as well as the pool for labor and talent in the media and how consumers respond to new technology. As with regulation, technology can have both positive and negative effects on media markets.

Understanding the criteria used in evaluating media industries presented in this chapter provides for a more comprehensive analysis of media markets and industries. Later chapters utilize this information in discussing specific media industries.

Discussion Questions

1. In order to analyze a media market, we must first define a market. How do we define a media market?
2. What are some of the resources we can use to find information about media industries? About different media companies?
3. Discuss the different types of concentration. What tools can we use to measure concentration of market share?
4. What is corporate diversification? How is it measured?
5. Discuss different types of financial ratios used to analyze firms and industries. What do the ratios tell us? How can they be used?
6. Why is regulation used in the media industries? What is the purpose for regulation?
7. How does technology affect the mass media? How does technology affect society?

Exercises

1. Find a media industry you are interested in researching, using *Standard and Poor's Industry Surveys*. Using the financial information on the firms listed in your industry, calculate the top four and top eight concentration ratios (if there are eight firms) and the HHI for your industry. Is your industry concentrated? Explain.
2. Obtain a copy of a corporate annual report for a media company you are interested in. Using the materials presented in this text and the financial data in the corporate report, calculate a diversification index and at least three different ratios (e.g., growth, performance, liquidity) for the company. What does this information tell you about the company?
3. Review a recent trade magazine for an industry you are interested in (e.g., *Broadcasting and Cable, Editor and Publisher, Radio and Records*) and look for articles dealing with current or pending regulation. What did you learn from your research?
4. Using the same trade magazine, look for articles that discuss new or anticipated advances in technology. What does the article suggest as to the impact of the new technology on the industry? What, if anything, does it say about the impact the technology may have on society?

References

Albarran, A. B., and J. Dimmick. (1996). Concentration and economics of multiformity in the communication industries. *Journal of Media Economics* 9 (4): 41–50.

Albarran, A. B., and J. Porco. (1990). Measuring and analyzing diversification of corporations involved in pay cable. *Journal of Media Economics* 3 (2): 3–14.

Bagdikian, B. H. (2000). *The Media Monopoly*. 6th ed. Boston: Beacon Press.

Bates, B. J. (1993). Concentration in local television markets. *Journal of Media Economics* 6 (1): 3–22.

Dimmick, J., and M. Wallschlaeger. (1986). Measuring corporate diversification: A case study of new media ventures by television network parent companies. *Journal of Broadcasting and Electronic Media* 30 (1): 1–14.

Litman, B. R. (1979). The television networks, competition and program diversity. *Journal of Broadcasting* 23:393–410.

———. (1985). Economic methods of broadcasting research. In *Broadcasting Research Methods*, edited by J. R. Dominick and J. E. Fletcher. Boston: Allyn and Bacon, pp. 107–122.

Owen, B. M., J. H. Beebe and W. G. Manning. (1974). *Television Economics*. Lexington, Mass.: D. C. Heath.

Picard, R. G. (1988). Measures of concentration in the daily newspaper industry. *Journal of Media Economics* 1 (2): 61–74.

———. (1989). *Media Economics*. Beverly Hills, Calif.: Sage.

Schiller, H. I. (1981). *Who knows: Information in the Age of the Fortune 500*. Norwood, N.J.: Random House.

III

The Broadcast,
Cable and Satellite
Television and
Internet Industries

5

THE RADIO INDUSTRY

After reading this chapter, you will understand:

- The major players, market structure and economic characteristics of the radio industry

- Key historical trends in the evolution of the radio industry

- How regulatory and technological forces are reshaping the radio industry

The radio industry is the oldest of the electronic media industries in the United States. Its roots extend back to the mid-1800s, when numerous inventors attempted to transmit the early dots and dashes of Morse code through the air. Eventually, the trials and tribulations of these early pioneers would harness the technology in order to create radio transmitters and receivers. By the 1920s, the new medium of radio would capture the imagination and attention of the American public and fundamentally change the way society consumes information and entertainment (Matelski 1993).

Eight decades later, the radio industry is still attracting audiences. The industry has changed considerably since KDKA, the first officially licensed radio station, broadcast the national election returns of 1920 to a handful of households in Pittsburgh. Today, more than 9,700 commercial stations operate in the United States, reaching an estimated 75 percent of the total population every day (Radio Advertising Bureau 2001).

Industry Trends

Throughout its history, the radio industry has been forced to change and adapt as various social, technological and regulatory trends have affected its economic viability. A discussion of the entire history of the radio industry is beyond the scope of this chapter. However, five trends illustrate the resilient qualities of the radio industry: (1) advertising, (2) the development of networks, (3) FM broadcasting, (4) the advent of television and (5) changes in ownership rules.

Advertising

The sale of time for advertising purposes—or *toll broadcasting*, as it was originally called—began in 1922 on WEAF, New York, a station owned by AT&T (Barnouw 1966). The ability of radio to attract local advertisers who desired access to audiences gave the nascent radio industry the economic base needed for growth. Prior to the use of advertising, the only way that radio stations made money was through the sale of radio receivers. Hence, many of the early companies involved in radio station ownership (e.g., Westinghouse, General Electric, American Marconi) manufactured radio receivers. Advertising gave radio stations another source of revenue, which would be far more lucrative than the sale of radio sets. In time, advertising would develop into national and regional, as well as local, markets.

Development of Networks

By the mid-1920s, radio stations were in a scramble for programming. Most of the early programming was live, and many stations operated only limited hours. The Radio Corporation of America (RCA), the electronics giant that was formed primarily to manufacture and sell radio receivers, developed a programming service that could be linked to other radio stations around the country. Not surprisingly, RCA hoped that the new service would sell more radio sets.

In 1926, the National Broadcasting Company (NBC) radio network debuted to provide programming to its affiliated stations (Albarran and Pitts 2001). A year later, the Columbia Broadcasting System (CBS) began operation. In later years, NBC would expand by developing an additional network (renamed the NBC "red" and "blue" networks). The growth of networks created a national market for radio, enabling advertisers to reach large audiences across the nation. The practice of networking stabilized the industry and created a national audience. Radio networks still exist today, although the programming primarily consists of news and feature materials.

FM Broadcasting

After years of experimentation, FM (frequency modulation) broadcasting began in 1941 (Matelski 1993). The FM signal quality was superior to the original AM (amplitude modulation) signals, although the audience shift to FM from AM would be very slow.

By 1978, the FM radio audience outnumbered the AM audience for the first time. Since then, FM radio has come to dominate the radio industry. As of 2001, FM listening accounted for about 85 percent of the total time spent listening to radio. FM stations typically rank as the most profitable stations in most radio markets.

Advent of Television

Television's emergence from the post-World War II years of the late 1940s to the rapid growth in the 1950s brought considerable hardships to the radio industry. Popular programs and performers, along with the advertisers who sponsored them, made the transition from radio to the new visual television medium. And as programs, performers and advertisers left radio, so did the audience—especially during prime-time hours. The radio industry was forced to adapt. No longer the primary distributor of national programming and advertising, the radio industry recognized that to survive, it had to rely on the local market for economic support. Radio stations began to differentiate themselves by adopting different formats—for example, news, talk or specific kinds of music, such as Top 40, country, "classic" rock, or "urban"—to appeal to different audiences and the local advertisers targeting those audiences.

Changes in Ownership Rules

The number of radio stations an individual or group could own changed numerous times during radio's history. The concept of scarcity was used by the Federal Communications Commission (FCC) to place limits on the number of stations controlled by a single owner. But during the 1990s, the ownership rules were modified several times, culminating with sweeping changes embodied in the Telecommunications Act of 1996. That legislation ended national ownership caps, instead enforcing limits at the local level. The result of this regulation has been rapid consolidation across the radio industry. These changes are discussed in more detail later in the chapter.

These trends illustrate some of the major changes the radio industry has encountered over the years. At the beginning of the 21st century, the radio industry enjoyed strong economic performance, with the 1990s having brought record levels of advertising sales.

The Radio Market

The contemporary radio industry consists of various markets operating simultaneously. The local market represents the geographic area or region where local radio stations target listeners and advertisers. And within each local market, smaller submarkets can be found, such as the submarket for a particular type of listener (in terms of demographic qualities) or the submarket for those stations carrying a similar type of format.

Consider the radio stations in the market where you currently reside. You likely will find a mix of AM and FM stations offering a variety of different music and talk formats. In one sense, all these stations compete against one another for listeners and advertisers. Upon closer analysis, however, you probably will find some stations targeting younger audiences, while others may target middle-aged and older listeners. Some stations will appeal more to men than women or vice versa. Others may target a certain ethnic group and perhaps even be broadcast in that group's primary language if it is something other than English. The stations differ in format, technical characteristics and demographic targets.

A second market that prevails in the radio industry is the national market. There are two possible ways to define the national radio market. One is by the total number of listeners reached on a national basis by radio group operators (see Table 5.1). The listing of the top 25 radio groups is in a constant state of flux due to mergers and acquisitions.

Another way to define the national radio market is by the national radio networks. There are approximately 25 radio networks, which together form a market that serves national advertisers and individual radio stations. The major national radio networks are listed in Table 5.2. Some of these networks provide specific types of news, features and other programs, whereas other networks provide a full, 24-hour schedule of programming. All of the national radio networks are fed by satellite to their affiliates. The market share of the national radio networks can be measured by the number of stations that are affiliated with each network, by the number of listeners each service can reach or by the amount of advertising dollars each network generates.

Demand by Consumers and Advertisers

There are three major types of demand observable in the radio industry: (1) demand by consumers, (2) demand by advertisers and (3) demand for the stations themselves by potential owners and investors. Here, we focus on the demand by consumers and advertisers. The demand for stations will be discussed later in the chapter.

Consumer demand is best indicated by statistics generated by the radio industry. According to the Radio Advertising Bureau (2001), 99 percent of all

Table 5.1. Radio industry group owners (2000)

Group	Number of Stations
ABC Radio, Inc.	52
Barnstable Broadcasting, Inc.	25
Beasley Broadcasting Group, Inc.	42
Bonneville International Corp.	18
Citadel Communications Corp.	207
Clear Channel Communication, Inc.	1018
Cox Radio, Inc.	83
Cumulas Media, Inc.	274
Emmis Communications Corp.	23
Entercom Communications Corp.	98
Entravision Communications Corp.	66
Greater Media, Inc.	14
Hispanic Broadcasting Corp.	46
Infinity Broadcasting Corp.	187
Inner City Broadcasting Corp.	17
Jefferson-Pilot Communication Co.	17
Journal Broadcasting Group, Inc.	36
Nassau Broadcasting Partners LP	31
Radio One, Inc.	51
Regent Communications, Inc.	47
Saga Communications, Inc.	51
Sandusky Radio	10
Spanish Broadcasting System, Inc.	25
Susquehanna Radio Corp.	29
Tribune Broadcasting Co.	4

Source: Adapted from Top 25 radio groups (2000, September 4). *Broadcasting and Cable*, pp. 50-62.

U.S. households have a radio, with an average of 5.6 radios per household. Radios are also found in 96 percent of all automobiles in the United States. Radio reaches an estimated 95 percent of all persons age 12 or older each week, with each individual averaging over 3 hours of daily listening and 5 hours of weekend listening.

One of the strong growth areas in the radio industry is Hispanic radio. The growth of the Hispanic population in the United States has increased demand for stations catering to Hispanic audiences. Advertisers need to help market products to Hispanic listeners. According to the Radio Advertising Bureau, listening among Hispanics age 12 or older ranks among the highest for all radio listeners.

Overall, radio advertising revenue has grown steadily. Table 5.3 lists radio revenues from selected years in the categories of local, spot (national advertising on local stations) and network advertising. Several trends are observable. First, total radio revenues more than doubled from 1980 ($3.541 billion) to 1990 ($8.839 billion), and doubled again by 1999 ($17.680 billion). Second, local ad revenues remain the most important, followed by spot and

Table 5.2. Examples of radio networks

ABC Radio Networks
    ABC Contemporary
    ABC Direction
    ABC Advantage Network
    ABC Entertainment
    ABC International
    ABC Rock
    ESPN Radio
    Radio Disney
American Urban Radio Networks
AP Radio Networks
    AP All News Radio
    AP Network News
CBS, Inc.
    CBS News
    CBS Sports
    CBS Station Group
Jones Radio Network
United Press International
USA Radio Networks
    Daily Programs
    Weekend Programs
    Best of USA @ Nite
    News Products
Westwood One
    News
    Talk
    Sports
    Entertainment
National Public Radio (NPR)

Source: Adapted from *Broadcasting and Cable Yearbook* (2000), pp. F-54-F-59.

network. Veronis, Suhler and Associates (2000) have projected that radio advertising revenues will grow at an annual rate of 9.5 percent by 2004 to reach just over $26 billion.

Major Players in the Radio Industry

Federal regulations historically have limited the number of radio stations a single group or individual could own. The passage of the Telecommunications Act of 1996 removed all national ownership limits in the radio industry while maintaining caps on local ownership in individual markets. In short, the larger the market, the more stations an individual or company may own.

For example, in markets with 45 or more commercial stations, a single company may own up to 8 stations, with no more than 5 in a single class (AM or FM). If the market has 30 to 44 stations, the number drops to a total of 7,

Table 5.3. Radio advertising revenues (millions of dollars)

Year	Local	Spot	Network	Total
1980	$ 2.643	$ 740	$ 158	$ 3.541
1985	4.915	1.319	329	6.563
1990	6.780	1.626	433	8.839
1991	6.578	1.573	440	8.591
1992	6.899	1.479	388	8.766
1993	7.526	1.627	407	9.560
1994	8.370	1.860	411	10.650
1995	9.120	1.920	430	11.470
1996	9.850	2.090	470	12.410
1997	10.740	2.410	650	13.800
1998	11.920	2.770	740	15.430
1999	13.590	3.210	880	17.680

Source: Adapted from Radio Advertising Bureau (2001).

with a maximum of 4 in the same class. For markets with 15 to 29 stations, the numbers drop to a total of 6 and a maximum 4 of a kind; for markets with 14 or fewer stations, the numbers drop further to 5 total and no more than 3 of a kind (or up to half the stations in the market). If a company also owns television stations in the same local market, the limits on radio ownership drop. For details on cross-ownership restrictions, see Sedman (2001).

Consolidation has slowed somewhat since the megamergers of the late 1990s have subsided. Still, consolidation is anticipated to increase in medium and smaller markets. As Table 5.1 illustrates, the top five companies in the radio industry are Clear Channel, Cumulus, Citadel, Infinity and Entercom. As for national radio networks, illustrated in Table 5.2, Disney-owned ABC Radio leads the industry through its multiple network divisions and its 10 national formats. Other leaders in the radio network market include Westwood One (owned by Infinity Broadcasting Corp.) and USA Radio Networks.

Market Structure

Two types of market structure are commonly found in radio: oligopoly and monopolistic competition. Because there are so many individual local markets, the type of structure is dependent on analyzing the number of owners in the market compared to the total number of stations. Since the passage of the Telecommunications Act of 1996, many local markets have moved away from a monopolistic competition structure toward an oligopoly structure. In fact, many stations in large and medium markets are part of clusters, where the activities of several stations are managed at one central location. In a limited number of cases during the late 1990s, the Antitrust Division of the U.S.

Department of Justice (DOJ) scrutinized some mergers because of concerns over control of the local advertising market. The DOJ consistently refused to approve any mergers where a single entity would control 75 percent or more of the local advertising revenue.

At the national market (radio networks), monopolistic competition is still evident. Although some consolidation of radio networks occurred in the 1990s, there are still enough different owners to maintain a monopolistic competition structure.

Market Concentration

Prior to the passage of the Telecommunications Act of 1996, market concentration measures in the radio industry routinely indicated lower levels of concentration at the local level because ownership was limited to a maximum of 40 stations under the old rules. This is no longer the case. In measuring concentration in the radio industry, the CR4 and CR8 ratios offer the easiest interpretation, particularly in assessing national concentration. In 1995, the top four radio companies controlled 58 percent of total industry revenue, while the top eight companies controlled 81 percent. By 1999, the CR4 ratio had increased to 77 percent, while the CR8 ratio had increased to 88 percent. Clearly, both the CR4 and CR8 measures reflect a highly concentrated industry at the national level.

With the increase in concentration, barriers to entry in radio are more formidable. In most markets, there are no available frequencies for new stations. Thus, the only way to enter the market is by acquiring an existing station. The frenzied pace of radio station mergers and acquisitions from 1996 through 1998 created significant demand among owners, resulting in higher prices for stations.

Demand for Radio Stations

Radio station sales from 1995 through 2000 are listed in Table 5.4. In 1995, there were a total of 568 radio station transactions. In February 1996, the Telecommunications Act was signed into law and the number of transactions jumped significantly, as did prices for stations. In 1996, a total of 254 AM stations were sold at an average price of $837,000. For FM stations, a total of 399 stations changed hands at an average price of $5.5 million, more than doubling the average price paid in 1995 ($2.15 million). Recognize that these are average prices—meaning that in larger markets, the sale of a radio station can reach well into the millions of dollars.

The consolidation of the radio industry has led to high prices for stations and to a decrease in the number of group owners. The growing consolidation

Table 5.4. Radio station transactions (AM/FM breakdown 1995–2000)

	AM		FM	
Year	Number of Transactions	Average Station Price	Number of Transactions	Average Station Price
1995	207	$497,196	361	$2,156,306
1996	254	837,877	471	5,554,318
1997	326	1,532,696	399	4,926,845
1998	243	2,389,151	339	3,011,710
1999	213	1,116,554	169	8,748,794
2000	133	3,023,168	192	8,593,256

Source: Compiled from industry trade sources and Federal Communications Commission data.

of the radio industry, along with the high prices for stations, pose significant barriers to entry for new competitors.

Government Regulation

Because the federal government through the FCC licenses radio stations, all stations must adhere to certain policies. Deregulation of the radio industry during the 1970s and 1980s eliminated many bureaucratic requirements for the industry, but several important policies remain. For example, radio stations must apply for renewal of their licenses every eight years in order to continue broadcasting. On an annual basis, stations must pay operating fees as required by the FCC, depending on the class of station they operate and their annual revenue. On a daily basis, stations must have operators on duty who carry restricted permits, maintain a public file of station information for inspection by local citizens, meet minimum programming requirements such as presenting a station identification at the top of each hour, and monitor and maintain technical facilities (transmitter power, operational tower lights, etc.).

During the late 1990s, the FCC attempted to create a new class of low-powered radio stations initially labeled "microradio." The idea was to allow new stations to begin broadcasting with power limited to 1,000 watts. From the outset, broadcasters fought against the new class of stations, arguing that the new service would cause technical interference and add to a heavily competitive radio marketplace. In the end, the lobbyists and industry prevailed. A new class of stations was established, known as LPFM (low powered FM), but with very limited power (maximum of 100 watts) and only noncommercial status. It will take several years to determine the success of LPFM as an FCC directive.

Technological Forces Affecting Radio

Two major technological forces that have had an impact on the radio industry are the launch of *digital audio radio services* (DARS) and the growth of the Internet and its ability to offer streaming (continuous transmission) of audio content and other enhanced services.

DARS

Originally approved by the FCC during the mid-1990s, DARS finally began limited operation in 2001. The two initial competitors, XM Radio and Sirius, offered a package of digital radio formats to subscribers for a monthly fee distributed via satellite. As the services debuted, the average monthly fee was around 0 to 2 a month. Designed initially for the automobile, DARS was expected to become standard equipment on new cars by about 2004.

Positioned as "commercial-free," the services provide multiple channels of digital music for commuters seeking an alternative to local radio stations or internal car stereo music. The radio industry is concerned about the potential of DARS to siphon away listeners if the services grow in popularity. The key questions are: Will consumers pay for the new service? Will they prefer DARS content to local radio?

The Internet

The Internet provides another means of distribution for the existing radio industry and another source of competition for listeners and advertisers. Most existing radio stations have web pages that detail programming, promotional activities and other features. Many stations now stream live content via the Internet, a practice that started in the late 1990s and was adopted by stations all over the world (Bulkeley 1998). Computer users can now listen to radio stations anywhere in the world with an Internet connection.

But the Internet has also brought along two new sources of competition for existing radio stations. A number of Internet-only radio stations are now in operation, with no offline counterpart. The number of Internet-only stations changes rapidly because stations frequently come and go. Internet-only stations know that to entice existing radio listeners, they must offer a qualitatively different product (Weber 1999).

Finally, the Internet has led to the development of *personal radio*. A personal radio service utilizes thousands of digital music files stored on a server. In a personal radio system, the user sets up a listener profile through an existing service. The user enters his or her music preferences by either choosing a genre or selecting individual artists. By adding a zip code to the profile, the listener can also obtain local weather. Eventually, the services can offer other types of information, such as news.

Internet-only stations and personal radio will take time to draw listeners away from traditional radio stations. But it is important to recognize that these new innovations represent other forms of competition for audiences and advertisers to the existing radio industry.

The Economic Future of Radio

As the oldest form of electronic media, the radio industry has adapted throughout history to various forces that have affected its economic potential. In every case, the radio industry has not only survived but also strengthened. The contemporary radio industry is a mature industry with a promising future.

Advertising revenue is expected to rise faster for the radio industry than for many other types of media industries through 2004 (Veronis, Suhler and Associates 2000). Radio remains an efficient advertising buy when compared with other media, and it is superior in its ability to target specific demographic groups through various program formats.

AM radio, which lost audience during the 1970s and 1980s, was rejuvenated by a host of syndicated talk shows emerging during the 1990s (e.g., Rush Limbaugh, Dr. Laura Schlesinger, Don Imus, Gordon Liddy) who brought listeners back to the medium. FM radio continues to hold audiences with a variety of music formats, and radio networks have expanded over the past decade to include 24-hour packaged formats and a range of feature programs and news.

The Telecommunications Act of 1996 radically altered the structure of the radio industry, leading to huge conglomerates owning hundreds of stations. This rapid expansion and geographical clustering has given the industry a stronger economic base in local markets. The radio industry has the opportunity to develop new revenue streams through the Internet and other new technologies.

Summary

The radio industry is the oldest of the electronic media industries and certainly the most resilient. The radio industry introduced and perfected the practices of advertising, networking and programming, which would form the basis of broadcasting. More than 10,000 commercial stations are in operation, reaching more than 99 percent of all households in the United States.

The radio industry operates in two distinct markets. At the local level, stations compete for local listeners and advertisers attracted to the programming formats used by individual stations. Nationally, radio networks compete for audiences and advertisers through news and programming services as well as 24-hour satellite formats.

Throughout the local and national markets, the radio industry is moving away from a monopolistic competitive structure to that of an oligopoly. Measures of concentration have risen significantly since 1996, indicating a shift in market structure.

In addition to the demand for radio by consumers and advertisers, there is also demand for the stations as investment properties. The high average prices for stations, coupled with the lack of open channels for broadcasting, create financial barriers of entry for new competitors in the industry.

Regulation has changed the structure of the radio industry, resulting in a number of companies consolidating into two major groups controlled by Clear Channel Communications and Infinity Broadcasting. In terms of technology, the new DARS poses a competitive threat to traditional radio. Likewise, the Internet offers the opportunity for stations to stream content while also offering opportunities for new competitors via Internet-only radio stations and personal radio services.

Estimates for advertiser demand through 2004 remain strong, with a projected 9.5 percent annual growth rate. With personalities like Dr. Laura and Rush Limbaugh, talk radio has flourished on AM radio, slowing the loss of listeners to FM. However, FM continues to dominate in terms of total listening. Further consolidation within the industry will be less dramatic, with most changes taking place in medium and small markets. Overall, the radio industry continues to adapt and change, as it has throughout its colorful history.

Discussion Questions

1. How has radio changed over the years? What factors have affected radio's economic development over time?
2. Discuss the types of markets in which the radio industry competes with other suppliers for audiences and advertisers.
3. How is demand observed in the radio industry? Discuss the types of demand and provide an example of each.
4. What impact have changes in radio ownership regulations had on the structure of the radio industry? What changes have you observed in the market where you live?

Exercises

1. Analyze the radio stations in the market in which you currently live by gathering the following information:
   a. Technical qualities of each station (class, power, etc.)
   b. Format of the station, call letters and logo

    c. Target audience

    d. Advertisers

    e. Promotion and marketing efforts to increase public awareness of each station

    f. Internet website, types of content offered via the Internet

    g. Owner of the station

2. Review local periodicals for your market for the past five years to determine how many radio stations have been sold, the price for each station and who the new owner is. How many of the owners in your market are found in Table 5.1?

3. Determine whether any stations in your market are managed as a cluster. If possible, try to talk with a member of station management to understand how cluster management works.

4. Determine how many radio networks are present in your market, and write a brief summary of the programming presented by one of the networks. The network can be a news and programming service, or it can be a satellite-delivered format.

References

Albarran, A. B., and G. G. Pitts. (2001). *The Radio Broadcasting Industry*. Boston: Allyn and Bacon.

Barnouw, E. (1966). *A Tower in Babel: A History of Broadcasting in the United States*. Vol. 1. New York: Oxford University Press.

Bulkeley, W. M. (1998). Radio stations make waves on the web. *Wall Street Journal*, 23 July, B1.

Matelski, M. J. (1993). Resilient radio. *Media Studies Journal* 7 (3): 1–13.

Radio Advertising Bureau. (2001). *Radio Marketing Guide and Factbook for Advertisers 2000–2001*. Available online at http://www.rab.com.

Sedman, D. (2001). Radio regulation. In *The Radio Broadcasting Industry*, edited by A. B. Albarran and G. G. Pitts. Boston: Allyn and Bacon, pp. 48–65.

Top 25 radio groups. (2000). *Broadcasting and Cable*, 4 September, 50–62.

Veronis, Suhler and Associates. (2000). *Communications Industry Forecast*. New York: Veronis, Suhler and Associates.

Weber, T. E. (1999). Web radio: No antenna required. *Wall Street Journal*, 28 July, B1, B4.

6

THE TELEVISION INDUSTRY

After reading this chapter, you should:

- Be able to identify the major players, market structure and economic characteristics of the television industry

- Understand how networks engage in vertical integration and economies of scale

- Recognize the different types of demand in the television industry

- Understand the importance of advertising to the television industry

- Recognize how regulatory decisions have previously limited but currently favor television industry economics

Despite a continual assault from new forms of video entertainment for audiences and advertisers since the 1970s, the broadcast television industry continues to dominate the electronic media landscape. The "big four" networks of ABC, CBS, NBC and Fox are the leaders of the television industry, operating in an interdependent and rather tenuous relationship with local affiliates who carry the majority of the network program schedule. The programming enables the networks to capture the majority of the viewers and the advertising dollars targeted for the television industry.

The television industry grew rapidly in the United States during the post-World War II years of the late 1940s, thanks to its older sibling, the radio industry. As discussed in Chapter 5, the radio industry established and refined the practices of networking, programming and advertising that would easily adapt to the new television medium. By the mid-1950s, television had become the primary source of entertainment and information in most households and had established itself as a major influence on American culture.

Network television became such a powerful social and economic force that by the early 1970s, a series of regulatory actions by the United States Congress and the Federal Communications Commission (FCC) were enacted to stimulate competition in the television industry and to limit network power. In 1970, the networks were stripped of any meaningful financial interest in the lucrative syndication programming market for off-network series. The following year, the prime-time access rule (PTAR) was adopted to limit the number of hours of network programming in prime time (8 to 11 p.m. Eastern Standard Time [EST]) and to encourage more local programming. Later, cable television systems were cleared of hurdles that restricted the importation of distant signals in local television markets.

Regulatory actions and new competition for audiences from cable television and the videocassette recorder (VCR) resulted in a loss of market share for the television networks throughout the 1980s. Further competition came from independent television stations, whose position was strengthened by the growth of cable television. Independents suddenly achieved visual parity with network affiliates in cable households. Independents were also able to utilize off-network series during the access time period, as well as to showcase first-run syndicated programs such as *Baywatch*.

Larger chains of television stations were created following a 1985 FCC decision to allow TV owners to increase the number of stations they could own from 7 to 12, or up to a maximum of 25 percent of the national television audience (Albarran 1989). Included among these new chains was Fox Broadcasting Company, which acquired the former Metromedia television stations in 1986 and would later become the cornerstone for the Fox network.

Capital Cities Communications Inc. merged with ABC in 1986, the same year NBC and parent company RCA were acquired by General Electric (Auletta 1991). CBS would undergo changes in its management structure in 1987, after fending off two hostile takeover attempts, including one from cable visionary Ted Turner (Auletta 1991). In 1987, the Fox network officially became a "fourth" network, offering a limited prime-time schedule, which would later grow to include all seven nights by the start of the 1994 season.

Competition for audiences and advertisers continued to intensify, and the recession years of 1991 and 1992 resulted in huge economic losses for the networks. Still, the networks were able to maintain at least a dominant share of the national television audience. In 1994, prime-time viewing of network affiliate stations was estimated at 72 percent across all television households (Nielsen Media Research 1994).

Unrest in the television industry continued through the 1990s. Fox established itself as a formidable power in the television industry, first by securing the coveted National Football League's National Football Conference games, which had aired on CBS for years, and then by acquiring a number of stronger affiliates in several major markets.

Fox added further upheaval in the television industry in May 1994 with the announcement that New World Communications would be switching all 12 of its television stations to the Fox network, secured by a $500 million investment from Fox. Ten of the 12 stations were in the top 50 markets. In several key markets, CBS, NBC and ABC were suddenly without affiliates. The announcement triggered a mad scramble during the summer of 1994 by all the networks to enter into long-term affiliation agreements to secure affiliate relations. Individual stations were able to negotiate stronger compensation payments as a result of Fox's move, improving their economic position.

Two new national broadcast networks began programming in January 1995: United/Paramount Network (UPN), and the WB (Warner Brothers) network. Paxson Communications launched PaxNet in 1998. Like Fox, these new "netlets" began with a limited prime-time schedule. Network ownership also evolved; in 1995 the Walt Disney Company acquired Capital Cities/ABC, while Westinghouse acquired CBS. In 1999, Viacom, by then the sole owner of UPN, acquired CBS, becoming the first company to be allowed to own two broadcast networks.

Much like the radio industry, the television industry has undergone a series of changes and transitions since the 1940s. The broadcast television industry faces many challenges in the years ahead as it continues to encounter competition from other video services. By 2001, television stations were struggling with ways to attract new revenue streams, making the transition to digital television and facing uncertainty with network-affiliate relationships.

The Television Market

The television industry consists of several different markets. At the local level, television stations (network affiliates, independents and public stations) compete with one another in the market for audiences, as well as with other close substitutes to the broadcast channels—most notably the cable channels. Commercial stations also compete with other stations and substitutes as a supplier of time for local advertisers. The number of competitors varies in local television markets depending on how many television channels are allocated to each market by the FCC. In general, larger markets are awarded a higher number of commercial television channels than are medium and small markets. The top 20 local television markets are listed in Table 6.1.

At the national level, the seven broadcast networks (ABC, CBS, NBC, Fox, UPN, WB and PaxNet) also compete in a dual product marketplace for

Table 6.1. Top 20 television markets

Location	Rank	TV Households
New York	1	6,692,370
Los Angeles	2	5,006,380
Chicago	3	3,070,830
Philadelphia	4	2,661,360
San Francisco–Oakland–San Jose	5	2,253,220
Boston	6	2,104,900
Washington, D.C.	7	1,855,440
Dallas–Ft. Worth	8	1,816,700
Detroit	9	1,735,340
Houston	10	1,510,580
Atlanta	11	1,510,340
Cleveland	12	1,446,970
Seattle–Tacoma	13	1,427,750
Minneapolis–St. Paul	14	1,389,420
Tampa–St. Petersburg, Sarasota	15	1,384,150
Miami–Ft. Lauderdale	16	1,296,800
Pittsburgh	17	1,141,830
St. Louis	18	1,109,090
Sacramento–Stockton–Modesto	19	1,099,950
Phoenix	20	1,097,480

Source: Adapted from *Broadcasting and Cable Yearbook* (2000).

audiences and advertisers. Demand for audiences at the national level is assessed by audience ratings compiled by Nielsen Media Research and other industry sources. Advertiser demand is available from different sources, including advertising agencies and independent firms.

Consumer Demand for Television

According to Nielsen Media Research (2000), 98 percent of all households in the United States have at least one television, with 76 percent having more than one set. These television sets on average are turned on for more than seven hours per day. Household viewing levels (referred to as households using television, or HUT) rise throughout the day for the television industry and peak during the prime-time hours of 8 to 11 p.m. EST. Sunday evening is the most popular night for TV viewing, followed by Monday evening. The least popular nights for watching television are Friday and Saturday.

Nielsen Media Research (2000) reports that across all TV households, approximately 54 percent of the total viewing time is divided among the networks and their affiliate stations. This is a major decline from the 1993–1994 season, when the network affiliates garnered 72 percent of the viewing. The drop shows the impact of cable and satellite households on the TV viewing audience.

Advertiser Demand for Television

Revenues from advertisers come from several markets. At the national level, advertisers buy time from the networks in a two-step process. In the *upfront market*, advertising time is purchased during the early summer months for the upcoming fall season (Albarran 2002). The networks want to sell as much of their inventory (spot purchases) as possible in the upfront market. Historically, the upfront market has presold as much as 80 percent of the total network time for the upcoming season. Unsold time is retained and offered during the television season; this market is called the *scatter market*. The scatter market functions throughout the television season and, depending on demand, may sell for higher or lower prices as compared to the upfront market.

Selling of advertising takes place throughout the year by local broadcast stations. Local advertising is offered to local businesses, whereas national spot advertising is available for national advertisers who purchase time in local markets through advertising agencies and representative firms. Certain time periods are more lucrative than others for local stations. In particular, the "sweeps" months of February, May, July and November represent good opportunities for advertisers, as programmers offer their best shows to the audience. Prices for advertising often rise during the sweeps period as a result of high demand by local advertisers.

Advertising on television is a billion-dollar industry. Table 6.2 lists advertising spent on television for selected years. Notice that all categories experienced steady growth through the second half of the 1990s. Veronis, Suhler and Associates (2000) have projected that television advertising at the network level will grow at a rate of 5.2 percent through 2004, compared with a growth rate of 4.1 percent for local stations, reaching a combined estimate of $48.1 billion.

Table 6.2. Television advertising (in billions of dollars spent)

Year	Network	Spot	Local	Total
1993	$10,209	$ 7,800	$ 8,435	$26,444
1994	10,942	8,993	9,464	29,399
1995	11,600	9,119	9,985	30,704
1996	13,081	9,803	10,944	33,828
1997	13,020	9,999	11,436	34,455
1998	13,736	10,659	12,169	36,564
1999	13,961	10,500	12,680	37,141

Source: Adapted from Television Bureau of Advertising website (www.tvb.org).

Major Players in the Television Industry

FCC regulations limit the number of stations a single group or individual may own by an audience *reach cap*. The reach cap limits a single owner to a maximum of 35 percent of the national audience. The reach cap is determined by totaling the percentage of television households available in each local market.

At the time of this book's publication, the FCC was considering modifying the cap. Any increase would result in further consolidation, especially among the networks. The reach cap became a major issue for the television industry in 2000–2001, leading to a dispute among networks and affiliates (Flint 2001). Affiliates did not want the networks to become larger by adding more stations; the networks wanted to grow. The issue led to several networks (CBS, NBC, Fox) leaving membership in the National Association of Broadcasters (NAB) after the NAB endorsed retention of the present cap. Most television stations are part of group ownership, with the networks holding strong positions in the industry. The top 25 television group owners are listed in Table 6.3.

Table 6.3. Top 25 television group owners (2001)

Group	Rank	Number of Stations
Paramount/CBS Group (Viacom)	1	35
Fox Television Stations, Inc.*	2	23
Paxson Communications Corp	3	60
Tribune Broadcasting Co.	4	23
NBC, Inc.	5	13
ABC, Inc.	6	10
Chris-Craft Industries/United Television Inc.*	7	10
Gannett Broadcasting Division	8	22
Hearst-Argyle Television, Inc.	9	32
USA Broadcasting, Inc.	10	13
Sinclair Broadcasting Group, Inc.	11	54
Belo Corp.	12	20
Univision Communications, Inc.	13	12
Young Broadcasting, Inc.	14	16
Telemundo Group, Inc.	15	8
Cox Broadcasting, Inc.	16	12
Meredith Broadcasting, Inc.	17	12
E. W. Scripps Co.	18	10
Shop at Home, Inc.	19	6
Raycom Media, Inc.	20	34
Post-Newsweek Stations, Inc.	21	6
Media General Broadcast Group	22	26
Pappas Telecasting Cos.	23	16
LIN Television Corp.	24	19
Benedek Broadcasting Corp.	25	26

Source: Adapted from Top TV Groups, *Broadcast and Cable* (April 10, 2000), pp. 72-98.
[a] A merger of Fox and Chris-Craft Television was complete prior to publication.

It should be no surprise to find the networks represented among the top six positions among television group owners. Each network needs a stable base of *owned and operated stations* (referred to as O&Os) to provide a strong audience for each network schedule. Network O&Os regularly clear the entire network schedule, giving each network a minimum reach of 20 to 25 percent of the national audience (Litman 1978, 1993).

Groups that have a strong presence in other media industries are also among the top owners of television stations. Tribune, Gannett, Belo, E. W. Scripps and Post-Newsweek all have significant interests in newspaper publishing. Interestingly, these types of companies are lobbying the FCC to eliminate cross-ownership restrictions that bar newspapers from owning television stations in the same market.

Market Structure

The market structure of the television industry resembles an oligopoly at both the local and national levels. Recall that in an oligopoly, there is more than one seller of a product, and the products offered may be either homogeneous (alike) or heterogeneous (differentiated). For the most part, the networks produce homogeneous products in that they each provide similar types of programming (e.g., situation comedies, dramas, reality programs, news, sports, etc.) and hours of service to affiliates.

Scholars have examined trends in prime-time programming over several decades. In general, these studies found a decline in the number and types of program categories offered by the networks, a direct indication of oligopoly behavior (Dominick and Pearce 1976; Wakshlag and Adams 1985).

Litman (1993) observes that the networks engage in several areas of cooperative behavior (or conduct) as an oligopoly. Litman claims that advertising inventory and prices, compensation agreements for affiliates and license fees for programming acquired from production companies reflect areas of conduct agreement among the networks, whereas television ratings, promotional activities and program quality represent areas that differentiate each network's products from one another.

The network oligopoly structure is further strengthened by vertical integration—the control of various aspects of production, distribution and exhibition. The networks are all involved in the production of television programming, and all but NBC (owned by General Electric) are aligned with film studios.

The similarity of television programming genres indicates high cross-elasticity of demand in the television industry. Early studies identified cross-elasticity of demand between the broadcast television industry and the cable television industry (e.g., Noll, Peck and McGowan 1973; Owen, Beebe and Manning 1974; Park 1971).

Market Concentration

Market concentration measures in the television industry have been utilized primarily in local television markets. As Bates (1993) suggests, clear definitions are needed in order to measure market concentration in the television industry precisely. Bates used different market definitions for both audiences and advertising in determining concentration in local television markets and found that over time, concentration levels declined slowly, due to the presence of new stations and cable television.

Concentration is more evident at the network or national level, particularly in the form of barriers to entry for new competitors. Litman (1993) explains that economies of scale form a major barrier in networking, as a competitor must reach approximately 70 percent of the national audience to be effective in the market for national advertising. Existing network affiliation agreements currently bind most television stations.

Demand for Television Stations

Historically, television stations have produced good returns for owners and investors, but the accelerating costs of programming, the conversion to digital television and a sluggish economy at the beginning of the 21st century all had a negative impact on the bottom line for many group operators. Studies assessing the value of a television station have found that market size, audience circulation, network affiliation and VHF (very high frequency) status increased the economic value of a television station (see Blau, Johnson and Ksobeich 1976; Cherington, Hirsch and Brandwein 1971; Levin 1980). Bates (1988) studied the impact of federal deregulation on television transactions and found the policies had little impact on the price paid for stations.

Table 6.4 summarizes television station transactions for selected years from 1990 through 1998. As the table illustrates, TV station prices soared during the decade, especially after the passage of the Telecommunications Act of 1996 that triggered a number of transactions. The average price of a television station nearly doubled from 1995 to 1999, from about $42 million to $79 million.

The high cost of purchasing television stations and the lack of open channels for new stations constitute significant barriers to entry for new competitors in the television industry. As such, any effort by the FCC to increase ownership limits would further impact concentration of ownership and help stifle entry of new competitors into the industry.

Table 6.4. Television station transactions for selected years

Year	Number of Transactions	Average Price (in millions)
1990	75	$ 9.29
1992	41	3.02
1994	89	24.72
1995	112	42.32
1996	99	50.59
1997	108	59.26
1998	90	79.10

Source: Data adapted from *Broadcasting & Cable Yearbook* (2000) and FCC website (www.fcc.gov).

Government Regulation

Television remains under the jurisdiction of the FCC, which has the power to renew the lucrative license necessary to operate a television station. Several major regulatory initiatives are creating structural changes in the television industry aside from ownership limits discussed in the previous section.

One of the most expensive regulatory burdens placed on the television industry is the required conversion to digital television (DTV) by 2006. Broadcasters were assigned a new digital channel while being allowed to continue to operate their traditional analog channel. At the end of the conversion period, broadcasters must give back their analog spectrum.

By mid-2001, only about 40 percent of all television stations had converted to digital, most in the top 25 markets. Many stations are expected to miss their conversion date for a number of reasons, including costs to convert, lack of digital equipment and technical issues. The industry continues to argue over the technical standards for digital television. Meanwhile, consumers—who would have to purchase new television sets capable of receiving digital broadcasts—have been leery about investing in the new equipment because of the limited availability of digital programming.

The digital channel can be used to provide from four to six compressed standard television (STV) signals or a single channel devoted to high-definition television (HDTV). Broadcasters seem interested in both options, and many are expected to eventually offer a hybrid service, programming STV during the day and an HDTV signal during prime time. The digital channels raised issues with cable and satellite operators over *must carry* (regulations that require cable operators to carry all local broadcast stations), but the courts have ruled that operators are not required to carry both types of signals, much to the chagrin of the broadcast television industry.

The FCC now allows duopoly ownership in the television industry provided the combinations are only VHF-UHF (traditional bandlengths in the ranges of very high frequency and ultra high frequency) and that after duopoly four independent "voices" (different owners) remain in the market (FCC revises, 1999). Previously, many TV stations controlled another station via *local marketing agreements* (LMAs) that did not involve transfer of control. Many of the former LMAs are in the process of moving to duopoly ownership.

In terms of programming, a controversial part of the 1996 act was the requirement that new television sets be equipped with a technology known as the "V-Chip," to enable parents to block out programs with violent or sexual content. A controversial voluntary ratings system was put in place by the networks in 1998 to warn parents about programs with violent or sexual content. However, NBC refused to participate in the system. By 2000, the first sets with V-Chip capability finally began to emerge, with little fanfare and little expectation that this technology would make any difference in television programming.

The broadcast networks came under fire in 1999–2000 by the National Association for the Advancement of Colored People (NAACP) over the lack of prime-time characters representing African-Americans and other people of color. Boycotts were threatened, and the networks responded with a series of new corporate appointments to address the concerns raised by the NAACP. By fall 2001, however, the NAACP was again threatening boycotts over the lack of progress by the networks.

The conversion and implementation of digital television, along with the possible expansion of ownership limits and elimination of cross-ownership provisions, remain the primary regulatory concerns of the television industry. The federal government will continue to play an important role in the formal regulation of television through the actions of the FCC and the interplay of the executive, legislative and judicial branches of government.

Technological Forces Affecting Television

In addition to the conversion to a completely digital system, other technological innovations continue to affect the television industry. One joint effort is the ongoing work and collaboration to develop interactive TV (Kerschbaumer 2000). Interactive TV is in its infancy, but it holds great promise for television of the future, allowing viewers the opportunity to engage in many activities, such as shopping, banking and playing games, with their television set. Several companies, including Microsoft and AOL Time Warner, are major players in the development of interactive TV applications.

Convergence between the personal computer and television is taking on new forms. Web TV, developed to use television to access the Internet, was one of the first technologies to integrate computing technology with the television set. TV video cards for personal computers enabled PC users to watch television on their PC monitor. Now, a number of PC/TV devices enable users to watch traditional television while also accessing the Internet. New personal video recorders (PVRs), such as Tivo and Ultimate TV, also blend the power of computing technology with traditional television viewing.

Improving and enhancing streaming media via the Internet is another area where more technological progress is needed (see Owen 1999). While streaming media is best realized via a broadband connection, the television industry is interested in improving the quality of streaming media as well as the possible marketing of television programming directly to a household for later viewing. In other words, television programmers (and film studios) want to offer programming on an a la carte basis to households, enabling viewers to download programs they want to view for a fee. Such a system would require strict copyright protection and include the inability to make copies of the digital programming for sale or illegal distribution.

The Economic Future of Television

The broadcast television industry continues to face intense competition from numerous competitors for audiences and advertisers. With combined prime-time viewing shares now in the 50s, the television audience has shrunk by nearly 25 percent since 1990 (Nielsen Media Research 2000). Yet, despite the erosion of the audience to cable, satellite and other technologies, advertising has retained slow and steady growth.

Advertising in the television industry is expected to keep growing at a modest 4 to 5 percent rate through 2004, with faster growth occurring at the network level in comparison to local television stations (Veronis, Suhler and Associates 2000). The conversion to digital television and the increasing cost of programming and personnel remain major expense categories for the industry. Stations and networks will continue to find ways to cut costs, including more joint partnerships to produce programming and share expenses. Likewise, TV operations will continue to seek out new revenue streams, especially via the Internet and e-commerce.

Regulatory reform has had a significant impact on the industry, and further actions could result in more consolidation of ownership. Changes to the audience reach cap or relaxation of cross-ownership rules barring newspaper ownership of TV stations would set off a wave of more divestitures and acquisitions, ultimately affecting the economic performance of the industry as a whole.

Summary

The television industry is still a powerful institution among mass media industries. The television industry includes four major networks (ABC, CBS, NBC and Fox) and three smaller networks (UPN, WB, Pax) that operate in an oligopoly structure in conjunction with their owned and operated stations (O&Os) and their individual network affiliates. Many of the networks are part of large media conglomerates, and many networks partner with movie studios, enabling economies of scale within their respective networking operations. The television industry has experienced bitter feelings between networks and their affiliates, primarily over issues of compensation and exclusivity of content.

The television industry functions in both national and local markets for audiences and advertisers. Consumer demand for television has declined in recent years due to competition from cable and satellite services. Still, broadcast television has the ability to attract millions of viewers at a single setting. Advertising demand remains strong in both markets, accounting for a total of nearly $38 billion in 1999. Demand for stations mushroomed after the Telecommunications Act of 1996, with station prices averaging more than $72 million by 1999.

Technology has had an impact on the television industry in a number of ways. The ongoing conversion to digital television is under way, as mandated by the FCC. Interactive TV, converging PC/TV appliances and improvements in streaming media over the Internet represent other ways to distribute television programs.

Economically, the television industry is expected to grow at a rate of 4.6 percent through 2004, when total revenues are projected to reach $48 billion. Regulatory actions led to significant structural changes in the television industry during the 1990s; further regulatory efforts could produce even more changes if ownership limits are relaxed or removed.

Discussion Questions

1. How has the television industry changed over the years? What factors have affected television's economic development?
2. In what ways does the television industry resemble an oligopoly market structure? How do the companies in the industry differentiate themselves?
3. How does networking encourage economies of scale? What are the barriers to entry into the television industry?
4. How have regulatory decisions had a negative impact on the television industry? How have regulatory decisions had a positive impact on the television industry? Should ownership provisions be further relaxed? What advantages would this hold for the industry? How might it affect you as a consumer?
5. What technological innovations are affecting the television industry? Do you think households will eventually move toward integrated PC/TV appliances or continue to use two separate devices? Why?

Exercises

1. Analyze the television stations in the market in which you currently live by gathering the following information:
   a. Technical qualities of each station (class, channel assignment, etc.)

    b. Network affiliation (if any)

    c. Market share (by audience ratings)

    d. Advertisers—local only

    e. Distinct programming (news, sports, etc.)

    f. Transition to digital television (currently broadcasting in digital?)

2. Review local periodicals for your market since 1996 to determine if how many television stations have been sold, the price for each station, and who became the new owner. Are any of the owners in your market found in Table 6.3?

3. Conduct a survey of TV households in your market, and find out the following information:

    a. How the household receives TV (antenna, cable, satellite)

    b. How many TV sets are in the home

    c. Whether the household owns a VCR

    d. Whether the household owns a personal computer

    e. Whether the household owns a personal video recorder

    f. About how many hours TV is viewed in the home each night

    What does this information tell you about broadcast TV usage compared to the use of other types of technologies?

4. Review local economic data to determine the amount of retail sales and advertising dollars spent in your market during the most recent year. If possible, determine how much money was spent on television for local advertising and what the individual market shares are for each TV station.

References

Albarran, A. B. (1989). The Federal Communications Commission's multiple ownership rules: Implications for program diversity and the public interest. *Arizona Communication Association Journal* 18:15–24.

———. (2002). *Management of Electronic Media.* 2d ed. Belmont, Calif: Wadsworth.

Auletta, K. (1991). *Three Blind Mice: How the TV Networks Lost Their Way.* New York: Vintage Press.

Bates, B. J. (1988). The impact of deregulation on television station prices. *Journal of Media Economics* 1:5–22.

———. (1993). Concentration in local television markets. *Journal of Media Economics* 6:3–22.

Blau, R. T., R. C. Johnson and K J. Ksobeich. (1976). Determinants of TV station economic value. *Journal of Broadcasting* 20:197–207.

Broadcasting and Cable Yearbook. (2000). New Providence, N.J.: R. R. Bowker.

Cherington, P. W., L. V. Hirsch and R. Brandwein. (1971). *Television Station Ownership: A Case Study of Federal Agency Regulation.* New York: Hastings House.

Dominick, J. R., and M. C. Pearce. (1976). Trends in network prime-time programming, 1953-1974. *Journal of Communication* 26 (1): 70–80.

FCC revises local television ownership rules. (1999). Available online: http://www.fcc.gov/Mass_Media/News_Releases/1999/nrmm9019.html. Release date 5 August, accessed 11 August.

Flint, J. (2001). Local TV stations seek investigation of big networks. *Wall Street Journal*, 9 March, B1, B5.

Kerschbaumer, K. (2000). Interactive television: Fulfilling the promise. *Broadcasting and Cable*, 10 July, 22–34.

Levin, H. J. (1980). *Fact and Fancy in Television Regulation: An Economic Study of Television Alternatives*. New York: Russell Sage.

Litman, B. R. (1978). Is network ownership in the public interest? *Journal of Communication* 28 (2): 51–59.

———. (1993). Role of TV networks. In *Media Economics: Theory and Practice*, edited by A. Alexander, J. Owers and R. Carveth. New York: Lawrence Erlbaum Associates, pp. 225–244.

Nielsen Media Research. (1994). Nielsen Report on Television. Northbrook, Ill.: Nielsen Media Research.

———. (2000). *2000 Report on Television*. New York: Nielsen Media Research.

Noll, R., M. Peck and J. McGowan. (1973). *Economic Aspects of Television Regulation*. Washington, D.C.: Brookings Institute.

Owen, B. M. (1999). *The Internet Challenge to Television*. Cambridge: Harvard University Press.

Owen, B. M., J. H. Beebe and W. G. Manning. (1974). *Television Economics*. Lexington, Mass.: D. C. Heath.

Park, R. E. (1971). Television station performance and revenues. *Educational Broadcasting Review* 5:43-49.

Television Bureau of Advertising. (2001). Available online: http://www.tvb.org. Accessed 20 August.

Top TV groups. (2000). *Broadcast and Cable*, 10 April, 72-98.

Veronis, Suhler and Associates. (2000). *Communications Industry Forecast*. New York: Veronis, Suhler and Associates.

Wakshlag, J. J., and W. J. Adams. (1985). Trends in program variety and the prime time access rule. *Journal of Broadcasting and Electronic Media* 29:23-34.

7

THE CABLE AND SATELLITE
TELEVISION INDUSTRIES

After reading this chapter, you should:

- Be able to identify the major players, market structure and economic characteristics of the cable and satellite television industries

- Understand how operators and programmers engage in economies of scale

- Recognize the different types of demand in the cable and satellite industries

- Recognize the impact of regulatory decisions on the cable and satellite television industries

- Understand how technology is increasing the number of channels in the cable and satellite television industries

This chapter centers on the economic aspects of the cable and satellite television industries. Together, these industries are also referred to as the *multichannel television* industries. These two industries provide television programming to more than 87 percent of all U.S. TV households (National Cable Television Association 2001). This means that most Americans pay to receive television service—a dramatic change from when television debuted in the 1940s (see chapter 6).

Cable television emerged in the United States in 1948 as a retransmission service of existing broadcast signals to households in rural areas that could not receive television signals with conventional antennas. These early systems were crude, saddled with poor technical quality and limited to a few broadcast channels. Cable grew very slowly until the 1970s, when satellite technology created a supply of new programming services in the form of basic cable networks, premium cable services and superstations.

In 2001, the National Cable Television Association (NCTA) reported that an estimated 87.5 million households subscribed to some form of multichannel television. Cable was the dominant provider, reaching 68.2 million households, while the direct broadcast satellite (DBS) providers totaled 14.8 million subscribers. The remaining subscribers received programming via C-band operators, satellite master antenna television (SMATV), multipoint multichannel distribution services (MMDS), local telephone companies or broadband competitors.

AT&T, AOL Time Warner and Comcast dominate the cable industry. Known as *multiple system operators* (MSOs), these companies provide different packages, or *tiers*, of programming to subscribers, along with the rental of converter boxes and remote-control devices. The MSOs have enjoyed a monopoly position in local markets for several years, but a combination of regulatory decisions and technological advances has opened the marketplace to new competitors. The most ambitious threat to cable's monopoly comes in the form of direct broadcast satellites (DBS). DirecTV and EchoStar are the leading providers of DBS services in the United States, serving 9.8 million and 5.7 million households, respectively, as of June 2001 (Higgins and Flynn 2001).

Cable television has operated as a monopoly in most local communities throughout its history. As cable began to diffuse in the United States, operators were granted a *franchise*, typically awarded on a competitive bid basis by the local franchising authority, in most cases the local government (see Baldwin and McElvoy 1991). The franchise gave the winning cable operator the right to offer exclusive cable television service in a specific geographical area. The franchising process created a de facto monopoly position for the cable operator, meaning that if a household wanted to subscribe to cable TV, it had only one choice of supplier. In some parts of the United States, *overbuilds* were allowed, meaning that an area could be served by more than one cable system. Overbuilds presently exist in 34 states, and rates in these areas tend to be lower than those of communities served by only one operator (Owen and Wildman 1992).

One reason the cable television industry developed slowly was due to successful lobbying by broadcasters to limit competition in local television markets (Owen and Wildman 1992). For years, the FCC restricted the growth of cable TV by imposing regulatory barriers that restricted the importation of any programming (referred to as distant signals) from outside the local TV market. Eventually, these regulatory barriers were removed, allowing the cable television industry to grow.

In 1984, the Cable Communications Act (more commonly called the 1984 Cable Act) deregulated many provisions and also gave cable operators the right to set their own rates for services without approval from the local franchising authority (Head, Sterling and Schofield 1994). Cable rates mushroomed between 1986 (when the law took effect) and 1990, outraging members of Congress and their constituents. The 1984 Cable Act also prohibited the broadcast networks from owning cable systems, and it limited telephone company ownership to system ownership outside their regions of service. These provisions increased the monopoly power of cable television operators.

In 1992, Congress passed the Cable Television Consumer Protection and Competition Act, which included several provisions to limit the unregulated monopoly power of cable TV operators. The most significant aspect of the new law concerned rates for basic service, with the FCC required to establish new rate structures for the industry. Additionally, TV stations were given the opportunity to negotiate with cable operators for carriage of their signals, known as *retransmission consent*. The 1992 act also required program providers to sell program services to competitors such as DBS, MMDS, and SMATV operations.

The Telecommunications Act of 1996 removed rate regulation from the FCC and left it to the local municipalities to work with their franchise holders to negotiate rates for basic service. The 1996 act also allowed telephone companies to own cable systems in their own areas of service. Cable TV operators were also cleared to offer telephony service, but they could not own local broadcast stations or a broadcast network.

Two other legislative acts helped promote the growing DBS industry. In 1998, Congress passed the Satellite Home Viewer Act, followed a year later by the Satellite Home Viewer Improvement Act (SHVIA). These acts, which will be discussed in greater detail later in the chapter, finally gave DBS operators the right to carry local television signals, spurring greater interest in DBS service.

Today cable television is a mature industry. Although more than two-thirds of the nation's television households (TVHH) subscribe to cable, the industry has passed approximately 97 percent of all TVHH (Cable Advertising Bureau 2001). In other words, approximately 97 percent of all TVHH have access to cable, but about one-third of the households choose not to subscribe for various reasons (e.g., don't want the service, cost, dissatisfaction with the service).

The Market for Cable and Satellite Television

Multiple markets exist in the cable television industry. As with broadcast television, there are separate local and national markets for audiences and advertisers for cable television. The most lucrative revenue market for the cable operator is basic cable TV service, which accounts for nearly 55 percent of total industry revenues (Industry Statistics 2001). Premium and pay services

Table 7.1. Growth of cable television systems (1970–1999)

Year	Systems
1970	2,490
1980	4,225
1990	9,575
1995	11,351
1999 (estimate)	10,700

Source: Adapted from National Cable Television Association (2001).

account for an additional 11 percent of revenues, and advertising, pay-per-view, equipment rental, installation fees, cable modems and other services account for the remaining 34 percent (Cable Advertising Bureau 2001).

The number of cable television systems operating in the United States has grown rapidly since 1970 (see Table 7.1), reflecting a relaxation in regulations limiting cable and an increase in the number of new cable networks (both premium and advertiser-supported). Although other types of program distributors exist in some local communities in the form of DBS, SMATV and MMDS services, the cable operator maintains a dominant share of the market for audiences. The top 20 local cable television markets are listed in Table 7.2.

Table 7.2. Top 20 cable television market systems (ranked by number of subscribers)

System Location	System Operator	Basic Subscribers	Rank
New York, NY	Time Warner	1,032,872	1
Long Island, NY	Cablevision Systems	683,718	2
Orlando, FL	TWE-A/N[a]	543,049	3
Bronx/Brooklyn, NY	Cablevision Systems	502,205	4
Phoenix, AZ	Cox Communications	450,303	5
Puget Sound, WA	AT&T Broadband	424,500	6
Pittsburgh, PA	AT&T	415,720	7
Chicago Suburbs, IL	AT&T	390,602	8
Denver, CO	AT&T	369,844	9
San Diego, CA	Cox Communications	354,500	10
Los Angeles, CA	AT&T	352,411	11
Tampa/St. Petersburg, FL	TWE-A/N[a]	336,954	12
Las Vegas, NV	Cox Communications	319,295	13
Cleveland, OH	Adelphia	309,674	14
San Antonio, TX	Time Warner	305,281	15
Houston, TX	TWE-A/N[a]	294,123	16
New Orleans, LA	Cox Communications	273,360	17
Broward/Dade Counties, FL	AT&T	269,448	18
Plam Beach County, FL	Adelphia	266,000	19
Hampton Roads, VA	Cox Communications	261,226	20

Source: National Cable Television Association (2001).
[a]TWE-A/N - Time Warner Entertainment and Advanced/Newhouse partnership.

Consumer Demand for Multichannel Television

Over the years, audiences have exhibited strong demand for multichannel programming. The number of cable television subscribers grew rapidly from 1970 to 1990 and then began to slow. Since 1990, the number of noncable multichannel households, primarily due to the introduction of DBS, has grown rapidly—from just over 3 billion TVHH in 1995 to more than 19 billion in 2000 (FCC 2001).

Several early studies found cross-elasticity of demand between cable and broadcast television (Comanor and Mitchell 1970; Park 1971; Noll, Peck and McGowan 1973). Later, Ducey, Krugman and Eckrich (1983) found differences in demand for basic and pay services. Bloch and Wirth (1984) found that consumer demand was influenced by demographics, price and quality of the programming. Childers and Krugman (1987) and Albarran and Dimmick (1993) examined competition between cable, pay-per-view, videocassette recorder (VCR) rentals and broadcast television, indicating high cross-elasticity of demand for these services. Studies by Crandall (reported in Owen and Wildman 1992) and Umphrey (1991) suggest that demand for basic cable is relatively elastic.

Premium cable television services, such as Home Box Office (HBO), Showtime, Cinemax and Starz represent other revenue streams for multichannel providers. Historically, the diffusion of premium services increased interest and demand for cable and DBS service. Premium services are offered to subscribers in various packages of services or a la carte. The average monthly price for a premium channel varies; most services charge about $8 to $10 a month for the first channel. The leading premium cable television services are listed in Table 7.3.

Premium cable TV services generated approximately $7.4 billion in 1999, with $5 billion going to cable operators and $2.4 billion to DBS providers (Veronis, Suhler and Associates 2000b). Premium revenue was expected to grow to $9.1 billion by 2004, with cable netting $5.6 billion and DBS $3.5 billion (Veronis, Suhler and Associates 2000a).

Table 7.3. Leading premium cable television services

Service	Start Date	Owner	Subscribers
Home Box Office	12/75	AOL Time Warner	36,000,000[a]
Showtime	3/78	Viacom	24,400,000[b]
Cinemax	8/80	AOL Time Warner	36,000,000[a]
Starz	7/94	Liberty Media	11,000,000

Source: National Cable Television Association (2001); Cable Advertising Bureau (2001).
[a]HBO and Cinemax subscribers are lumped together.
[b]Showtime Networks subscribers include The Movie Channel (TMC), Showtime and Flix.

Pay-per-view (PPV) services represent another market and potential revenue stream for multichannel operators. Pay-per-view consists of programming that is paid for by consumers on a per-event basis. Programming consists of two categories: movies and events (sports, concerts and specials). In the cable TV industry, not all households have the ability to receive PPV programming. Signals for PPV typically are scrambled to prevent viewing by those who have not paid for the service, and thus *addressable technology*—special equipment capable of deciphering scrambled signals—is required to receive PPV programming. As the industry continues to upgrade its systems, more households will acquire addressable technology and become able to receive the programming available from operators. In 2001, only about 49 percent of all U.S. TVHH had addressable technology (National Cable Television Association 2001).

PPV revenues are smaller than premium cable TV revenues but still represent an important revenue stream. In 1999, PPV revenue totaled $1.7 billion, with $1.185 billion spent on movies and $520 million spent on events (Veronis, Suhler and Associates, 2000b). PPV revenues were expected to reach just over $3 billion by 2004, with movie revenue expected to lead event revenues by a three-to-one margin (Veronis, Suhler and Associates 2000a).

PPV demand varies greatly. There are few studies available that examine audience demand for pay-per-view programming. Studies by Childers and Krugman (1987) and Albarran and Dimmick (1993) indicate that competition exists between pay-per-view programming, other cable programming and VCR usage, suggesting cross-elasticity of demand for these services. The leading PPV services and their potential numbers of subscribers are found in Table 7.4.

Other revenue markets exist for the cable industry, including digital cable service (an expansion of existing channels and greater variety), Internet service via the rental of cable modems, and equipment rental (converters, remote control devices). These multiple revenue streams, coupled with the sale of

Table 7.4. Leading pay-per-view services and potential subscribers

Service	Start Date	Systems	Addressable Subscribers
BET Action Pay Per View	9/90	462	8,000,000
Cine Latino	N/A	28	200,000
The Filipino Channel	N/A	17	38,000
ESPN Extra	9/99	N/A	N/A
iN DEMAND	11/85	1,700	N/A
Playboy TV	11/82	550	11,900,000
Viewer's Choice	11/85	1,700	28,000,000

Source: Compiled from various sources by the author.

advertising, give the cable industry a strong competitive position compared to broadcast television.

Demand for Advertising

Advertising on cable television continues to grow at both the national and local levels, as can be seen in Table 7.5. There are two significant trends in the data presented in Table 7.5. First, advertising on various national networks (e.g., ESPN, MTV, CNN) continues to attract annual increases in national advertising dollars, reflecting their ability to draw audiences from the broadcast networks. Veronis, Suhler and Associates (2000a) project that cable TV advertising will grow at an annual compounded rate of 13.4 percent through 2004 to reach approximately $21 billion.

Second, local cable advertising continues to achieve steady growth. At the local level, cable systems compete directly with other local media outlets (e.g., newspapers, radio and broadcast television stations) for advertising revenue.

Many cable systems sell advertising through *interconnects*. An interconnect exists when two or more operators join together to distribute advertising simultaneously over their respective systems. Interconnects increase advertiser effectiveness by offering the efficiency of a multiple-system buy and save time in that only one contract must be initiated (Cable Advertising Bureau 2001). Numerous interconnects are in operation in the United States.

One of the more popular forms of local cable advertising is *insertion advertising*. Insertion advertising occurs when national cable networks such as ESPN, MTV and USA offer advertising availabilities to local systems for their local commercials. It enables local clients to advertise on popular cable networks, usually at a rate comparable to that of local radio stations and much

Table 7.5. Cable television advertising revenue (millions of dollars)

Year	Local/Spot Revenue	Cable Networks	Regional Revenue	Total Revenue
1980	$ 8	$ 50	$ 0	$ 58
1985	167	634	14	815
1990	634	1,802	103	2,539
1995	1,433	3,974	216	5,623
1996	1,662	4,827	195	6,684
1997	1,850	5,843	231	6,684
1998	2,092	6,932	361	9,385
1999	2,546	8,298	351	11,195

Source: Adapted from National Cable Television Association (2001) website (www.ncta. com).

cheaper than broadcast television. Clients usually purchase insertion advertising for one or more weeks at a time; spots are rotated around various cable networks on a random basis several times a day.

Major Players in Cable and Satellite Television

The top 10 cable and satellite television operators as of June 2001 are listed in Table 7.6. AT&T and AOL Time Warner are the two largest operators; together they account for more than 28 million subscribers in the United States. In regard to DBS operators, DirecTV is the third largest operator with 9.8 million subscribers, while EchoStar has 5.7 million subscribers.

The 1990s brought increasing consolidation to the cable and satellite industry. *Clustering*, the merging of smaller cable systems into geographic groups, became a common practice in the cable television industry. Clustering allows companies to utilize economies of scale more effectively to lower average costs. Economies of scale also enable large operators to negotiate lower prices for software (programming) and hardware (equipment). Efficiencies in marketing and advertising are another advantage. DBS operators have also consolidated to the point that there are now only two national operators.

Further consolidation may be forthcoming. In March 2001, a federal appeals court overturned FCC ownership regulations on cable systems that capped ownership at 30 percent of all cable/satellite households (Dreazen and Solomon 2001). AT&T and AOL Time Warner challenged the rules, arguing

Table 7.6. Top 10 cable and satellite operators (ranked by number of subscribers in millions)

Operator	Subscribers	Rank
AT&T Broadband	15.9	1
AOL Time Warner	12.8	2
DirecTV	9.8	3
Comcast Corporation	7.3	4
Charter Communications	6.3	5
Cox Communications	6.2	6
Adelphia Communications	5.7	7
EchoStar (Dish Network)	5.7	8
Cablevision Systems	2.9	9
Insight Communications	1.4	10

Source: Higgins & Flynn (2001). At the time of publication AT&T Broadband and Comcast Corporation planned to merge, as well as DirecTV and EchoStar.

that the 30 percent cap was arbitrary and capricious. Industry observers expected the FCC to offer new rules that would expand or possibly eliminate ownership limits.

In addition to ownership of cable TV systems, many operators practice *vertical integration*—that is, they control different aspects of production, distribution and exhibition of their products—by maintaining interests in various networks. For example, AT&T owns part of several program services through its subsidiary Liberty Media. At the time of publication, AT&T was in the process of selling off Liberty. AOL Time Warner has ownership of several services, including pay services HBO and Cinemax, as well as TBS, TNT, CNN, CNN Headline News and the Cartoon Network. Viacom owns Showtime, MTV/VH1, Nickelodeon, TV Land and BET. The top 20 national cable television networks (ranked by number of subscribers) are listed in Table 7.7.

Many other companies involved in the electronic media have ownership interests in cable television programming, including but not limited to Disney (Disney Channel, ESPN, ESPN2), General Electric (CNBC, MSNBC) and Fox (FX, Fox News, Fox Sports). These companies offer their programming to cable TV systems in return for a monthly fee per subscriber and, like the broadcast networks, sell access to these audiences to national advertisers.

Table 7.7. Top 20 cable networks (ranked by number of subscribers)

Network	Number of Subscribers (millions)	Origination Date	Rank
TBS Superstation	80.6	12/76	1
Discovery Channel	79.8	06/85	2
ESPN	79.0	09/79	3
Nickelodeon/Nick at Nite	78.0	04/79 (07/85)	4
USA	78.0	04/80	5
CNN (Cable News Network)	78.0	06/80	6
Lifetime Television for Women	78.0	02/84	7
A & E (Arts and Entertainment)	77.0	02/84	8
CNBC	77.0	04/89	9
C-Span (Public Affairs Network)	77.0	03/79	10
TNT (Turner Network Television	76.8	10/88	11
FOX Family Channel	75.7		12
TLC (The Learning Channel)	75.6		13
TNN (The Nashville Network)	75.0	03/81	14
The Weather Channel	74.0	05/82	15
MTV: Music Television	73.2	08/81	16
CNN Headline News	72.5		17
QVC	72.2	11/86	18
AMC (American Movie Classics	71.0	10/84	19
VH1 (Video Hits One)	68.3	01/85	20

Source: Adapted from National Cable Television Association (2001) website (www.ncta. com).

Market Structure

The market structure for multichannel programming reflects an oligopoly. Despite efforts to increase competition, most U.S. households have only one option for local cable service (depending on the franchise for the local community) and no more than two choices for DBS service (DirecTV and Dish Network/EchoStar). Fewer than 3 million subscribers receive programming from C-band, SMATV, MMDS, local telephone operators or other broadband competitors (Broadband 2001). Some 84 million subscribers receive programming via an entrenched cable operator (AT&T, AOLTW, Comcast) or DBS (DirecTV/Dish Network).

Regulators had hoped that by introducing competition, more providers would emerge. This has not happened, and the growing consolidation within the cable and satellite industries indicates little movement away from an oligopoly market structure.

Market Concentration

The cable and satellite television industries are heavily concentrated. The top 10 cable and satellite operators in June 2001 (listed in Table 7.6) collectively served 74 million subscribers out of an estimated universe of 87.5 million households (Higgins and Flynn 2001). Using this same data, the author calculated CR4 and CR8 ratios and found that the CR4 ratio was equal to 52.8 percent, while the CR8 was equal to 80 percent, both exceeding the definition of heavy concentration.

When the FCC-imposed subscriber reach cap of 30 percent was found unconstitutional in March 2001, the stage was set for further industry concentration and consolidation. To what extent further consolidation will occur and how quickly it could happen will depend on a number of different economic and political factors. The prospects for greater competition in the cable and satellite television industries appear dim. If the industry engages in monopolistic behavior, regulators may step in, especially if consumers complain over rates for services.

Demand for Cable Systems

Cable systems are normally sold based on some multiple of cash flow (revenues minus expenses plus depreciation, interest and taxes) and an estimated dollar amount per subscriber. Between 1997 and 1999, systems were selling at multiples of 10 to 20 times cash flow, or from $2,000 per subscriber

Table 7.8. Data on aggregate cable system transactions, 1997–2000

Year	Seller	Transactions	Total Value/ Millions	Price/ Subscriber
1997		109	$21.5	$ 2,038
1998		119	64.6	2,875
1999		90	75.8	3,884
2000[a]		22	55.0	6,259

Source: FCC Annual Assessment of the status of competition in the market for the delivery of video programming (2001). Available on line: http://www.fcc.gov/Bureaus/Cable/Reports/fcc01001.pdf

[a]2000 data for first six months of 2000 only (January–June)

to as much as $6,000 per subscriber. Annual data for cable system transactions from 1997 through mid-2000 are listed in Table 7.8.

Impact of Regulatory Forces on Cable and Satellite TV Industries

Many aspects of regulation involving the cable and satellite industries have been discussed earlier in the chapter. This section will focus on key regulatory issues facing these industries, including dual must carry, forced access regarding Internet connectivity, pole attachments, and interactive TV.

Dual must carry is a major issue for both the broadcast television industry and the cable and satellite industries. Currently, the must carry provisions require operators to provide local television signals as part of their basic service. But since must carry passed, TV stations are engaged in upgrading to digital television (DTV) service. Congress allowed broadcasters to operate both an analog and a digital channel until the conversion to a nationwide digital system is complete. In the interim, broadcasters want the cable TV industry to carry both channels—hence the term *dual must carry*. Cable does not want to give up the additional channel capacity for the broadcaster's digital channel but instead wants to negotiate with broadcasters for carriage rights as they would another provider of programming, such as ESPN or the Weather Channel.

The cable industry is threatened by telephone company efforts to have the government force cable television operators to allow open access for high-speed Internet access. By gaining open access to the cable industry's broadband networks, telephone companies could offer Internet services without having to invest billions of dollars in creating new broadband networks. Open access became a key issue in resolving concerns with the merger of AOL and Time Warner, by forcing the new company to offer competing Internet service to companies other than AOL.

Pole attachments represent another issue that poses economic harm to the cable industry. In many communities, cable TV shares the same utility poles that provide other types of services to homes. But with electric companies now offering communication services and cable operators in some areas offering telephone and Internet access, circumstances have changed. Utility operators, which own most of the poles, want to charge more money to cable operators for access to the poles—in some cases increasing the price by as much as 8 to 10 times the regular monthly fee. The U.S. Supreme Court was scheduled to hear arguments on this case in the fall of 2001.

Interactive TV may raise other issues for cable and satellite providers. With the ability to offer "two-way" communication between a household and a program provider, many types of services could potentially be offered, ranging from commerce and banking to home security and community issues. The technology is available, but the demand for many of these services is limited at present.

Impact of Technological Forces on Cable and Satellite TV Industries

The cable and satellite television industries are technologically intensive, with millions of dollars invested in both physical plants and satellite transponders. No doubt, the biggest technological force driving the cable industry is upgrading to a digitally based delivery system. DBS providers already offer digital distribution.

The cable television industry has made great strides in upgrading to digital technology. As of March 2001, there were approximately 10 million digital subscribers across the cable industry (Broadband 2001). Digital cable not only offers extended programming, but also a host of CD-quality audio channels. The NCTA expects digital cable subscribers to grow to 48 million by 2006 (Broadband 2001). If these projections hold, digital cable would represent a significant growth opportunity for the cable industry.

Coupled with the diffusion of digital cable are the continuing advances in *digital compression*. Digital compression allows multiple channels to be compressed into the existing space of a standard 6 MHZ analog channel, increasing capacity for the cable provider. Another continuing technological innovation is the growth of high definition television programming, found on both the broadcast networks and cable/DBS providers. As more households adopt new digital receivers, it will help increase demand for this type of programming.

The cable television industry also has benefited from the consumer rush to the Internet. As of 2001, there were an estimated 4 million households subscribing to broadband access (Broadband 2001), which allows users to surf the net at speeds 50 to 100 times faster than dial-up access. Plus, the service is directly connected to the network, making access faster and more pleasurable for the user.

The Economic Future of Cable Television

The cable and satellite television industries find themselves in a strong economic position at the beginning of the 21st century. The entrenched players have become bigger and stronger thanks to consolidation, and new competitors face a daunting task in trying to secure market share.

In terms of revenues, the picture is extremely rosy. Veronis, Suhler and Associates (2000b) expect total industry revenues to grow from $56 billion in 1999 to over $86 billion in 2004, a compound growth rate of just under 9 percent. Advertising and PPV are expected to experience double-digit growth during this time period, with basic and premium services growing at rates of 8.8 and 7.8 percent, respectively. DBS will continue to grow faster than cable in terms of new subscribers, but to date DBS has tended to attract new subscribers as opposed to siphoning subscribers away from cable.

Future consolidation could become a reality, resulting in greater economic power being concentrated among the leading providers. As this chapter was going to press, there was growing speculation that DirecTV and EchoStar would merge to form one giant DBS provider to compete with cable. With the FCC's cap on ownership thrown out by the courts, the stage is set for more consolidation.

The growth of new revenue streams in the form of digital cable and Internet access via cable modems are other economic bright spots for the cable television industry. All of this good news comes to the chagrin of broadcasters, who lack the multiple revenue streams and growth potential of the cable and satellite industries.

Summary

Cable television grew rapidly in the 1970s, following the elimination of a series of regulatory barriers and an increase in the number of new services available through satellite technology. By 2001, 68 million television households subscribed to basic cable television service, while another 19 million subscribed to other services led by DBS. Nationwide, cable and satellite has passed 97 percent of all television households.

The cable and satellite industries draw revenues across several different markets, including subscriptions to basic and expanded tiers of service, premium channels and pay-per-view services. For cable operators, advertising, digital cable and cable modems provide other revenue streams. Cable operators, represented by large MSOs such as AT&T, AOL Time Warner, Comcast,

Charter and Cox dominate cable, while DirecTV and EchoStar dominate the DBS market. Many of the MSOs engage in vertical integration through ownership interests of various cable programming services and networks, increasing their economic power.

The cable industry represents an oligopoly structure. Consolidation increased during the 1990s, even though new competitors (AT&T, Charter) emerged as new players. There are limited choices for service providers in most communities, with at least one cable operator competing against DBS and broadcast television.

Consumer demand for cable television has been found to be relatively elastic. Demand by advertisers continues to grow at both the local and national levels. Demand for cable systems has also increased due to clustering of cable systems and consolidation, resulting in higher prices paid per subscribing household.

Regulatory issues of concern to the cable industry are uncertainty over ownership limitations, as well as dual must carry, pole attachments, forced access to its broadband networks and issues related to interactive television.

Technological forces are creating more channels and more services for the cable TV operator to offer customers. Digital cable, compression technology and the upgrading of cable physical plants have resulted in greater channel capacity for cable television operators.

Economically, the cable and satellite television industries are well positioned to experience growth over the next decade.

Discussion Questions

1. Discuss revenue streams for the cable television industry. Which revenue areas are the most lucrative for the cable TV operator? Why?
2. What factors have led to the cable television operator enjoying a monopoly position in most local communities? How is the market structure for cable and satellite television likely to change in the years ahead?
3. How would further consolidation affect the cable and satellite television industries? How might it affect consumers?
4. What impact have regulatory decisions had on the cable and satellite television industry?
5. What impact will technological innovations have on the economic development of the cable television industry? What will digital cable offer to the operator? To the subscriber?

Exercises

1. Analyze the cable television system in the market in which you currently live by collecting the following information:
   a. Technical capacity of the system

    b. Tiers of service and fees (programming)

    c. Number of subscribers

    d. Advertisers—local only

    e. Rental costs for cable modems, addressable converters, remote control devices and other accessories

2. Analyze the DBS providers in the market in which you currently live by collecting the following information:

    a. Technical capacity of the system

    b. Tiers of service and fees (programming)

    c. Number of subscribers

3. Review the history of cable television in your market. When was the system started? Has the system ever been sold? If so, when and at what price? How has the system been changed or upgraded over the years?

4. Determine if any of the competitors to cable discussed in this chapter (DBS, SMATV, MMDS) exist in your market. Try to determine the types of services they offer that are similar to the cable system, as well as those that are different. Why would people choose one system over the other? Compare programming, costs and other features.

References

Albarran, A. B., and J. Dimmick. (1993). Measuring utility in the video entertainment industries: An assessment of competitive superiority. *Journal of Media Economics* 6 (2): 45–51.

Baldwin, T. F., and P. S. McElvoy. (1991). *Cable Communications*. 2d ed. Englewood Cliffs, N.J.: Prentice Hall.

Bloch, H., and M. O. Wirth. (1984). The demand for pay services on cable television. *Information Economics and Policy* 1:311–32.

Broadband. (2001). National Cable Television Association. Available online: http://www.ncta.com/broadband.

Cable Advertising Bureau. (2001). *Cable Industry Facts 2001*. Available online: http://www.cabletvadbureau.com.

Childers, T., and D. Krugman. (1987). The competitive environment of pay per view. *Journal of Broadcasting and Electronic Media* 31 (3): 335–42.

Comanor, W. S., and B. M. Mitchell. (1970). Cable television and the impact of regulation. *Bell Journal of Economics and Management Science* 2:15–212.

Dreazen, Y. J., and D. Solomon. (2001). Court overturns FCC's ownership caps in victory for AT&T, AOL, cable firms. *Wall Street Journal*, 5 March, A3, A10.

Ducey, R., D. Krugman and D. Eckrich. (1983). Predicting market segments in the cable industry: The basic and pay subscribers. *Journal of Broadcasting and Electronic Media* 27 (2): 155–61.

Federal Communications Commission (FCC). (2001). Annual assessment of the status of competition in the market for the delivery of video programming. Available online: http://www.fcc.gov/Bureaus/Cable/Reports/fcc01001.pdf. Release date January, accessed 10 June.

Head, S. W., C. H. Sterling and L. B. Schofield. (1994). *Broadcasting in America: A Survey of Electronic Media*. 7th ed. Boston: Houghton Mifflin.

Higgins, J. M., and G. Flynn. (2001). Cable slows, DBS sprints. *Broadcasting and Cable*, 4 June, 30–42.

National Cable Television Association. (2001). Available online: http://www.ncta.com.

Noll, R. G., M. J. Peck and J. J. McGowan. (1973). *Economic Aspects of Television Regulation*. Washington, D.C.: Brookings Institute.

Owen, B. M., and S. Wildman. (1992). *Video Economics*. Cambridge: Harvard University Press.

Park, R. E. (1971). *Prospects for Cable in the 100 Largest Television Markets*. Santa Monica, Calif.: Rand.

Satellite Home Viewer Improvement Act (SHVIA). (1999). Available online: http://www.fcc.gov/csb/shva/shviafac.html.

Umphrey, D. (1991). Consumer costs: A determinant in upgrading or downgrading of cable services. *Journalism Quarterly* 68:698–708.

Veronis, Suhler and Associates. (2000a). *Communications Industry Forecast*. New York: Veronis, Suhler and Associates.

———. (2000b). *Communications Industry Report*. New York: Veronis, Suhler and Associates.

8

THE INTERNET INDUSTRY

After reading this chapter, you should:

- Be able to identify the key markets that make up the Internet industry

- Recognize the major companies involved in the various Internet markets

- Understand the different types of market structure found in the Internet markets

- Understand the impact of regulation on the Internet

This chapter, devoted to the Internet, is new to this second edition. Some readers may wonder why a chapter devoted to the economics of the Internet is included in a book entitled *Media Economics*. The rationale is that the Internet has been a transforming force across the media industries represented in this book. Further, while the audience for a single website may be small compared to the audience for a prime-time television program or the daily circulation of a national newspaper like *USA Today*, the cumulative impact of the Internet on traditional media activities is unique (Chan-Olmsted 2000). The Internet is not a mass medium in the same sense as books, magazines or television, but the Internet certainly has the ability to distribute content to audiences in many different forms, as well as attracting advertising and other forms of revenues from companies that desire access to those same audiences.

This chapter does not attempt to cover all aspects of the Internet in a few pages but rather focuses on those key market segments that are most visible to audiences and advertisers. The discussion will focus on the following areas: Internet Service Providers (ISPs), Internet portals, content providers, including both traditional media companies and Internet-only content providers, and Internet advertising.

The *Internet* is a vast network of computers connecting many of the world's businesses, institutions and individuals. The word Internet means *interconnected network of networks*. The Internet exploded in consumer awareness and interest with the introduction of the World Wide Web (WWW) in 1994. Before that time, the Internet contained only text-based information. The Web, however, utilized a computer programming language called *hypertext markup language* (HTML), which was capable of conveying audio and visual material as well as text and graphics.

The actual work on hypertext language had been started in 1989 by Tim Berners-Lee and Robert Cailliau at the European Laboratory for Particle Physics (known by the acronym CERN from its name in French, *Conseil Européen pour la Recherche Nucléaire*). Berners-Lee and Cailliau decided to make their language code available to other developers for free, enabling faster innovation and improvement over the initial hypertext code (see Klopfenstein 2000 for a good summary of Web development).

From 1990 to 1994, a series of steps led to the development of the Web as we know it today. The WWW library of common code was established in 1991, and a year later, physicists around the globe began running web servers. In 1993, Marc Andressen and Eric Bina developed the first *browser* (a piece of software used to access websites), known as Mosaic, at the University of Illinois. Andressen would later move on to develop the Netscape Navigator browser, much improved over Mosaic.

By 1994, the Web began to take off in numerous directions. The first commercial sites began to appear on the Web, leading to a new term for buying and selling via the Internet—*electronic commerce*, or *e-commerce* (Albarran 2000; Schwartz 1997). Web browsers were offered for free to users and also bundled (included) with the software package in new computers. Schools and colleges rushed to offer courses related to information technology, web page authoring, and e-commerce. Just about every business and organization—including the White House—debuted a *home page*, the starting page of a website that functions as a sort of electronic table of contents and helps users navigate the site.

But the Internet was not just a U.S. phenomenon. The introduction of the Web triggered worldwide interest in the technology, leading to a massive global adoption of personal computers and Internet access. With so many people able to interconnect via the Internet, it seemed as if media theorist Marshall McLuhan's concept of a "global village" introduced in the 1960s had finally came of age.

By 1998–1999, consumer adoption continued to move at a dizzying rate, and businesses followed as websites offered new ways to search for information (Yahoo!, Alta Vista, Excite) buy books and recordings (Amazon), purchase tickets for travel (Expedia and Travelocity) and buy or sell personal merchandise (eBay). Unfortunately but not surprisingly, pornographic and "hate" websites mushroomed, raising concerns about access by children and youth. Other concerns also emerged, ranging from privacy and security issues to the fear of a "digital divide," with low-income and less-educated individuals unable to gain access to the Web due to the prohibitive costs of obtaining a computer and Internet access.

Still, Web euphoria had gripped the world by the late 1990s, leading to a number of Internet-related services and companies labeled *dot-coms* to signify the commercial suffix of many websites. Many scholars argued that the Web was in the process of transforming society; virtually everything would change (see, e.g., Evans and Wurster 2000; Shapiro and Varian 1999). But just as quickly as the Internet revolution started, things seemed to fall apart. Many of the dot-coms had been started with venture capital at a time when the economy was very strong and interest rates were low. But the economy began to falter in January 2000, a time when many dot-coms had yet to produce a single dollar of profit. The crash that followed was ugly, and many Internet millionaires who had seen their stock prices soar quickly lost the entire value of their portfolios, leading to a major shake-up in the commercial expectations of the Web.

By 2001, numerous dot-coms were out of business. Thousands of commercial websites were operating, but few were profitable. Many companies cut back on their Web departments, some eliminating them entirely. Everyone seemed to agree that the Internet offered many competitive advantages compared to other forms of technology, but everyone was still looking for a workable business model (The failure of new media 2000). The media industries, quick to jump on the Web bandwagon, began rethinking their business strategy and trying to determine how to turn their Web units into revenue streams instead of expense centers.

It is in this environment that we now turn our attention to the Internet as an industry, looking at the primary market segments that have emerged since 1990, when the first hypertext markup language made its debut. Again, the focus in this chapter will be on the following market segments: Internet Service Providers (ISPs), Internet portals, content providers and Internet advertising. Differing slightly from the framework in other chapters, each market discussion will also identify the leading companies operating in the market and analyze market structure and market concentration.

Key Internet Markets

Internet Service Providers (ISPs)

Internet service providers (ISPs) offer online access to users, either free or for a fee. Users access the Internet in one of several ways: through a paid or free dial-up connection using a modem, via a broadband connection such as those offered through a cable modem or a digital subscriber line (DSL), through an Internet TV device such as Web TV or via satellite. Wireless cable provides a limited form of access to specially equipped cellular phones as well as personal digital assistants.

Online access generates some of the largest revenues related to the Internet. For example, in 1994, online access reached just over $1 billion. By 1999, online access had jumped to $9 billion, with expectations of reaching $14 billion by 2004 (Veronis, Suhler & Associates 2000a, 2000b). In mid-2001, an estimated 70.1 million households subscribed to an Internet Service Provider (Pastore 2001).

An estimated 9,400 companies offer online access throughout the country, but the largest is America Online, owned by AOL Time Warner. In mid-2001, the number of AOL subscribers exceeded 22 million. Microsoft, through its Microsoft Service Network (MSN) is the second-largest provider, serving 5 million subscribers, while Earthlink is the third largest ISP, serving 4.8 million subscribers (Fusco 2001). The top 10 ISPs as of June 2001, are listed in Table 8.1.

The top 10 ISPs account for more than 76 percent of all subscribers, indicating a market that is increasingly concentrated. Using the estimated market share, the CR4 ratio equals 52.6 percent, while the CR8 equals 71.3 percent. What we have is essentially a two-tiered market structure, with the top 10 companies controlling more than 76 percent of all subscribers and the remaining companies fighting for less than one-fourth of the available market.

There is considerable volatility among ISP subscribers. Quality of service is an important issue for users, as is price. Demand is highly elastic, and price clearly has an impact on subscribers. Users try different services before deciding which service to adopt that best meets their needs. The growing influ-

Table 8.1. Top Internet service providers (as of June 1, 2001)

Company	Subscribers (In millions)	Estimated ISP Market Share
AOL	22.7	32.5
MSN	5.0	7.2
Earthlink	4.8	6.9
Juno	4.1	6.0
NetZero	3.7	5.4
Excite@Home	3.2	4.6
Prodigy	3.1	4.4
CompuServe	3.0	4.3
BlueLight.com	2.0	2.4
Gateway.net	1.7	2.4

Source: Adapted from Fusco, 2001. This data changes monthly; consult the Internet for the latest numbers.

ence of broadband subscribers will also affect the ISP market. As broadband diffuses, more dial-up users are likely to switch, possibly leaving behind companies like AOL, MSN and Earthlink.

Internet Portals

While ISPs provide the online access link to the Internet, most users' browser opens to an Internet *portal*, the starting point for a Web session. Portals initially gained popularity among users for their search capabilities, and today they offer many different types of features, including the ability to personalize the page to get information wanted the most by the user.

Some ISPs (such as AOL and MSN) also function as portals in that they offer entry points to the Internet. But because their primary function is as an ISP, this section will focus on those websites that are not involved in selling online access.

Veronis, Suhler and Associates (2000b) track only eight public reporting companies in the portal segment, but in reality there are many more. In 1999, these eight companies generated $946 million in revenues, more than doubling their 1998 revenue of $419 million. However, operating losses for these companies grew as well, with few firms producing any profits. Most of the revenues obtained by Internet portals come primarily from the sale of advertising, with some revenues from e-commerce.

Yahoo! is the largest portal on the Internet and the most popular, with 1999 revenues reaching $588 million. According to Jupiter Media Metrix, which measures Web activity, Yahoo! draws more than 50 million *unique visitors* (different individuals as opposed to repeat visits by the same individuals) from each month to its site (see http://www.mediametrix.com for the most current data). Yahoo! made two major acquisitions in 1999, broadcast.com (now Yahoo! Broadcast Services) and GeoCities.

Terra Lycos, owned by the Spanish telecommunications company Telefonica, is the next largest portal, with 1999 revenues of $135 million. Other popular portals include Ask Jeeves, Excite, Goto.com, Looksmart, Verity and the National Information Consortium, which operates the government portals eFed and NIC Conquest.

Portals are among the most popular sites on the Internet. Table 8.2 lists the top 10 sites for a typical week during August 2001, with the average time spent by each unique visitor. As the sample week in Table 8.2 illustrates, the amount of time varies considerably among websites, with the exception of eBay, which averages a higher usage pattern in comparison with other sites.

In terms of market structure, the portal submarket is perhaps best identified as an oligopoly simply due to the limited number of companies qualifying as actual portals. With Yahoo! dominating the segment in terms of

Table 8.2. Top Internet sites and average time spent (August 6, 2001)

Website	Time Spent (Minutes: Seconds)
AOL Time Warner Networks[a]	16:11
Yahoo![a]	29:21
MSN	24:52
Microsoft[a]	4:37
Lycos	9:02
Excite@Home	11:50
eBay	38:51
Disney Interactive[a]	15:38
About.com	6:57
Google	6:41

Source: Adapted from Nielsen NetRatings (2001). (www.nielsen media.com). This data changes weekly; consult the website for the latest information.

[a]Data is aggregate user time compiled from multiple web sites controlled by the same company.

revenues, the company is the clear leader among those entities identified solely as an Internet portal. Again, this definition of a "pure" portal must be taken lightly, because some economists would consider AOL and MSN portals as well as access providers.

Content Providers

Content providers range from traditional media companies with an online presence to Internet-only entities. For example, there are many websites associated with traditional media companies, such as ESPN, MTVi and the online version of the *Wall Street Journal*, wsj.com. Likewise, there are sites that offer content that are not affiliated with any brick-and-mortar establishment, including C/Net, Salon.com, Expedia and ZD Net. Content providers are distinct from retail sites (e.g., Gap, Sears).

For consistency of presentation, we again consult the Veronis, Suhler and Associates (2000b) data on Internet content providers for details on revenues for this submarket of Internet activity. According to these data, 1999 revenues for content providers totaled $1.1 billion, up from $479 million in 1998. However, only one publicly reporting content provider, ZDNet, reported positive operating income for 1999. In other words, all publicly reporting content providers in the Veronis, Suhler and Associates report lost money in 1999, except for ZDNet.

C/Net generated the largest revenues ($112 million) in 1999 to lead the segment. C/Net completed several mergers in 1999, acquiring NetVentures,

Winfiles.com, KillerApp Corp. and Auction Gate Interactive. The company also initiated a joint venture with AOL to provide exclusive software and hardware buying guides on the service (Veronis, Suhler and Associates 2000b).

ZDNet was the second largest content provider in terms of revenue, with $104 million in 1999, and the only company to post a profit. Travelocity.com, USA Networks and Sportsline.com rounded out the top five companies in the segment, totaling approximately $402 million, or about 36 percent of the total revenues for the segment (Veronis, Suhler and Associates 2000b). Other recognizable content providers operating in this segment of the Internet include InfoSpace.com, TheStreet.com, Playboy.com, iVillage and NBC Internet.

Like the ISP market, there are hundreds of content providers trying to make money on the Internet, but just about all companies continue to operate in the red. The market would best be described as a monopolistic competitive market, but that could change if the economy grows bullish on the Internet.

Advertising

Like many media industries, the Internet depends on advertising dollars to operate. Most commercial websites sell advertising, and it is a very important revenue stream for the entire Internet industry. Advertisements on the Internet come in many different forms, but for the most part *banners, clickthroughs* and e-mail are the primary methods used to attract Internet users to sample ad messages.

As the Internet turned into a commercial medium in the 1990s, advertisers slowly began to allocate dollars to the online world. In 1995, only $50 million was spent in the United States for online advertising, out of a total of nearly $120 billion spent on advertising across all media (Veronis, Suhler and Associates 2000b). Internet advertising topped $1 billion in 1998, swelling to over $4 billion in 1999. Veronis, Suhler and Associates (2000a) projected that online advertising will grow to just over $24 billion by 2004. Another source, eMarketer (2001), projected that online advertising would reach $23 billion in 2004. Should these projections hold, online advertising would become the fourth largest category of U.S. ad spending, behind newspapers, television and radio.

TOP ADVERTISING CATEGORIES AND TOP ADVERTISERS   Many companies participate in online advertising. Categories and the top advertisers vary from year to year. Table 8.3 lists the top five advertising categories for 1999 and the amount of spending for online advertising for each category.

Considering that online advertising is designed to attract Internet users, it is understandable that computer- and technology-related websites and e-commerce sites would encompass the two largest categories of online ad spending.

Table 8.3. Top five Internet advertising categories

Category	Advertising Spent (in millions)
Computers and technology	$663
Electronic commerce	278
Financial services	192
Local services	133
Media and advertising	127

Source: Veronis, Suhler and Associates (2000a).

Financial services also spend a lot of money on online advertising, knowing that online users are likely to fall in the middle- and upper-income categories and would have the ability to utilize financial services such as investment and brokerage sites. Media and advertising, the fifth largest category of ad spending, reflects the need for media companies to reach consumers involved in different types of media consumption.

The top 10 online advertisers vary from week to week and from year to year, although many individual advertisers can be found within the top five categories of advertiser spending on the Internet. Table 8.4 lists the top 10 online advertisers for a representative week in August 2001.

The companies listed in Table 8.4 consist of six companies involved in computers or technology and e-commerce; two sites devoted to retailing and two sites devoted to financial services. Rankings for the top advertisers on websites are based on the number of impressions generated from web pages.

Table 8.4. Top Internet advertisers (as of August 6, 2001)

Rank	Company
1	Microsoft Web Sites
2	AOL Time Warner Sites
3	Yahoo!
4	EBay
5	Sony
6	Classmates Online
7	Providian Bank Corporation
8	Barnesandnoble.com
9	Gap
10	J. P. Morgan Chase & Company

Source: Adapted from Jupiter Media Metrix (2001) (www.mediametrix.com) and Nielsen Net Ratings (www.nielsenmedia.com) websites.

Note: This data changes weekly; consult the web sites for the latest information.

Whenever a unique visitor sees a banner ad or other type of advertising message, this is counted as a single impression.

PLACEMENT OF ADVERTISING DOLLARS   With an understanding of how much money is spent for online advertising and recognizing the top categories and top individual advertisers, our focus now turns to where the advertising dollars are being placed. Portals receive most of the advertising dollars, no doubt because they account for the largest number of Internet users. It is estimated that portals such as Yahoo!, Excite and others account for 49 percent of all online advertising (Veronis, Suhler and Associates 2000b).

Content providers such as C/Net, ZDNet and other niche sites collected about 22 percent of online advertising revenues in 1999 (Veronis, Suhler and Associates 2000b), followed by traditional general content providers (e.g., media and entertainment companies). A breakdown of 1999 online advertising revenues by type of site is listed in Table 8.5.

Internet advertising will likely experience cyclical behavior for the next four to five years due to a sluggish economy and a general slowdown in ad spending. Of all categories of media-related advertising, online advertising offers the greatest growth potential through 2004.

Impact of Regulatory Forces on the Internet

There are numerous regulatory issues associated with the Internet. For users, concerns over privacy and security are of utmost concern (Lee 2000). While encryption technology and secure websites continue to improve, many consumers are still very concerned about submitting personal information on a web page, whether it is credit card information used to order a product or storing preferences for a particular site. Too many websites are victims of hackers, and the fear of personal information falling into the hands of strangers

Table 8.5. *Placement of online advertising revenues (1999)*

Type of Site	Estimated Expenditure (in millions)
Internet portals	$2,254
Content providers	1,010
General content/Media & entertainment	568
Other sites	609

Source: Adapted from Veronis, Suhler and Associates (2000b).

is of great concern. Privacy and security issues are a major impediment to e-commerce growth among consumers (Albarran 2000).

For content makers and providers, issues of intellectual property represent another area of concern. Content owners are threatened by illegal piracy, duplication and distribution of copyright-protected works over the Internet (Lee 2000). The Napster controversy (see Chapter 10) in the recording industry demonstrated the problems of protecting intellectual property when content is converted to a digital file. The motion picture industry is trying to avert some of these problems by offering a film-on-demand service to computer users (Orwall 2001). No one is precisely sure how much of an economic loss is caused by illegally duplicated works, but it is likely to be in the billions of dollars.

Taxation of items purchased over the Internet is another issue, especially for state governments that fail to collect state and local taxes from e-commerce activities. In 1998, the Internet Tax Freedom Act established a three-year ban on any new Internet sales taxes as a way to spur e-commerce activity. Congress in 2001 extended the moratorium on Internet taxation for two more years, to 2003.

As a collection of global interconnected networks, the Internet is impossible to regulate per se. Some countries have tried to limit Internet access for certain types of sites. For example, France was able to get eBay to restrict French citizens' access to Nazi memorabilia, while Islamic nations try to control access to pornography. We can expect regulators to monitor developments and enact policies to try to protect consumers and content providers as the Internet continues to diffuse.

Impact of Technological Forces on the Internet

It is almost an oxymoron to talk about the impact of technology on the Internet since the Internet is all about technology. Instead, the focus in this section will be on Internet access.

Use of the Internet depends on access, and access varies considerably around the globe. Online statistics are found in many places on the Internet, but one website often cited is www.nua.com. As of August 2001, the site projected total online population worldwide at about 513 million. The breakdown by regions of the world is detailed in Table 8.6.

Given that the total population of the world is somewhere around 5.9 billion people, obviously there is considerable growth potential for more users to access the Internet. As the data in Table 8.6 illustrate, the developed regions of the world are much farther along than the developing regions in providing access. Online access, while important, may be of less use in regions where people lack adequate water, electricity, and food supplies. Total global online access will take many more years.

Table 8.6. Online users in millions (as of November 2000)

Africa	4.15
Asia/Pacific	143.99
Europe	154.63
Middle East	4.65
USA/Canada	180.68
Latin America	25.33
Worldwide	513.41

Source: How many online? (2001) (www.nua.org).

Turning back to the United States, the growth of broadband technology adds to the ease of use and satisfaction with the Internet. A study released in August 2001 by the Federal Communications Commission (FCC) found that the United States has made considerable progress in the diffusion of broadband. For example, in 1999 high-speed Internet service was found in 56% of all zip codes, but a year later had grown to 75% of all zip codes (Broadband adoption 2001). Critical to electronic commerce and online or streaming media, there are about 3.6 million high-speed households using cable modems, and 2 million DSL subscribers. The FCC projected that as many as 9.4 million households may have high-speed access by early 2002 (Broadband 2001).

Wireless access will also provide an increasing path to the Internet, whether available via cell phones or *personal digital assistants* (PDAs), such as organizers and handheld computers. Wireless access will improve with the implementation of the new 3G technologies, an improved standard for wireless transmission.

The Economic Future of the Internet

Internet access via broadband technology, Internet advertising and electronic commerce will together push the Internet industry toward new heights in the first three to five years of the 21st century. According to Veronis, Suhler and Associates (2000a), online access and advertising could reach $38.9 billion by 2004, making the industry the fastest-growing segment among media-related industries.

Electronic commerce, or e-commerce, comes in different models such as business-to-business (B2B), business-to-consumer (B2C), and consumer-to-consumer (C2C, as with sites such as eBay that facilitate consumer transactions with one another). The first category, B2B, encompasses electronic data exchange among business partners, the sale of items via corporate intranets and extranets and traditional selling. B2C occurs whenever individuals purchase items from the Internet, be it software and books to clothing and gifts.

Electronic commerce data are difficult to compile. Forrester Research (2001) reported that U.S. e-commerce reached $488 billion in 2000, and was projected to grow to an astounding $3.45 trillion by 2004 to lead the world market. Worldwide, e-commerce revenues were projected to grow from $657 billion in 2000 to a total of $6.8 trillion by 2004.

This section really illustrates who makes money from the Internet, at least in these continuing early stages. ISPs make money by providing online access. Portals and other heavily used sites capture the majority of the advertising dollars. Business-to-business commerce accounts for the majority of e-commerce revenues.

As reported in many chapters of this text, the challenge for many media industries is finding the best business models to draw revenues from consumers. Only a limited number of categories have attracted significant consumer dollars: adult, gambling, sports, gaming and music. Television and film companies; newspapers, books and magazines; and the recording industry are all attempting to use the Internet to effectively sell products and services to consumers. When companies identify the most efficient methods to accomplish this task, the economic growth of the Internet will progress to another level.

Summary

The introduction of the World Wide Web forever changed the Internet, resulting in massive worldwide adoption of computer technology and online access. Today, more than 500 million people worldwide are connected to the Internet, engaged in a variety of behaviors ranging from e-mail to instant messaging to shopping and surfing.

The Internet industry is made up of several different markets of activity. Online access, dominated by Internet service providers (ISPs), enables users to connect with the Internet. Portals offer a variety of search and information services to visitors. Content providers offer information and entertainment products and services to consumers. Advertisers invest in the online world to reach consumers who are using the Internet, often to the detriment of traditional media.

Access is still a major issue in Internet adoption, especially for developing regions of the world. High-speed Internet access via cable modems and digital subscriber lines (DSL) will diffuse rapidly in the 21st century, enabling users to have a faster and more gratifying experience with the Internet. Privacy and security issues will keep some potential users from ever engaging in e-commerce. Preserving copyright and intellectual property in a digital world will continue to be a major challenge for content creators.

A booming economy during the mid-1990s helped lead the surge of consumer and business activity moving toward the Internet. The economic collapse in 2000–2001 brought the world back to reality. The Internet is well positioned for future economic growth via online access, advertising and e-commerce.

Discussion Questions

1. How did the introduction of the World Wide Web affect the Internet?
2. Discuss the different markets for the Internet. What markets are the most lucrative in terms of revenues?
3. How does a portal differ from an ISP? Is AOL a portal or an ISP?
4. What are some of the regulatory issues impacting the Internet?
5. How does access to the Internet vary around the world?

Exercises

1. Consider the types of Internet access available in your area. Gather research on the different companies, the features they offer and the price they charge for their service. Explain why consumers would choose one service over another.
2. Compare AOL, Yahoo!, MSN, Excite and Lycos. How are these sites similar? How are they different? How do these portals differ in other countries? Which portals are the most popular in other developed countries?
3. Conduct a survey of Internet users to determine the type of Internet access they have and their level of satisfaction, especially with different types of services (e.g., dial-up versus broadband). Determine if they have ever engaged in electronic commerce. For those who have never purchased information over the Web, find out why they have avoided e-commerce.
4. Keep a log for a week to record your own time spent with the Internet. Record the time spent online in terms of hours and minutes each day. Then in a separate column, write down the primary activity (e-mail, research, financial, surfing). Ask a few friends and family members to do the same. What patterns did you observe in your own log? How does your usage compare to that of your friends and family members? How does your usage compare to those with or without high-speed access?

References

Albarran, A. B. (2000). Electronic commerce. In *Understanding the Web: Social, Political and Economic Dimensions of the Internet*, edited by A. B. Albarran and D. H. Goff. Ames: Iowa State University Press, pp. 73–94.

Broadband. (2001). National Cable Television Association. Available online: http://www.ncta.com/broadband.

Chan-Olmsted, S. (2000). Marketing mass media on the World Wide Web. In *Understanding the Web: Social, Political and Economic Dimensions of the Internet*, edited by A. B. Albarran and D. H. Goff. Ames: Iowa State University Press, pp. 95–116.

eMarketer. (2001). *eCommerce Revenues 2001–2004*. Available online: http://www.emarketer.com. Accessed 28 August.

Evans, P., and T. S. Wurster. (2000). *Blown to Bits: How the New Economics of Information Transforms Strategy*. Boston: Harvard Business School.

Forrester Research. (2001). Available online: http://www.forrester.com. Accessed 15 August.

Fusco, P. (2001). Top 20 ISPs by subscribers. Available online: http://www.isp-planet.com/research/rankings/usa.html. Release date 11 June, accessed 13 August.

How many online? (2001). Available online: http://www.nua.org. Accessed 4 August.

Jupiter Media Metrix. (2001). Available online: http://www.mediametrix.com. Accessed 6 August.

Klopfenstein, B. C. (2000). The Internet phenomenon. In *Understanding the Web: Social, Political and Economic Dimensions of the Internet*, edited by A. B. Albarran and D. H. Goff. Ames: Iowa State University Press, pp. 3–22.

Lee, L. T. (2000). Privacy, security and intellectual property. In *Understanding the Web: Social, Political and Economic Dimensions of the Internet*, edited by A. B. Albarran and D. H. Goff. Ames: Iowa State University Press, pp. 135–164.

Nielsen NetRatings. (2001). Available online: http://www.nielsenmedia.com. Accessed 6 August.

Orwall, B. (2001). Film studios join venture for video on demand. *Wall Street Journal*, 17 August, A3-A4.

Pastore, M. (2001). Number of U.S. households online grows in second quarter. Available online: http://www.internetnews.com/isp-news/article/0,,8_862411,00.html. Release date 8 August, accessed 12 August.

Schwartz, E. (1997). *Webonomics*. New York: Broadway Books.

Shapiro, C., and H. R. Varian. (1999). *Information Rules*. Boston: Harvard University Press.

The failure of new media. (2000). *Economist*, 19 August, 53–55.

Veronis, Suhler and Associates. (2000a). *Communications Industry Forecast*. New York: Veronis, Suhler and Associates.

———. (2000b). *Communications Industry Report*. New York: Veronis, Suhler and Associates.

IV

The Motion Picture and Recording Industries

9

THE MOTION PICTURE INDUSTRY

After reading this chapter, you should:

- Be able to identify the major players, market structure and economic characteristics of the motion picture industry

- Understand the exhibition windows important to motion picture revenues

- Understand the oligopoly practices used in the motion picture industry

- Know how self-regulation is used in the motion picture industry

- Realize how technology is affecting the motion picture industry

The motion picture industry continues to serve as a major source of entertainment for audiences worldwide (Litman 1996). Movies are produced along a range of genres and capture the attention of audiences across many age groups and cultures. The motion picture industry draws audiences and revenues through several different forms of exhibition—beginning with the box office and continuing through other *windows* such as home video, pay-per-view, premium cable, syndication sales and international distribution.

The leading companies associated with the Hollywood motion picture industry have been in operation for several decades. The early movie companies attempted to establish market power through *vertical integration*—controlling all aspects of production, distribution and exhibition, the latter through the ownership of individual theaters. Eventually the government forced the larger studios to divest themselves of either the distribution or exhibition functions through the Paramount antitrust case. The studios wisely retained the lucrative distribution operations in lieu of exhibition (Litman 1990).

Gomery (1998b) points out that the companies that make up the movie industry have faced numerous challenges over the years, ranging from the introduction of television, cable television and home video to numerous technological, social and demographic changes. The industry has remained stable because the major companies in the movie industry have adopted one of two operational strategies. Some companies are horizontally integrated across different media industries (e.g., Vivendi Universal and Sony) and draw revenues through other business segments, which helps subsidize other divisions. Others, such as AOL Time Warner and Viacom, have adopted a strategy of vertical integration in which a movie produced by their studios will eventually be seen on their premium cable services and cross-promoted via publishing outlets.

The economics of the motion picture industry, the focus of this chapter, are fascinating to examine. For the most part, the motion picture industry is a healthy media industry, drawing revenues through several important exhibition streams. Box-office receipts have grown at an average rate of nearly 8 percent every year since 1996 (see Table 9.1) and were expected to grow to $10.3 billion by 2004 (Veronis, Suhler and Associates 2000a). The movie business is also risky. In 1999, it cost an average of $51 million to produce and market a movie, and some films with lavish production budgets (e.g., *Titanic*) cost several times the average amount. In Hollywood, a film is not considered a success unless box-office sales surpass $100 million.

Movie production costs began to stabilize during the late 1990s (see Table 9.2). In 1980, the average production cost per feature film was approximately $8.5 million. By 1990, average costs had more than tripled, to $26.8 million; in 1999, the costs declined from the two previous years to an average price of $51.5 million (MPAA 2000).

Table 9.1. U.S. box office receipts (millions of dollars)

Year	Total Admissions
1970	$ 1,162
1975	2,115
1980	2,750
1985	3,749
1990	5,021
1995	5,494
1996	5,912
1997	6,366
1998	6,949
1999	7,448

Source: Motion Picture Association of America (2000).

Table 9.2. Production costs—average U.S. feature film (millions of dollars)

Year	Total Costs
1980	$ 8.5
1985	16.8
1990	26.8
1995	36.4
1996	39.8
1997	53.4
1998	52.7
1999	51.5

Source: Compiled by author from Motion Picture Association of America (2000).

The returns on a hit film can be staggering. *Titanic*, released in 1997, collected $601 million in domestic ticket sales alone (Top 50+ films 2001). Total revenues from the movie, videos and international distribution easily generated another $1 billion. The Paramount studio film *Snow Day*, a comedy released in 2000, cost only $13 million to produce yet returned nearly $105 million in ticket sales. Rentals and purchases of the movie netted another $19.5 million. In contrast, the movie *Mission Impossible II*, another Paramount film starring popular actor Tom Cruise, cost $125 million to produce and returned $215 million in ticket sales, plus another $51.5 million in purchases and rentals. The 10 all-time highest-grossing U.S. movies are presented in Table 9.3.

The motion picture industry does more than simply make movies. Hollywood studios are also heavily involved in producing television movies and

Table 9.3. Top U.S. feature films (as of May 2001)

Film	Date	Box Office Gross (millions)
Titanic	1997	$601
Star Wars	1977	$461
Star Wars: The Phantom Menace	1999	$431
E.T.	1982	$400
Jurassic Park	1993	$357
Forrest Gump	1994	$330
The Lion King	1994	$313
Return of the Jedi	1983	$307
Independence Day	1996	$306
The Sixth Sense	1999	$293

Source: Top U.S. feature films, www.movieweb.com/movie/alltime.html (2001, May 31)

Table 9.4. Feature film studio ownership by top media groups

Media Group	Revenue (in billions)	Film Studios Owned
AOL Time Warner	$34.2	Warner Bros. Pictures; New Line Cinema: New Line Cinema, Fine Line Features, New Line International, New Line Television; Castle Rock Entertainment; Telepictures Productions
The Walt Disney Co.	23.4	Miramax Films, Buena Vista Filmed Entertainment, Walt Disney Feature Animation, Buena Vista International, Touchstone Films
Vivendi Universal	22.6	Universal Pictures, Working Title (50%), Universal Pictures International, United International Pictures (50%), CANAL + Le Studio CANAL + (company plans to spin off)
Viacom	20.3	Paramount Pictures, Nickelodeon Movies, MTV Films, United International Pictures (33%)
Sony Corp.	16.9	Sony Pictures Entertainment, Columbia TriStar Motion Picture Group, Columbia TriStar Home Video, Columbia TriStar Television Group
News Corp.	14.3	20th Century Fox, Fox 2000, Fox Studios, Fox Searchlight, Fox Animation Studios

Source: Adapted from Special Report, Top Media Groups, *Broadcasting and Cable* (2000, August 8), pp. 32-40.

programming for broadcast networks and stations (Gomery 1998b). Several of the major studios have merged with broadcast networks (see Table 9.4). In fact, Sony and Vivendi Universal are the only two studios not directly tied to a major broadcast network.

The Market for Motion Pictures

The motion picture industry draws revenues from a number of different markets. Our discussion in this chapter centers on four markets: (1) consumer demand for movies as represented by the sale of box-office tickets, (2) home video, (3) international distribution and (4) product placement. Another important revenue stream is the revenue derived from the licensing of movies to premium cable and pay-per-view services, as discussed in Chapter 7; that information is not repeated here.

Consumer Demand at the Box Office

Demand for box-office tickets is influenced by a number of microeconomic and macroeconomic factors. Disposable income, marketing and promotion, demography and competition with other types of entertainment all affect consumer demand for motion pictures.

Box-office sales (see Table 9.1) have kept pace with the rising costs of making movies. In 1995, domestic ticket sales totaled $5.4 billion, improving to $7.4 billion by 1999 (MPAA 2000). Admission ticket prices have also increased along with the cost of making movies. In many large markets, the ticket for an evening performance averages around $7.

Annual surveys conducted by the Motion Picture Association of America (MPAA 2000) find that movie companies continue to attract audiences across demographic groups. According to the most recent MPAA survey, people over the age of 40 accounted for 40 percent of attendance in 2000, followed by the 25-to-39 age group (32 percent) and the 12-to-24 age group (28 percent). The increase in the over-40 age group is critical; in 1990, only 32 percent of the people in this age group attended movies. With the aging of the baby boomers, it is critical that the motion picture industry continue to attract older audiences.

Home Video

The home video market often generates revenues that can surpass the box-office runs. The majority of the companies that distribute the movies also own the home video distribution rights. The home video industry, manifested in the rental and sale of prerecorded videotapes (and videodiscs), exploded during the 1980s with the rapid diffusion of the VHS-formatted videocassette recorder (VCR). Another push for home video came with the introduction of digital videodiscs (DVDs) during the 1990s. Videos can be purchased and rented in a number of different retail establishments, from chain stores such as Blockbuster to supermarkets and convenience stores.

Home video revenues grew to approximately $19 billion in 1999 and were expected to exceed $26 billion by 2004 (Veronis, Suhler and Associates 2000a). Not all sales and rentals of videos are necessarily feature films, but there is little argument that movies capture the bulk of the revenues in the home video market. On average, rental activity accounts for approximately 65 percent of revenues, and the sale of video material has captured the remaining dollars. A profile of the U.S. home video market is found in Table 9.5.

Home video sales and rentals benefited from the entry of DVD in 1997. In 1999, total spending on cassettes reached $17.7 billion, while DVD spending reached $1.6 billion, for a grand total of $19.3 billion (Veronis, Suhler and Associates 2000b). Top rental titles in 2000 were *The Sixth Sense, Double Jeopardy, The Green Mile*, and *Runaway Bride*.

Table 9.5. U.S. home video market

Year	U.S. VCR HH (millions)	% of TVHH with VCRs	Videocassette Sales Prerecored (millions of units sold)	Videocassette Sales Blank (millions of units sold)
1999	85.5	85.1	742	410
1998	84.1	84.6	701	420
1997	80.4	82.0	674	398
1996	78.8	82.2	641	408
1995	75.8	79.5	522	384
1994	72.8	77.3	435	385

Source: Adapted from Motion Picture Association of America, (2000).

International Distribution

The international market is an important part of revenues for the motion picture industry (Storper 1989). Movies are popular around the world, and the international market represents great revenue potential for film companies. The reason is simple; the U.S. population is roughly 280 million, whereas the rest of the world totals over 6 billion people.

The United States continues to be the leading exporter of filmed entertainment among the major developed countries, giving it a strong position in trade. Hollywood studios frequently enter into distribution rights with companies overseas to share in revenues in the international market.

International piracy and illegal copying and distribution of filmed material, especially videotapes, is a major problem in many foreign countries. The actual loss attributed to international film and video piracy is difficult to determine, but estimates suggest a value exceeding $2 billion annually.

Product Placement

Product placement refers to the payments that companies make to movie studios for having their merchandise appear in the studios' films. It was not due to chance that the namesake alien in *E.T.* enjoyed Reese's Pieces or that James Bond drove a BMW, and Coke and Pepsi are notorious for getting their sodas into the hands of movie actors. Although it may look like free advertising, those companies paid for the placement of their products on screen. Prices vary, and product placement has become an important source of revenue for motion picture companies.

Related to product placement is the use of advertiser promotional tie-ins with feature films. Advertisers pay for the exclusive rights to exhibit movie characters with their products and are often also part of product placement agreements. Companies such as Pepsi, Coca-Cola, Taco Bell, Pizza Hut,

McDonalds, Burger King and various automakers regularly use product placement as a means of extending brand identity and awareness for their goods.

There are no composite statistics regarding the amount of revenues obtained from product placement and promotional tie-ins for the motion picture industry. Any major *search engine* (a computer program for locating information on the Internet, such as Google) will produce a list of companies engaged in marketing product placement in the motion picture and television industries.

Major Players in the Motion Picture Industry

Six companies, many of which have interests in other media industries, dominate the motion picture industry. The leading motion picture studios together control the market. Following is a brief look at each company and its parent owner, if applicable.

- Warner Brothers (AOL Time Warner). One of the first companies in the movie business; produced the first "talking" picture—the *Jazz Singer* in 1926, in cooperation with Western Electric.
- Paramount (Viacom). Viacom acquired the assets of Paramount Communications in 1994 for $9.7 billion. Paramount is one of the oldest names in the motion picture industry.
- Buena Vista/Touchstone/Miramax/Walt Disney Filmed Animation (The Walt Disney Company). The Disney studios are a major force in the motion picture industry. Disney was the leading film studio in terms of market share in both 1998 and 1999.
- Universal (Vivendi Universal). The Universal studios have changed owners several times in their history. Vivendi, a French company, merged with Seagram and renamed itself Vivendi Universal. The company plans to become a leading provider of different types of media content.
- Twentieth Century Fox (News Corporation). Acquired by media tycoon Rupert Murdoch in the mid-1980s, the studio became the backbone for the Fox television network, which began operation in 1986.
- Columbia Tri-Star/Sony Pictures Entertainment (Sony). Sony acquired Columbia Pictures from Coca-Cola in 1989 for $3.4 billion. Sony has considered selling the studios after several lackluster years but still retains ownership.

In addition to the six major companies, a number of independent studios also make up the motion picture industry. DreamWorks SKG, founded in 1994 by Oscar-winning director Stephen Spielberg, former Disney executive Jeffrey Katzenberg and recording industry executive David Geffen, has delivered a number of major hits in just a few years, including *Saving Private Ryan, Gladiator, American Beauty, Cast Away* and *Shrek*. MGM (Metro Goldwyn Mayer) used to be one of the major studios, but financial troubles and management problems have plagued the studio in recent years.

A number of smaller, independent film companies had found success by the end of the 1990s. Alliance Atlantic Communications was the largest independent in 1999, with revenues of $438 million (Veronis, Suhler and Associates 2000b). Pixar, which coproduced both *Toy Story* movies with Disney, was the second-largest independent in 1999, followed by Trimark Holdings.

Market Structure

The motion picture industry represents an oligopoly structure, with more than 95 percent of the market share divided among the six leading companies. The motion picture oligopoly holds a host of advantages that limit the market power of newcomers (see Gomery 1998a, 1998b; Litman 1996). The major studios engage in cross-subsidization (drawing revenues from other business activities), reciprocity (cooperative behavior), horizontal and vertical integration and price discrimination in establishing fees for various exhibition windows.

Market Concentration

Several studies have examined concentration in the motion picture industry, and all have found the industry to be heavily concentrated, with market power clustered among the top companies regardless of the methods used to measure concentration (e.g., concentration ratios, Herfindahl-Hirschman Index [HHI]). Litman (1990) reported concentration ratios and HHIs for selected years in his analysis of the motion picture industry. The top four ratio (CR4) measures ranged between 53 percent and 68 percent; the top eight ratio (CR8) measures ranged from 79 percent to 96 percent, and the HHI ranged from a low of 1,100 to a high of 1,600 (Litman 1990).

Based on 1999 industry data, the author calculated recent financial ratios for the motion picture industry. The CR4 measured 78 percent, and the ratio for the top six firms totaled 99 percent. These ratios are a further indication of an oligopoly market structure.

The Impact of Regulatory Forces on the Motion Picture Industry

The motion picture industry has been subjected to both public (governmental) and private (self-initiated) scrutiny since its inception. Early governmental regulation and court actions were designed to promote competition in the industry. Local and state governments have from time to time censored films by preventing their exhibition in certain communities. Austin (1989) points out that one of the earliest cases of movie censorship involved the 1896 "peep-show" film *Dolorita in the Passion Dance*. This provocative film was removed because it featured bare ankles and "suggestive" posturing!

Over time, the industry has adopted its own regulatory policing in dealing with issues of morality as a means to avoid state and federal censorship. Today, the self-regulatory efforts of the film industry are manifested in the motion picture codes of the MPAA, well known to domestic movie audiences. The current system features the following rating system: G for general audiences; PG for parental guidance suggested; PG-13 for parental guidance suggested especially for children under age 13; R for restricted audiences, which means that no one under age 17 is admitted without an accompanying parent or guardian; and NC-17 for no children under 17, which means no one under age 17 is admitted under any circumstances (Monush 1994). The NC-17 rating has been used infrequently, as the label signifies a major problem in marketing a motion picture. Motion picture producers will often modify film content in order to achieve an R rating, because many theaters will refuse to show NC-17 movies.

Self-regulation remains the primary regulatory influence in the motion picture industry. During the fall of 2000, the MPAA produced a new set of "self-policing mechanisms" to stem criticism from Washington after a Federal Trade Commission report condemned the industry for the way it marketed violent films. Among the guidelines were providing detailed information to consumers as to why films were rated R and preventing any previews for R-rated films from playing before any G-rated film (Orwall 2000).

The Impact of Technological Forces on the Motion Picture Industry

Technology continues have an impact on the motion picture industry in terms of both production and exhibition. Regarding production, new innovations appear every year in the making of motion pictures, helping to draw audiences from around the world. One of the more significant changes is the rapid adoption of the Linux operating system as an alternative to workstations using software from Microsoft or Silicon Graphics Inc. (SGI). (Avery 2001).

Several companies are converting to Linux, including DreamWorks, Pixar, and Industrial Light and Magic, the production company established by *Star Wars* creator George Lucas. Linux is a free software platform that can run on machines that cost an average of $5,000, as compared with a Silicon Graphics Inc. machine with a price tag of over $20,000. Animators in particular are very pleased with the products created using Linux, such as the film *Shrek*.

But it is the exhibition area that may experience the greatest degree of change in the motion picture industry in the years ahead. Movie studios are interested in partnering with theater chains to equip movie theaters with the needed technology to show digital films (Mathews and Orwall 2001). Presently, the motion picture industry spends millions of dollars distributing reels of film to theater operators around the globe. Moving to a digital environment would eliminate this expense, as the movies would be distributed electronically to large servers from which the movies could be shown to audiences.

The cost to convert thousands of theater screens across the country to an all-digital environment will be enormously expensive, however. Hence, the studios are willing to discuss cost-sharing proposals with the theater operators to see if agreements can be reached to change the way films are distributed in the United States. The new technology would not only eliminate many distribution costs but also have a major impact on the economics of the motion picture industry. How soon or when this might happen is unknown, but the studios appear to be interested in moving forward with plans to revamp film distribution.

In the short term, a consortium of studios (Sony, Warner Brothers, Universal, Paramount and MGM) announced plans in August 2001 to deliver feature films to consumers via the Internet for a fee (Orwall 2001). Using encryption and compression technology, the films would be downloaded to the purchaser and must be played within 30 days. Once the file is actually opened, the film must be viewed within 24 hours. The studios, well aware of the problems digital downloading brought to the recording industry (as will be discussed in the next chapter), hope to offer a legitimate service that will ease concerns over piracy and illegal distribution of feature films.

The Economic Future of Motion Pictures

The motion picture industry has a mixed outlook in regard to its economic potential. While revenues have escalated, production and marketing costs have soared, leaving operating margins at record lows in both 1998 and 1999 (Veronis, Suhler and Associates 2000b). Growth rates for the industry from 2000 to 2004 were expected to be about the same as the preceding five-year period: around 6 to 7 percent for box-office receipts and 6 percent for home video.

The Internet has become an important tool for marketing new releases. Most films released now have an accompanying website that helps promote the film to audiences. Interest in DVD will expand this market in the years ahead, as many homes bypass VHS tapes in favor of DVDs that can be accessed on both traditional DVD players and computers equipped with DVD drives.

The motion picture industry will continue to be concerned with issues regarding governmental oversight or investigations, international piracy and constant technological change. Like many media industries, the motion picture industry competes in a crowded marketplace for consumer attention, with many products considered close substitutes for movie entertainment.

Summary

The motion picture industry participates in several different markets, with the bulk of revenues drawn from different exhibition windows such as the box office, home video, premium cable and pay-per-view, international distribution and syndication. The industry generates a lot of revenues, but operational costs are also very high, leading to low profit margins and a flat economic outlook.

Consumer demand has remained strong, and industry surveys suggest that people are attending movies across age groups, especially adults over the age of 40. Home video sales and rentals have been stimulated by the introduction of DVD and are expected to grow to a $26 billion business by 2004. International distribution, product placement and promotional tie-ins are other important streams of revenue for the movie industry.

Six companies dominate the movie industry, together accounting for more than 95 percent of the market. The six major companies are AOL Time Warner Viacom, Walt Disney, Vivendi Universal, News Corporation and Sony. Smaller companies include DreamWorks SKG, MGM, Alliance Atlantis, Pixar and Trimark Holdings.

The motion picture industry is an oligopoly. Although products are differentiated, movie studios engage in similar practices of cross-subsidization, horizontal and vertical integration and price discrimination. The industry is heavily concentrated according to concentration ratios and poses significant barriers to entry for new competitors.

Most of the regulatory activities in the motion picture industry are internal, coordinated by the Motion Picture Association of America. The public is most familiar with the MPAA rating codes of G, PG, PG-13, R and NC-17. Technological forces are having an impact on the motion picture industry in the areas of production and distribution. New entertainment technologies are competing for the attention and disposable income of movie audiences.

Revenue projections for the movie industry suggest that box-office receipts will be sluggish through 2004, averaging only about 6 percent growth. Home video and syndication will produce stronger growth estimates for the industry. Total industry revenue is expected to reach approximately $36 billion by 2004.

Discussion Questions

1. What does the term *windows* mean? How is it used in the motion picture industry?
2. Discuss the different revenue streams for the motion picture industry. Why are box-office sales expected to be sluggish?

3. How are product placement and promotional tie-ins used in the film industry? Give examples.
4. What countries hold ownership in Hollywood film studios?
5. What is the MPAA? What are the principal activities of the MPAA as discussed in the chapter?

Exercises

1. With other class members, conduct a small-scale survey of movie patrons. Determine how many times they attend a movie in a month, their age and other demographic characteristics, and other information as warranted. Compare your findings with those of other class members.
2. Review the movie listings in the daily newspaper. How many current films do the major studios produce? How many films are the products of independent companies?
3. Schedule an interview with a theater owner or manager. Determine how he or she decides which films will be shown in the theater, the length of the run and other information. Report on your findings.
4. With other class members, conduct a survey of home video rental or purchase activity, similar to the survey described in exercise 1. Share your findings with other class members.

References

Austin, B. A. (1989). *Immediate Seating: A Look at Movie Audiences*. Belmont, Calif.: Wadsworth.

Avery, S. (2001). Linux takes Hollywood as Microsoft, SGI Trail. *Wall Street Journal*, 17 May, B5, B9.

Gomery, D. (1998a). Media ownership: Concepts and principles. In *Media Economics: Theory and Practice*, 2d ed., edited by A. Alexander, J. Owers and R. Carveth. New York: Lawrence Erlbaum Associates, pp. 45–52.

———. (1998b). The economics of Hollywood. In *Media Economics: Theory and Practice*, 2d ed., edited by A. Alexander, J. Owers and R. Carveth. New York: Lawrence Erlbaum Associates, pp. 175–183.

Litman, B. R. (1990). The motion picture entertainment industry. In *The Structure of American Industry*, 8th ed., edited by W. S. Adams. New York: Macmillan, pp. 183–216.

———. (1996). *The Motion Picture Mega-Industry*. Boston: Allyn and Bacon.

Mathews, A. W., and B. Orwall. (2001). Major studios discuss plan to equip theaters to show digital films. *Wall Street Journal*, 17 May, A1, A8.

Monush, B., ed. (1994). *The International Motion Picture Almanac*. New York: Quigley.

Motion Picture Association of America (MPAA). (2000). Available online: http://www.mpaa.org. Accessed 6 June 2001.

———. (2001). Available online: http://www.mpaa.org. Accessed 6 June.

Orwall, B. (2000). Film industry to unveil self-policing mechanisms. *Wall Street Journal*, 26 September, B10.

———. (2001). Film studios join venture for video on demand. *Wall Street Journal*, 17 August, A3–A4.

Special Report: Top Media Groups. (2000). *Broadcasting and Cable*, 8 August, 32–40.

Storper, M. (1989). The transition to flexible specialization in the U.S. film industry: External economics, the division of labour, and the crossing of industrial divides. *Cambridge Journal of Economics* 13:273–305.

Top 50+ films of all time. (2001). Available online: http://www.movieweb.com. Accessed 31 May.

Top U.S. feature films. (2001). Available online: http://www.movieweb.com/movie/all-time.html. Accessed 31 May 2001.

2000 attendance study. (2000). Motion Picture Association of America (MPAA). Available online: http://www.mpaa.org/useconomicreview/2000AttendanceStudy/index.htm. Accessed 6 June 2001.

Veronis, Suhler and Associates. (2000a). *Communications Industry Forecast*. New York: Veronis, Suhler and Associates.

———. (2000b). *Communications Industry Report*. New York: Veronis, Suhler and Associates.

10

THE RECORDING INDUSTRY

After reading this chapter, you should understand:

- The major players, market structure and economic characteristics of the recording industry

- The historical development of the recording industry

- Factors influencing consumer demand for recordings

- The role the Recording Industry Association of America (RIAA) plays in regulating the industry

- The impact of the Internet on the recording industry

The recording industry plays an important role in both the commerce and the culture of a society. In this chapter, the focus is on sound recordings in consumer-oriented formats. As a leading source of entertainment, sound recordings bring pleasure to millions of listeners through a variety of different prerecorded formats such as compact discs and cassettes. As a source of culture, sound recordings have served as a catalyst for change and a reflection of cultural values (Vivian 1995). Historically, the recording industry has been one of the most profitable media industries in the world, but the growth of the Internet has led to new ways to access music and thus made the economic future of the recording industry less certain. This chapter begins with a brief discussion of the historical development of the recording industry and then examines the economic characteristics of the industry.

Historical Development of the Recording Industry

The Mechanical Era

The ability to reproduce sound has captured the imagination of engineers and scientists since the 19th century. Early pioneers, such as the great American inventor Thomas Edison, were only interested in reproducing speech. Edison patented a device in 1877, which he called a phonograph, that was capable of mechanically reproducing sound using a tin foil cylinder. Vivian (1995) explains that although Edison's invention was fascinating for its time, it lacked commercial success because the crude recordings could not be duplicated.

Eventually a wax disc was perfected that could record sound and also play it back. The discs also could be manufactured in quantity and distributed (sold) to people. A hand-cranked device called the Gramophone appeared around 1887, to be followed years later by the Victrola, which debuted in 1925. The Victrola, manufactured by the Victor recording company, was later acquired by the Radio Corporation of America (RCA) and renamed RCA Victor. Today, RCA still exists in the recording industry but under different ownership.

The Electronic Era

The electromagnetic or electronic phase for recordings eliminated the hand-cranked appliances by the early 1930s. Recordings could now be enhanced through electronic components by improving and amplifying the sound. Early recordings operated at a speed of 78 revolutions per minute (RPM), which became the standard phonograph speed.

Recording technology continued a number of enhancements through the 1940s and 1950s. Wax discs were replaced by vinyl, which produced a better quality of sound. The long-playing (LP) record, operating at a speed of 33 RPM, eliminated the constant changing of discs associated with the old 78 recordings. Magnetic tape recording was perfected in the mid-to-late 1940s, following World War II, and master recordings could be made on tape and then transferred to discs. Single vinyl recordings called 45s were introduced in 1949 and became popular with teens because of their low prices. The radio industry embraced the 45 RPM format during the 1950s with the rock 'n' roll revolution.

Stereo sound was perfected by 1961, replacing the old high-fidelity, or hi-fi, system. Stereo recordings were eagerly received by consumers and served as a major force in the development of FM radio. In fact, stereo sound gave FM a distinct identity over AM radio and led to a gradual shift toward FM dominance (Albarran and Pitts 2001). Formats for recordings also expanded with the introduction of the eight-track tape and the cassette. The tape formats represented a major change for consumers; for the first time, listening to their favorite recordings could now take place away from their stereo set.

The Digital Era

During the 1970s, digital technology was perfected, leading to the next great wave of change in recording music formats. Using a computer binary code of 1s and 0s, scientists could capture and record individual sound waves in millisecond intervals and play them back in the same way, using laser technology that reads each recorded bit of information. The result was a new format produced on a 4.7-inch platter known as the compact disc, or CD. Compact discs were introduced to consumers in 1983, and today the CD is the primary format for sound recordings, followed by cassettes and then vinyl.

In November 1992, the Motion Pictures Experts Group introduced the MPEG-1 format as the standard for storage and retrieval of moving pictures and audios on various types of storage media—including computer servers. By 1994, the original MPEG format had been refined, and MPEG-3, also known by the more common name of MP3, came into existence.[1] MP3 would cause major concern for the recording industry, because the new format allowed individuals to convert and copy audio tracks from a CD to MP3, and the files could then be shared with other users. This innovation led to the growth of a number of websites devoted to sharing MP3 files, and a huge controversy with the recording industry.

Music Videos

Music videos—short films based on popular songs, showing the musicians playing the song and sometimes including other images to create a mood or tell a story—were introduced to U.S. consumers in 1981 with the debut of the Music Television (MTV) cable channel. Although some observers feared that the video versions of popular recordings would economically harm the recording industry, the opposite occurred. Music videos became very popular with younger listeners and bolstered the sale of recorded music.

The original music videos were based on rock music. Today, the music video industry has expanded into other formats, including country, urban, rap and hip-hop. In addition to MTV, other channels showing music videos include Video Hits 1 (VH-1), Country Music Television (CMT) and Black Entertainment Television (BET).

Recording Industry Activities

Recordings are produced and manufactured by major recording companies and their subsidiary labels and then distributed to the public through retail establishments. The recording industry tracks the number of units (expressed in CDs, audiocassettes, vinyl and video formats) shipped each year, as well as the total revenues collected from retailers.

The recording industry operates in an interdependent relationship with the radio industry, as well as music video programmers such as MTV, Country Music Television (CMT) and Black Entertainment Television (BET). Radio stations and music video channels use recordings as a form of programming. This exposure helps showcase and promote new recordings and aids in the marketing efforts of the recording companies. Consumers hear recordings on radio stations and watch music videos, which creates demand for the products.

Radio stations and video channels pay royalties to independent licensing firms such as American Society of Composers, Authors and Publishers (ASCAP), Broadcast Music Incorporated (BMI) and the Society of European Stage Authors and Composers (SESAC) to use the copyrighted products manufactured by the recording industry. The bulk of the royalties derived from these fees goes to the composers and authors of various recordings, with a small portion retained by the recording industry firms.

Markets in the Recording Industry

Although other media industries are characterized by a number of different markets in which they offer products and services, the recording industry derives the majority of its revenues from a single market—consumers. Most consumer purchases are made at various retail establishments such as chain music stores (e.g., Blockbuster Music, Sam Goody, Musicland, Tracks), general merchandise stores (e.g., Wal-Mart, Kmart, Target) or independent record shops. Customers can purchase a number of products, including CD albums, CD singles, cassette albums, cassette singles, LPs and DVDs.

CDs lead the consumer market, accounting for 89.3 percent of all sales in 2000 (RIAA 2000). Consumer demand for recordings is influenced by a number of microeconomic and macroeconomic factors, including demography, discretionary income, promotion, advertising and marketing of new recording products, radio station or video channel acceptance and the impact of the Internet.

Demand statistics for recordings from 1995 to 2000 are presented in Table 10.1. The number of units shipped each year has been relatively flat since 1995, although the value of shipments has increased. Expectations for future growth are sluggish. Veronis, Suhler and Associates (2000a) predict only a 2.1 percent growth rate through 2004, with the value of shipments expected to reach $16 billion.

According to data compiled by the London-based International Federation of the Phonographic Industry (IFPI), the global music market revenues reached $36.9 billion in 1999. Overall units shipped remained level, with a growth of 3 percent in the CD market offset by a 10 percent decline in cassette

Table 10.1. Demand for recordings (in millions of dollars)

Year	Units Shipped	Value of Shipments
1995	1,112.7	$12,533.8
1996	1,137.2	12,533.8
1997	1,063.4	12,236.8
1998	1,124.3	13,723.5
1999	1,160.6	14,584.5
2000	1,079.3	14,323.0

Source: Recording Industry Association of America (2001).

album sales and an 11 percent decline in sales of cassette singles (*Recording Industry World Sales* 2000).

The United States dominates the global market, with a 38 percent share of world sales. The nine next largest markets and their approximate market shares are Japan (16.7%), the United Kingdom (7.6%), Germany (7.4%), France (5.2%), Canada (2.3%), Brazil, Australia and Spain (1.7% each) and Mexico (1.6%) (*Recording Industry World Sales* 2000).

Major Players in the Recording Industry

Five major companies dominate the recording industry. Most companies hold interests in other types of media. These five companies are referred to in the recording industry as the "majors." A list of the companies and some of the individual labels they represent follows.

- AOL Time Warner. This is the only U.S. firm holding a dominant position in the recording industry. Among the Time Warner labels are Warner Brothers, Atlantic and Elektra as well as numerous smaller labels.
- Sony Corporation. The Japanese electronics firm entered the recording industry in 1988 with the acquisition of CBS records. Major labels include Columbia records, Epic, Legacy and Tri-Star Music.
- Bertelsmann. This German company acquired RCA records in 1988 from General Electric. RCA, Arista records and some 30 smaller labels make up what consumers recognize as the BMG Music Group.
- EMI Group. Formerly Thorn EMI, EMI Group of England has several labels, including Chrysalis, Capitol, Virgin, Blue Note, Credence and Food Label. In 2000, Time Warner tried to acquire EMI but was rebuffed by European regulators over antitrust concerns. Bertelsmann also made a play for EMI but was unsuccessful (Ordonez 2001).

- Universal/Polygram. This company resulted from the merger of Seagram and Polygram, both of which are now part of the larger conglomerate Vivendi Universal. Universal/Polygram consists of a number of labels, including MCA, Motown, Decca, Interscope and Geffen Records.

Each of the five majors produces, manufactures and distributes its own recording products through its major labels and a host of smaller, subsidiary labels. The organization of a typical record company is illustrated in Figure 10.1.

In addition to the five majors, there are other suppliers in the recording industry, although together they account for only a small percentage of total industry revenues. These companies include mini-major labels, major-distributed independent labels and true independent labels. *Mini-major labels* produce and manufacture recordings but are not involved in distribution; this is done by one of the major labels. A *major-distributed independent label* primarily signs artists to contracts with majors or mini-majors and is responsible for everything except the actual recording. *True independent labels* have no affiliation or connection with majors or mini-majors and market their products through independent distributors.

Market Structure

The small number of companies that dominate the recording industry indicates an oligopoly market structure. Alexander (1994) uses two models of product release behavior to illustrate how the recording industry reflects an oligopoly structure. The products produced by each of the major labels use the

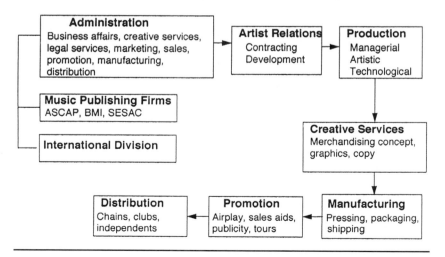

FIGURE 10.1. *Record company organization.*

same formats (e.g., CDs, cassettes, music videos, vinyl) and sell for approximately the same price to retailers. The companies also share similar distribution functions. These similar practices are typical in an oligopoly market structure.

Each recording is different from one another, however, which makes the recording industry oligopoly interesting to observe. Individual packaging, promotion and format establish product differentiation. Further, the individual signing of recording artists to exclusive labels further differentiates one company from another in the mind of the consumer.

Market Concentration

With five companies dominating revenues in the recording industry, the market is heavily concentrated. It is difficult to determine the actual revenues for each of the five major companies due to several factors. First, only one player (AOL Time Warner) is a publicly owned company based in the United States; the other major companies are all international corporations. Second, individual reporting of company revenues varies; some of the companies report their recording revenues separately, whereas others report recording revenues along with other lines of business.

Using data from Veronis, Suhler and Associates (2000b), the author calculated CR4 and CR8 concentration ratios for 1999. The CR4 ratio reached 98 percent, while the CR8 ratio measured 99 percent. These market shares represent significant barriers to entry for new competitors, in that the five majors control the majority of recording artists and distribution methods. Over the years, these data reflect the steady consolidation in the music industry as the larger companies have consistently acquired small and medium-size labels.

Regulatory Forces in the Recording Industry

The recording industry encounters regulatory forces in several different areas. The industry attempts self-regulation through the RIAA in an effort to stave off governmental regulation. The RIAA represents the interests of the recording industry as a lobbying force in Congress and has been successful in gaining copyright and anti-piracy regulation while fighting off censorship challenges.

Over the years, controversial lyrics of musical recordings have brought about public criticism and calls for governmental intervention. Songs that alluded to drug usage during the 1960s, such as the Doors' "Light My Fire" and Jefferson Airplane's "White Rabbit" were easy targets of watchdog organizations. During the 1980s, the Parents Music Resource Center

(PMRC) was formed in Washington, D.C., and called for immediate censorship of controversial lyrics, especially those related to sex, drugs and violence (Vivian 1995). Working within the industry, the RIAA was able to develop self-policing policies in which record companies placed warning labels on controversial material and restricted the sale of some recordings to persons age 18 or older.

Payola—the practice of influencing the selection and play of certain types of recordings in the radio industry through compensation in the form of cash or other gifts—is prohibited. Payola represents an example of the interdependent relationship between the recording industry and the radio industry. In an effort to get the produced material aired on radio stations, bribes in the form of payola have been offered by recording companies to secure an unfair advantage. Payola is harmful to the programmer and the recording industry, and both may be subject to fines by the Federal Communications Commission (FCC) and the Federal Trade Commission (FTC).

Most consumers have made their own home recordings (referred to as "home dubbing") either from taping directly off a radio station or by borrowing a friend's recording and making a copy of it in another format (such as CD to cassette). Whenever recordings are reproduced at home, the record industry loses money, because most consumers will not purchase material that they have already copied. The debut of MP3 technology, along with the development of Napster and related websites that allow for the sharing of audio files, created a nightmare for the recording industry, leading to questions about the industry's ability to protect copyrighted material.

Interestingly, Napster's introduction came after the passage of the Digital Millennium Copyright Act in December 1998. The legislation implemented two 1996 World Intellectual Property Organization (WIPO) treaties: the WIPO Copyright Treaty and the WIPO Performances and Phonograms Treaty. The act also addressed a number of other copyright-related issues, including copying of computer-related files (see Digital Millennium Copyright Act 1998). However, this legislation is being challenged in federal court by opponents who claim that the law stifles scientific exploration of technologies designed to "prevent illicit copies of digital music" (Hamilton 2001). The outcome of this litigation could pose new challenges for the recording industry in its efforts to limit the economic impact of the Internet. These areas are discussed further in the following section.

New Technologies in the Recording Industry

Napster founder Shawn Fanning released software in May 1999 that allowed individuals with Internet access to identify and trade songs stored on the MP3 format with one another. Over the next few months, Napster users mushroomed by the millions. Many college campuses were forced to block access to Napster because having so many students accessing the popular site caused Internet access to bog down. Interest in other file-sharing sites such as MP3.com and Gnutella also grew. But Napster generated the most attention, leading to a lawsuit by the five majors claiming that the service could potentially rob the companies of billions of dollars in profits (Robinson 2001). A legal battle ensued, leading to the Ninth U.S. Circuit Court of Appeals ruling that Napster infringed on copyrights controlled by the recording companies (Harris 2001). The court required Napster to block access to copyrighted materials archived by its users. Other "Napster clones" are also being targeted by the recording industry (Gomes 2001a, 2001b).

Napster's introduction brought with it both blessings and curses for the recording industry. The technology that led to interest in downloading music via Napster will not go away. For the recording companies, the issue was how to be able to draw revenues from Internet distribution, as opposed to illegal copying of recordings by computer users.

The recording companies responded by creating their own Internet services. AOL Time Warner, Bertelsmann and EMI launched MusicNet in conjunction with Real Networks. Vivendi Universal and Sony Music teamed up to create an Internet music platform called PressPlay to distribute music through the portal Yahoo! In an effort to reposition itself as a legitimate service, Napster reached a licensing accord with MusicNet in June 2001 (Peers 2001).

The Economic Future of the Recording Industry

The recording industry has shown stagnant growth in the past few years, and future projections anticipate continued slow growth. Most industry analysts expect a growth rate of 2 to 3 percent due to the uncertainty of Internet downloads that may siphon away paying customers. Veronis, Suhler and Associates (2000a) offer a very conservative growth rate of 2.1 percent through 2004.

In terms of shipments, CDs will continue to outsell cassettes in the future. CDs will contribute to industry growth, but at a slow pace. DVDs will become more important over the next five years as more video material featuring musicians becomes available.

International markets will continue to be important for industry revenues. Most of the successful recording artists in the world are from the United States, and thus America's industry leadership position will remain unchallenged abroad. Concerns over the continuing impact of technology, the Internet and court decisions create an uncertain economic environment in the recording industry.

Summary

The recording industry for many years was one of the most profitable media industries in the United States and abroad. In the immediate future, concerns over technology through the sharing of music files via the Internet, along with flat consumer demand, impose limitations on growth. But the recording industry has always been marked by technological change and progress, having evolved from a mechanical system to an electromagnetic system to the current system employing digital technology. At the beginning of the 21st century, the industry finds itself in a position to evolve once again.

Recordings are produced and manufactured by major companies and their subsidiary labels and then distributed to the public through retail establishments. The recording industry maintains an interdependent relationship with the radio industry. The recording industry supplies needed programming to radio stations, and stations provide much needed exposure to consumers. Music video services also enjoy a similar relationship with the recording industry.

Consumers form the primary market for recordings, which are acquired from chain music stores, retailers, independent record shops and the Internet. Demand for recordings varied through the 1990s; units shipped and revenues were relatively flat from 1995 through 2000. Revenues for the domestic recording industry reached $14.3 billion in 2000, out of a total of $36 billion worldwide. The recording industry is expected to grow at about a 2 percent rate through 2004.

The recording industry is dominated by five major companies: AOL Time Warner, Sony, Bertelsmann, EMI and Universal/Polygram, a subsidiary of Vivendi Universal. The five companies compose an oligopoly market structure and account for more than 95 percent of industry revenues. The market is heavily concentrated, with significant barriers to entry for new competitors.

The recording industry is primarily self-regulated through the RIAA, its industry association. The RIAA has been successful in securing copyright and anti-piracy regulation. The organization was critical in working with its members to limit the impact of Napster on the industry.

The Internet will continue to have an impact on the recording industry. Other file-sharing sites will continue to exist, posing the threat of loss of revenues. In the interim, the recording industry is developing an online distribution presence through two partnerships: MusicNet and PressPlay. Their success depends heavily on their ability to attract paying customers via the Internet.

Discussion Questions

1. How did the three eras of development (mechanical, electronic, digital) change the recording industry?

2. What are the various functions of a recording company?
3. The recording industry primarily serves a single market, that of consumers. How does this aspect differ from other media industries examined in this text?
4. What challenges and opportunities does the Internet pose for the recording industry? How successful do you think the recording industry will be in distributing music online? What factors might influence Internet distribution? What factors will limit Internet distribution?
5. The recording industry represents an oligopoly structure. Why is it unlikely that any new competitors will emerge to challenge the five major recording companies?

Exercises

1. Pick out one of the five major labels identified in the chapter and answer the following:
   a. What are the sublabels under this company?
   b. What recording artists appear on these labels?
   c. In what formats (e.g., CD, cassette, DVD) are products released?
   d. Where (locally) can you find this company's recordings for sale?
   e. Are products licensed under ASCAP, BMI or SESAC?
2. Find a list of top-selling recordings in your area, and compare it with a national listing in a publication such as *Billboard* or *Radio and Records*. What recordings are similar on the list? Which ones are different?
3. Compare the costs for recordings sold at several local retail establishments. Are prices lower at one type of location than another? How do local prices compare with prices offered by music clubs such as BMG and Sony? How do prices compare with music available over the Internet?
4. Which current recordings contain controversial lyrics or parental advisory labels? Do these recordings appear on the local top-seller list?

Note

1. MP3 does not really stand for MPEG-3, but rather MPEG1 layer 3. The "layer 3" part refers to the compression algorithm developed at the University of Erlanger by Dr. Dieter Sietzer. Many people and publications refer to the new format simply as MP3.

References

Albarran, A. B., and G. G. Pitts. (2001). *The Radio Broadcasting Industry*. Needham Heights, Mass.: Allyn and Bacon.

Alexander, P. J. (1994). Entry barriers, release behavior and multi-product firms in the music recording industry. *Review of Industrial Organization* 9:85–98.

Digital Millennium Copyright Act. (1998). U.S. Copyright Office Summary. Available online: http://www.loc.gov/copyright/legislation/dmca.pdf. Accessed 20 May 2001.

Gomes, L. (2001a). "Open Napster" clones feel industry heat. *Wall Street Journal*, 23 February, B9.

———. (2001b). Entertainment firms target Gnutella. *Wall Street Journal*, 4 May, B6.

Hamilton, D. P. (2001). Digital copyright law faces new fight. *Wall Street Journal*, 7 June, B10.

Harris, R. (2001). Court says Napster must stop. Available online: http://www.ap.com/topstories. Accessed 12 February 2001.

Ordonez, J. (2001). Twice jilted, EMI faces the music alone. *Wall Street Journal*, 6 June, B2.

Peers, M. (2001). Napster reaches licensing accord with MusicNet. *Wall Street Journal*, 6 June, B6.

Recording Industry Association of America. (2000). 2000 consumer profile. Available online: http://www:riaa.org. Accessed 5 June 2001.

———. (2001). Available online: http://www.riaa.org.

Recording Industry World Sales 2000. (2000). Available online: http://www.ifpi.org. Accessed 5 June 2001.

Robinson, S. (2001). Online music companies outplayed. *Interactive Week*, 10 January, 27–30.

Veronis, Suhler and Associates. (2000a). *Communications Industry Forecast*. New York: Vernonis, Suhler and Associates.

———. (2000b). *Communications Industry Report*. New York: Veronis, Suhler and Associates.

Vivian, J. (1995). *The Media of Mass Communication*, 3d ed. Needham Heights, Mass.: Allyn and Bacon.

V

*The Print
Industries*

11

THE NEWSPAPER INDUSTRY

After reading this chapter, you should understand:

- The major players, market structure and economic characteristics of the newspaper industry

- The types of advertising found in newspapers

- How newspaper chains dominate the industry

- How economies of scope and barriers to entry have led to single newspapers in many cities

- How newspapers have embraced the Internet

The newspaper industry represents one of the oldest forms of mass media in the United States, second only to the book publishing industry. Throughout its colorful history, the newspaper industry has been an important source of social, political and cultural information to generations of readers. The newspaper industry has also played a pivotal role in commerce, serving as a major commercial entity linking advertisers and consumers.

Newspapers offer something for every type of reader. Local, national and international news represent the major categories of newspaper content sought by most readers. Sports, weather, editorials, advice, columns and features, comics, puzzles and games, advertising and other types of data are among the regular sections found in many metropolitan and hometown newspapers. Unlike other forms of publishing, the daily newspaper is a product that has a life of only 24 hours or less!

Newspapers remain popular as an important source of news and information, even in today's saturated electronic media environment. Statistics from the Newspaper Association of America (NAA) indicate that 55.1 percent of all adults read a daily newspaper on an average weekday. The Sunday newspaper has an even higher reach. It is estimated that 65 percent of all adults read a Sunday newspaper during an average week (Newspaper Association of America 2001). Nationally distributed newspapers, such as the *Wall Street Journal, New York Times* and *USA Today*, are regularly read by thousands of people every day.

In addition to daily and Sunday papers, weekly newspapers (also known as suburban papers) reach millions of readers. More than 1,000 online newspapers have emerged in the United States alone, giving readers another means of reading a newspaper.

Newspapers continue to be among the most profitable forms of mass media in the United States. Newspapers routinely attract the largest percentage of advertising revenues when compared with television and radio, although the margin between newspapers and television narrowed during the 1990s. In 1999, total newspaper advertising revenue (national, retail and classified) was estimated at $46.2 billion (Newspaper Association of America 2001). Combined with weekly subscriber fees and the sale of papers through newsstands and other outlets, the newspaper industry currently attracts over $50 billion through advertising and circulation sales (Newspaper Association of America 2001).

The newspaper industry grapples with a number of issues, including sluggish circulation, the opportunities and threats provided by the Internet, the cyclical cost of newsprint and a competitive media marketplace. As this chapter will illustrate, newspapers are different from other mass media industries in terms of their characteristics and market structure.

The Market for Newspapers

The newspaper industry operates in a dual product market, selling the same product to both consumers and advertisers. Daily newspapers, which consist of morning and evening newspapers and Sunday editions, represent the most visible form of newspaper activity. Weeklies, or suburban papers, make up a second, smaller market. Online newspapers have emerged as the newest market.

Daily Newspapers

There were approximately 1,483 daily newspapers in operation in the United States in 1999, compared with more than 1,600 in 1990 (Veronis, Suhler and Associates 2000b). Picard (1993) found that 90 percent of these papers exist as the only newspaper in their city of operation. Table 11.1 reports data for morning, evening and Sunday newspapers for selected years between 1950 and 1999. Several trends are apparent when examining the table. First, the total number of daily newspapers has dropped since 1950, experiencing a steady decline since 1980. Second, evening papers continue to outnumber morning papers, although the gap separating morning and evening papers has narrowed over the years. Finally, the number of Sunday newspapers grew steadily through 1995 but has remained relatively flat since then.

According to Veronis, Suhler and Associates (2000b), total annual circulation for morning papers was 45.9 million in 1999, the highest figure reported in newspaper history. Annual circulation for evening papers was 9.9 million the same year, a drop of nearly 10 million papers from 1990. Evening newspaper circulation has fallen steadily since 1965, in conjunction with the decline in the number of evening papers. Sunday circulation has remained relatively steady since 1995. In 1999, Sunday circulation was reported at 59.8 million papers.

Average daily circulation (ADC) is the best indicator of consumer demand for daily newspapers. The 20 largest daily newspapers are listed in Table 11.2. The two largest papers, the *Wall Street Journal* and *USA Today*, are considered national newspapers in the sense that they do not serve a specific geographic area, or *retail trading zone* (RTZ), a term commonly used in the newspaper industry. Other papers on this list are also available in many parts of the country and thus widely read, including the *New York Times, Washington Post,* and *Chicago Tribune.* Industrywide, weekday circulation accounts for approximately 11 percent of all newspaper revenues, and Sunday circulation accounts for 5 percent of total revenues.

Table 11.1. Number of U.S. daily newspapers

Year	Morning	Evening	Total M&E	Sunday
1950	322	1,450	1,772	549
1955	316	1,454	1,760	541
1960	312	1,459	1,763	563
1965	320	1,444	1,751	562
1970	334	1,429	1,748	586
1975	339	1,436	1,756	639
1980	387	1,388	1,745	735
1985	482	1,220	1,676	798
1990	559	1,084	1,611	863
1995	656	891	1,533	888
1996	686	846	1,520	890
1997	705	816	1,509	903
1998	721	781	1,489	897
1999	736	760	1,483	907

Source: Newspaper Association of America (2001).

Table 11.2. Largest U.S. dailies by average daily circulation

Paper	Daily Circulation	Edition
The Wall Street Journal	1,752,693	m
USA Today	1,671,539	m
The New York Times	1,086,293	m
Los Angeles Times	1,078,186	m
The Washington Post	763,305	m
New York Daily News	701,831	m
Chicago Tribune	657,690	m
Newsday (New York)	574,941	m
Houston Chronicle	542,414	m
The Dallas Morning News	490,249	m
Chicago Sun-Times	468,170	m
The Boston Globe	462,850	m
San Francisco Chronicle	456,742	m
New York Post	438,158	m
The Arizona Republic	433,296	m
The Star-Ledger (Newark)	407,129	m
The Philadelphia Inquirer	399,339	m
Denver Rocky Mountain News	396,144	m
The Plain Dealer (Cleveland)	386,312	m
The San Diego Union-Tribune	376,604	m

Source: Newspaper Association of America (2001).
Note: m = morning edition.

Elasticity of demand, or the "circulation spiral," is one of several factors contributing to the decline of daily newspapers (see Gustafsson 1978). In cities served by more than one newspaper, one paper usually emerges as the market leader in terms of circulation and advertising linage. Advertisers tend to place more dollars in the paper that attracts the most readers; thus, other papers in the market will receive a disproportionally lower share of advertising dollars. As the leader attracts more readers and advertisers over time, the competitor faces a downward-sloping circulation spiral. Picard (1993) claims that once the leading paper attracts as much as 55 to 60 percent of the circulation in a market, serious financial problems will result for the other paper.

Weekly Newspapers

The Newspaper Association of America estimates that there are 8,138 weekly newspapers, with an average circulation of 5,754 across the United States (Newspaper Association of America 2001). Total weekly circulation is estimated at 74 million papers. Data for U.S. weekly newspapers between 1960 and 1999 are included in Table 11.3.

Table 11.3. U.S. weekly newspapers

Year	Total Weekly Newspapers[a]	Average Circulation	Total Weekly Circulation
1960	8,174	2,566	20,974,338
1965	8,061	3,106	25,036,031
1970	7,612	3,660	27,857,332
1975	7,612	4,715	35,892,409
1980	7,954	5,324	42,347,512
1985	7,704	6,359	48,988,801
1990	7,550	7,309	55,181,047
1995	8,453	9,425	79,668,266
1996	7,915	10,307	81,582,295
1997	7,214	9,763	70,434,299
1998	8,193	9,067	74,284,112
1999	8,138	5,754	74,457,621

Source: Newspaper Association of America (2001).
[a]Includes paid and free newspapers

Weekly newspapers are popular in both rural and suburban communities, where local news and events are emphasized. Large metropolitan cities can devote only a limited amount of space to news in suburban areas, giving weekly papers an eager market for readers desiring more local news coverage. Local retail advertisers find that ad rates at weekly newspapers are cheaper than at their larger metropolitan counterparts and provide greater efficiency in reaching target audiences.

Online Newspapers

Publishing firms were quick to embrace the Internet as a new method for distributing papers and reaching new readers. Online newspapers take one of two forms, either Web versions of daily newspapers or Internet-only papers. The number of online newspapers is a constantly changing variable; in 2001, there were an estimated 1,000 online newspapers in the United States, and more than 4,000 online newspapers worldwide. Most domestic online newspapers attract fewer than 50,000 viewers, and daily subscribers make up most of the audience for online newspapers (Newspaper Association of America 2001). Online newspapers for the most part generate little revenue, but publishers are hopeful that the online editions will improve in their ability to attract revenues. One exception is the online version of the *Wall Street Journal*, which is available on a subscription basis. In 1999, revenues at wsj.com topped $30 million (Veronis, Suhler and Associates 2000a). Studies on online newspapers are beginning to emerge, offering mixed findings on consumer usage (see Chyi and Sylvie 1998; Newspaper Association of America 2001).

The Market for Newspaper Advertising

Newspapers capture a large percentage of advertising dollars among media industries in the United States. In 1999, newspapers accounted for 21.5 percent of all advertising expenditures (Newspaper Association of America 2001). Advertising content takes up about 50 to 60 percent of the total space in a daily newspaper; that proportion is slightly higher on Sundays.

Newspapers draw advertising revenues across three separate areas. National advertising represents the smallest category of revenues and is used primarily by major companies to help market products and services that are distributed nationally. Retail advertising is the most lucrative area for newspapers and is derived from local businesses in the same RTZ as the newspaper. Classified advertising is sold to individuals and small businesses to reach buyers and sellers across different categories (help wanted, housing, automobiles, appliances, garage sales, miscellaneous, etc.).

Newspaper advertising revenues for selected years are detailed in Table 11.4. Total daily and weekly advertising was expected to grow at an average rate of 6.5 percent through 2004, to reach an estimated $71 billion (Veronis, Suhler and Associates 2000a).

Table 11.4. U.S. daily newspaper advertising expenditures (millions of dollars)

Year	National	Retail	Classified	Total Advertising
1950	$ 518	$ 1,175	$ 377	$ 2,070
1955	712	1,755	610	3,077
1960	778	2,100	803	3,681
1965	783	2,429	1,214	4,426
1970	891	3,292	1,521	5,704
1975	1,109	4,966	2,159	8,234
1980	1,963	8,609	4,222	14,794
1985	3,352	13,443	8,375	25,170
1986	3,376	14,311	9,303	26,990
1987	3,494	15,227	10,691	29,412
1988	3,821	15,790	11,586	31,197
1989	3,948	16,504	11,916	32,368
1990	4,122	16,652	11,506	32,280
1995	4,251	18,099	13,742	36,092
1996	4,667	18,344	15,065	38,075
1997	5,315	19,242	16,773	41,330
1998	5,721	20,331	17,873	43,925
1999	6,732	20,907	18,650	46,289

Source: Modified from Newspaper Association of America (2001).

Major Players in the Newspaper Industry

Corporations or groups own most newspapers in the United States. In the newspaper industry, the term *chain* is used to represent group-owned newspapers. The practice of acquiring newspaper chains began in the 1880s, when larger publishers began acquiring a number of newspapers.

The largest chains are listed in Table 11.5, ranked according to daily circulation statistics. Chain ownership surged during the 1970s and 1980s, with record prices paid for many newspapers. The 1990s brought further consolidation among newspaper companies. A major transaction in 2000 involved the Tribune Company's acquisition of Times Mirror (Veronis, Suhler and Associates 2000b).

Many of the companies found in Table 11.5 are among the most profitable companies in the world. As observed in earlier chapters, many of these companies (e.g., Gannett, Tribune, Cox and Belo) also have ownership interests in other media industries. Thomson Newspapers, a Canadian company, is the largest single foreign owner, with approximately 48 dailies.

Table 11.5. *Largest U.S. newspaper chains, ranked by circulation*

Company Name	Daily Circulation	Number Dailies
Gannett Co. Inc.	6,377,565	74
Knight-Ridder Inc.	3,641,410	34
Advance Publications Inc.	2,776,774	23
Times Mirror Co.[a]	2,392,306	9
The New York Times Co.	2,368,193	21
Dow Jones & Co. Inc.	2,311,305	14
MediaNews Group	1,794,362	50
E. W. Scripps Co.	1,412,061	21
McClatchy	1,323,256	11
Hearst Newspapers	1,295,600	12
Tribune Co.[a]	1,244,587	4
Cox Entertainment Inc.	1,106,698	16
Thomson Newspapers Inc.	1,097,967	48
Belo	943,884	9
Freedom Communications Inc.	918,929	26
Washington Post Co.	816,563	2
Central Newspapers	799,129	7
Media General Inc.	790,854	18
Copley Newspapers	717,713	10
Hollinger International	716,732	15

Source: Modified from Newspaper Association of America (2001).
[a]The Tribune Company acquired Times Mirror in the spring of 2000.

Market Structure

The newspaper industry represents a monopolistic market structure across most of the country. The number of cities with two or more competing newspapers has declined as consolidation among newspaper publishers has escalated. Many major metropolitan cities are now served by only one daily newspaper.

The cost structures of producing a newspaper have helped promote a monopolistic structure for newspapers (Picard 1988b). The "first copy" costs to produce a newspaper include considerable fixed and variable costs. Once the first copy is produced, the publisher is able to lower the actual cost per issue through the mass production and distribution of other copies of the paper. Economies of scale lower the costs as more and more papers are produced (Rosse and Dertouzous 1979).

For a rather simplistic example, let's assume that it costs a publisher $10,000 to produce a single copy of the newspaper. As succeeding copies of the paper are reproduced, the cost per issue drops rapidly. Producing 1,000 papers lowers the cost per paper to $10; producing 100,000 papers would lower the cost per paper to just 10 cents each. No doubt, producing 100,000 papers would also increase some of the variable costs associated with newspaper publishing (e.g., ink and newsprint), but economies of scale would still be realized.

Picard (1993) claims that scholars sometimes incorrectly consider newspapers to be natural monopolies. In reality, natural monopolies are able to engage in continuous economies of scale, which is rare in the newspaper industry. Litman (1988) adds that such a situation is possible only where a single firm produces a newspaper in a market, controls the entire market and exercises significant power.

Market Concentration

Newspaper markets are highly concentrated due to a monopolistic market structure. Picard (1988a) calculated concentration ratios for national and local newspaper markets based on circulation data. Picard found that although newspaper markets are highly concentrated, concentration increases as the size of the market decreases. The author calculated concentration ratios using 1999 data for daily newspapers and found that the CR4 equaled 48 percent, while the CR8 equaled 69 percent.

Concentration is a particular concern in the newspaper industry, because newspapers "operate not only in the marketplace for goods and services but also in the marketplace for ideas" (Picard 1988a, 62). The rise in chain ownership, coupled with market concentration, has raised industry concerns about the push for profits at the expense of journalistic endeavors, diversity of expression and balanced presentation. Dertouzous and Trautman (1990) argue that the lack of direct competition in many cities is the result of scale economies in production, advertising, circulation and news.

The concentration of newspaper markets as well as the start-up costs required to develop a new newspaper pose considerable barriers to entry for new competitors desiring to enter the market. Wirth (1986) has shown that it is easier to enter the market for local broadcasting than to begin a newspaper.

The Impact of Regulatory Forces on Newspapers

Newspapers are subject to few regulatory policies at either the local, state or federal levels. In fact, most policies directed toward newspapers have been designed to enhance the economics of the industry. Included are such provisions as exemptions from sales taxes on advertising and relaxation of wage and hour laws for employees.

The most significant legislative reform to affect the newspaper industry was the 1970 Newspaper Preservation Act. Congress passed the act to promote a diversity of expression in those communities where the market could no longer support two competing newspapers. The act allows the establishment of *joint operating agreements* (JOAs) among newspaper firms. Under a JOA, editorial operations remain separate, but all other operations (printing, advertising, distribution, etc.) are combined. According to the NAA, there were 13 JOAs in operation in the United States as of 2001 (Newspaper Association of America 2001). The largest cities with JOAs include San Francisco, Detroit, Seattle, Cincinnati and Las Vegas. At one time there were nearly 30 JOAs in operation, but consolidation eliminated many of those agreements.

The Newspaper Preservation Act has been highly controversial since its inception and has been repeatedly challenged in the courts as to the manner in which the act has been both implemented and interpreted (Picard 1993; Watkins 1990). The act permits the attorney general of the United States to allow new JOAs, provided that one of the newspapers is "in probable danger" of failing (Watkins 1990). In the 1980s, two major judicial challenges concerned the approval of JOAs in Seattle and Detroit. In both cases, the courts allowed the JOAs to remain. With the exception of those papers engaged in JOAs, all newspapers are subject to antitrust laws that prohibit anti-competitive practices and behavior.

Concerns over the increasing size of major newspaper chains, concentration of control and foreign ownership remain important issues in the newspaper industry. However, it is unlikely these events will result in any type of regulatory actions for the newspaper industry. Newspaper publishers are hoping that the Federal Communications Commission (FCC) will relax cross-ownership restrictions that currently bar publishing companies from owning TV stations. Should the FCC act in favor of the publishers, it may trigger further consolidation.

The Impact of Technological Forces on Newspapers

Newspapers have been greatly affected by technological changes in the way papers are prepared, printed and distributed. A number of new technologies have had an impact on production in the newspaper industry. The most significant of these changes was the conversion from the old Linotype (also referred to as hot type) method of typesetting to the use of photocomposition (also called cold type) made possible with computer-linked video display terminals (VDTs). Over the years, improvements in computing technology and software have streamlined the production process for newspapers.

Picard (1993) claims that new technologies have had two major effects on the newspaper industry. First, a newspaper can be produced today with fewer employees. Using computers, writers and editors in the various departments can directly place stories and advertisements on a page without the use of typesetters. Many news and syndicated features are distributed in electronic form and can simply be plugged in to the proper layout position. Second, the newspaper can be produced much faster, allowing for longer deadlines and the ability to provide late-breaking news coverage. This has enabled newspapers to remain more competitive with the electronic media in their ability to cover the news.

Photojournalism has also been affected. Newspapers process photographs directly from the camera, using electronic darkrooms equipped with the appropriate computer hardware and software. Newspapers now have the ability to use digital processing to provide sharper, clearer pictures.

There are positive and negative aspects of adopting new technologies in newspaper production. On the plus side, newspapers can be created more efficiently, with faster processing and distribution. On the down side, new technologies usually require significant outlays of capital, in turn requiring several months or even years to recapture the return on investment. As such, newspaper managers must weigh the benefits against the anticipated costs when considering new technologies.

The Internet will continue to have an impact on the newspaper industry in many ways. Publishing companies will continue to try to build new audiences via their online editions as well as additional revenue streams. Individual time spent with the Internet has the potential to affect newspaper usage from a competitive media perspective.

The Economic Future of the Newspaper Industry

Newspapers remain one of the most profitable forms of mass media in the United States, but concerns remain about the economic future of the newspaper industry. Although circulation data paint a favorable picture of newspaper use, the fact is that fewer members of the population are reading newspapers today. Picard (1993) points out that although newspaper circulation grew nearly 19 percent between 1950 and 1990, the nation's population increased by 70 percent. As a result, newspaper penetration has in reality declined over time. A growing number of younger people (those under age 18) have little interest in reading a newspaper. Likewise, those Americans who either cannot read at all or cannot read very well tend to use radio and television for the bulk of their news and information.

Another continuing problem for the newspaper industry is the cyclical cost of newsprint, which has soared in price since 1970 (see Table 11.6), peaking in 1990 and declining only slightly since then. Recycling of newspapers has helped curb newsprint costs. Approximately 34 percent of all recycled newspapers are reconverted to new newsprint (Newspaper Association of America 2001).

The newspaper industry is expected to grow at a rate of 5.8 percent through 2004 (Veronis, Suhler and Associates 2000a). Veronis, Suhler and Associates expected total newspaper advertising to reach $71 billion by 2004 and overall newspaper revenues (combined daily, Sunday and weekly circulation and advertising) to reach $83.9 billion by 2004. Among the traditional print industries, newspaper growth is expected to exceed that of magazines and consumer books.

Table 11.6. Newsprint prices

Year	Price (per metric ton)
1970	$179
1975	287
1980	440
1985	535
1990	685
1995	658
1996	632
1997	546
1998	587
1999	515

Source: Newspaper Association of America (2001).

Summary

The newspaper industry is one of the oldest forms of mass media in the United States. Newspapers play an important role in society as a source of news and information as well as a commercial entity linking advertisers and consumers.

As an industry, newspapers remain one of the most profitable of all mass media industries, and the most profitable among traditional print industries. Newspapers draw revenues from national, retail and classified advertising as well as through daily and Sunday circulation. Daily papers have declined since the mid-1990s, but weekly papers have flourished, reflecting the population shift of households to the suburbs and the desire for local news in the suburban communities in which they reside. Online newspapers have grown at an astonishing rate at both the domestic and worldwide levels.

Most daily newspapers are part of large chains. Among the leading newspapers publishers in the United States are Gannett, Knight-Ridder, Tribune and Thomson. Most cities in the United States have only one daily paper. Most newspapers operate under a monopolistic market structure. Economies of scope exist in newspaper production, circulation and advertising, creating significant barriers to entry for new competitors. As such, newspaper markets tend to be heavily concentrated.

Newspapers are subject to few regulations at the local, state or federal level. The 1970 Newspaper Preservation Act allows a failing newspaper to combine operations with a stronger competitor in forming a joint operating agreement. Under a JOA, editorial departments remain separate, but all other departments are consolidated. Only 13 JOAs were in operation by the end of 1999.

New technology is changing the way newspapers are created, distributed and consumed. Many newspapers have started online editions to attract Internet users. The cyclical costs of newsprint are a continuing concern for the industry. Newspapers continue to seek ways to expand by offering new products in expanding markets.

Discussion Questions

1. What factors have led to a decline in the number of daily newspapers?
2. What factors have led to an increase in the number of weekly newspapers?
3. Discuss the types of advertising found in the newspaper industry. Which category is the most important to daily newspapers?
4. Discuss the following terms as they relate to the newspaper industry: (a) chain, (b) retail trading zone (RTZ), (c) joint operating agreement (JOA), (d) online newspaper.

Exercises

1. Compare copies of the local daily paper(s) serving your market to the weekly suburban paper(s) serving your market and to any online newspapers produced locally in regard to the following criteria:
   a. amount of space devoted to news
   b. amount of space devoted to advertising
   c. types of advertising found in each paper
   d. circulation
2. Obtain a copy of *USA Today* and the *New York Times*. How are these two papers similar to each other? How are they different? Describe the type of audience each paper serves.
3. Make arrangements to visit a local newspaper. Write a summary of your experiences, noting in particular what you observed in the way of technological enhancements used in producing the paper.
4. Arrange a guest speaker from your local newspaper—ideally a reporter or someone involved in the editorial department.

References

Chyi, H. I., and G. Sylvie. (1998). Competing with whom? Where? And how? A structural analysis of the electronic newspaper market. *Journal of Media Economics* 11 (2): 1–18.

Dertouzous, J. N., and W. B. Trautman. (1990). Economic effect of media concentration: Estimates from a model of the newspaper firm. *Journal of Industrial Economics* 39:1–14.

Gustafsson, K. E. (1978). The circulation spiral and the principle of household coverage. *Scandinavian Economic History Review* 26:1–14.

Litman, B. R. (1988). Microeconomic foundations. In *Press Concentration and Monopoly: New Perspectives on Newspaper Ownership and Operation*, edited by R. G. Picard, M. McCombs, J. P. Winter and S. Lacy. Norwood, N.J.: Ablex, pp. 3–34.

Newspaper Association of America. (2001). *Facts about Newspapers*. Available online: http://www.naa.org. Accessed 19 March 2001.

Picard, R. G. (1988a). Measures of concentration in the daily newspaper industry. *Journal of Media Economics* 1 (1): 61–74.

———. (1988b). Pricing behavior of newspapers. In *Press Concentration and Monopoly: New Perspectives on Newspaper Ownership and Operation*, edited by R. G. Picard, M. McCombs, J. P. Winter and S. Lacy. Norwood, N.J.: Ablex, pp. 55–69.

———. (1993). Economics of the daily newspaper industry. In *Media Economics: Theory and Practice*, edited by A. Alexander, J. Owers and R. Carveth. New York: Lawrence Erlbaum Associates, pp. 181–204.

Rosse, J. N., and J. N. Dertouzous. (1979). The evolution of one newspaper cities. In Federal Trade Commission *Proceedings of the Symposium on Media Concentration*, vol. 2. Washington, D.C.: Government Printing Office.

Veronis, Suhler and Associates (2000a). *Communications Industry Forecast*. New York: Veronis, Suhler and Associates.

———. (2000b). *Communications Industry Report*. New York: Veronis, Suhler and Associates.

Watkins, J. J. (1990). *The Mass Media and the Law*. Englewood Cliffs, N.J.: Prentice-Hall.

Wirth, M. O. (1986). Economic barriers to entering media industries in the United States. In *Communication Yearbook*, vol. 9, edited by M. McLaughlin. Beverly Hills, Calif.: Sage, pp. 423–442.

12

THE MAGAZINE INDUSTRY

After reading this chapter, you should understand:

- The major players, market structure and economic characteristics of the magazine industry.

- The two types of divisions in magazine publishing.

- The various markets for magazines.

- How postal rates and economic downturns affect magazine publishing.

- The impact of the Internet and technology on the magazine industry.

Magazines have been an important source of news, information and literature in the United States since the early 1800s. Magazines have contributed to the transmission of culture, while introducing new journalistic approaches and innovations to the American public (Vivian 1995). As a visual medium, magazines have captured history in their pages. Articles and photographs have informed generations of readers from the Civil War to the Gulf War, charting the growth of America, the collapse of communism, and a changing world culture.

The growth of magazines as a mass medium provided those who could not afford the high price of books the opportunity to read literature from some of the great authors of the world. Magazines such as the *Saturday Evening Post*, the *New Yorker, Atlantic, Look, Life* and *Reader's Digest* are but a few of the magazines that have educated and influenced thousands of readers throughout their publishing history.

Magazine publishing is the work of two separate divisions (Worthington 1994). The business division handles all of the business aspects of the publication, including such areas as marketing, advertising, finance and personnel. The editorial division is charged with producing the content of the magazine and encompasses all of the editors, writers, photographers, graphic artists and other staff needed to create it.

Magazines have changed and adapted through the years, along with other forms of mass media. Magazines no longer attract the large, homogeneous audiences that they did in the pretelevision world. The contemporary magazine industry is specialized, with most publishers targeting smaller markets of readers. The magazine industry increasingly is targeting audiences with products designed to meet specific interests and needs. Evidence of this trend is found in the number of magazine titles published in the United States. According to the Magazine Publishers of America, more than 17,000 magazines are published in the United States (Magazine Publishers of America 2000).

The magazine industry finds itself in a relatively strong economic position at the beginning of the 21st century. Overall, circulation and advertising have increased since the mid-1990s, and projections are that the trend will continue. While some individual titles have experienced declines in both circulation and advertising revenues, overall the industry is healthy.

Magazines draw revenues from two important sources: advertising and circulation. Advertisers represent the largest source of revenue for the magazine industry. According to Veronis, Suhler and Associates (2000b), magazine advertising in 1999 accounted for approximately 56 percent of industry revenues, compared to 44 percent for circulation. Circulation revenues are obtained from consumers who purchase magazines through annual subscriptions or at the newsstand. Single-copy magazines are usually priced higher than the per-issue price through an annual subscription. Single-copy sales were down in both 1998 and 1999, and projections suggested that single-copy sales will continue to decline through 2004 (Rose 2001; Veronis, Suhler and Associates 2000a, 2000b).

Magazines compete for audiences and advertisers with other forms of publishing as well as with the electronic media. With numerous choices available for advertisers and growing leisure-time options for consumers, magazine publishers are aggressively pursuing new products and revenue streams, including the Internet. Magazine publishers recognize the value of using the Internet to extend their brands, and some publishers have been successful in attracting additional advertising dollars through their online counterparts.

The Market for Magazines

As with other media industries, the magazine industry operates in several markets. Magazines can be broken into identifiable submarkets, such as the markets for particular categories of magazines (i.e., consumer magazines, business or trade magazines and professional journals). We could also consider the circulation interval—whether published monthly, bimonthly or weekly—of individual publications as separate markets. Finally, we could consider the U.S. domestic market as compared with magazines designed for global markets.

The magazine industry can also be analyzed by examining the market for advertisers as well as the market for publishing (acquisition of magazines by other publishers). Because of the number of potential submarkets to consider, this section will focus on the market for magazines in three categories of demand: (1) consumer demand for magazines, which will encompass all types of magazines, (2) demand for magazine advertising and (3) demand for magazine acquisitions.

Consumer Demand for Magazines

According to studies conducted for the Magazine Publishers of America (*MPA Handbook* 2001), typical magazine readers tend to be college graduates, work full time, have annual income of $75,000 or greater, own a home and actively use the Internet. Most magazine readers are under the age of 55, however, 18-to-24-year-olds tend to be among the heaviest users of magazines. About two-thirds of all magazines sold are by subscription and one-third by single copy. Some magazines have considerable success with single-copy issues, such as the annual *Sports Illustrated* swimsuit edition and *People* magazine's "Most Beautiful People" issue. The top four locations to buy single-copy issues of magazines are (1) supermarkets, (2) mass merchant retailers such as Wal-Mart, Target and Kmart, (3) drugstores and (4) bookstores.

Consumer, or general-interest, magazines are the most popular publications among readers. The *AARP Bulletin* is the leading monthly consumer magazine in the Unites States in terms of total circulation, primarily because it is provided as a benefit to members of the American Association of Retired Persons (AARP), with the cost included in the organization's annual membership fee. Other leading magazines include *Modern Maturity, Reader's Digest, TV Guide, National Geographic, Better Homes and Gardens, Family Circle, Good Housekeeping* and *Ladies' Home Journal* (see Table 12.1). A total of 10,171 new magazines have debuted since 1985; about 55 percent of these titles were quarterly publications (Veronis, Suhler and Associates 2000b). But not all of these magazines have survived. Since 1990, only 27 percent of all

Table 12.1. Top 20 magazine circulation leaders

Rank	Magazine Title	Circulation
1	*NRTA/AARP Bulletin*[a]	20,554,989
2	*Modern Maturity*	20,419,458
3	*Reader's Digest*	12,962,369
4	*TV Guide*	11,461,612
5	*National Geographic Magazine*	8,566,453
6	*Better Homes and Gardens*	7,605,845
7	*Family Circle*	5,002,547
8	*Good Housekeeping*	4,588,161
9	*Ladies' Home Journal*	4,512,930
10	*McCall's*	4,205,992
11	*Woman's Day*	4,177,306
12	*Time*	4,103,799
13	*People Weekly*	3,599,198
14	*Sports Illustrated*	3,266,553
15	*Home & Away*	3,231,059
16	*Playboy*	3,203,087
17	*Newsweek*	3,162,551
18	*Prevention*	3,148,299
19	*Cosmopolitan*	2,866,794
20	*Westways*	2,666,925

Source: Adapted from Magazine Publishers of America (2000).
[a]Provided as a membership benefit to AARP members.

new titles have remained in publication. Existing titles, some published for several years, also fail to survive. Among titles that ceased publication in 2000 and 2001 were *Sport, Mirabella, Mademoiselle, New Woman, George* and *Today's Homeowner.*

There are magazines for virtually every age group, lifestyle and hobby. General-interest magazines include publications devoted to news, business and finance, entertainment, sports, women, men and general editorial. Special-interest publications consist of magazines devoted to such topics as computers, cars and trucks, health and fitness, participation sports, home, travel and other categories. Cross-media marketing and branding has increased in recent years. Magazines built on established television programming includes A&E's *Biography, ESPN The Magazine, American Movie Classics* and the PBS Series *This Old House.* Established publications have also successfully spawned cable programs or in some cases cable networks, including *National Geographic, People, Better Homes and Gardens, Sports Illustrated for Kids* and *Family Circle* (Veronis, Suhler and Associates 2000b). Celebrities such as Oprah Winfrey and Martha Stewart have been successful producing media content across several media, including magazines.

Prices for magazines increased from 1995 through 1999. Single-copy prices increased an average of 8.3 percent during this time period, while sub-

Table 12.2. Magazine industry statistics

Year	Average Number of U.S. Periodicals	ABC Titles[a]	ABC Single-copy Revenue	ABC Yearly Subscription Revenue
1990	14,049	587	$2,448,191	$4,983,340
1991	14,256	600	2,540,249	5,262,392
1992	14,870	617	2,632,350	5,431,864
1993	14,302	631	2,690,986	5,655,103
1994	15,069	643	2,776,809	5,807,466
1995	15,996	668	2,713,333	5,971,039
1996	17,195	711	2,867,696	6,297,682
1997	18,047	751	3,013,413	6,320,280
1998	18,606	758	3,095,804	6,827,508
1999	17,970	750	3,058,967	6,877,128

Source: Magazine Publishers of America (2000).
[a]Top titles by circulation reporting to Audit Bureau of Circulation (ABC).

scription prices increased 4.6 percent (Veronis, Suhler and Associates 2000b). Prices for both single copies and subscriptions were expected to rise between 2 and 3 percent in both 2001 and 2002 due to anticipated increases in postal fees. Table 12.2 charts the number of magazines published in the United States from 1990 through 1999, along with single-copy and circulation revenue using data compiled from the Audit Bureau of Circulation (ABC) and the Magazine Publishers of America. Note that subscription revenue outpaces single-copy revenue by a nearly 2-to-1 margin throughout the time period presented in the table.

Demand for Magazine Advertising

Of all dollars spent on advertising in the United States, magazine advertising has averaged around 6.8 percent of total advertising revenues since 1995. Advertising revenue for all magazines totaled $11.465 billion in 1999; revenues are expected to reach $16 billion by 2004 (Veronis, Suhler and Associates 2000b).

Magazine advertising is dominated by 10 categories that account for approximately 55 percent of total magazine advertising. The top 10 categories, based on complete 1999 data (Veronis, Suhler and Associates 2000b) are:

1. automotive accessories and equipment
2. technology
3. home furnishings and supplies
4. cosmetics and toiletries
5. direct response
6. apparel and accessories
7. financial, insurance and real estate
8. food and food products
9. drugs and remedies
10. media and advertising

Demand for Magazine Acquisitions

Publishing mergers and acquisitions operated at a frenzied pace through much of the 1980s. According to data compiled by Greco (1993), some 584 transactions took place, with several major U.S. periodicals (e.g., *New Yorker, U.S. News and World Report, TV Guide*) changing ownership during this time. News Corporation's acquisition of *TV Guide, Seventeen* and the *Daily Racing Form* for $3 billion in 1988 remains the largest magazine transaction to date (Greco 1993).

Among key transactions during the latter half of the 1990s were Willis Stein and Partners' acquisition of Ziff-Davis Publishing ($780 million), Conde Nast Publications' acquisition of Fairchild Publications ($650 million) and Bertelsmann's majority purchase of Springer-Verlag ($577 million). The most significant transaction since the new millennium has been Primedia's $515 million acquisition of the U.S. magazine assets of Emap PLC, a British company (Rose and Deogun 2001). The New York Times Company has indicated that it may sell its magazine division (Interconnect 2001).

Major Players in the Magazine Industry

There are many publishers in the magazine industry, ranging from large-scale international conglomerates to small publishing houses producing single publications. Four publishers, however, together accounted for more than 75 percent of all magazine revenues in 1999 (Veronis, Suhler and Associates 2000b). Following is a brief look at these top four magazine publishers in the United States, some of which also have interests in other media industries.

1. AOL Time Warner. The largest publisher of magazines in the United States, AOL Time Warner owns popular consumer titles such as *Time, Life, Fortune, Money, People, Sports Illustrated, Entertainment Weekly, In Style* and *Teen People*. AOL Time Warner is also a major player in the cable and satellite television, Internet, motion picture and recording industries.
2. Bertelsmann. Based in Germany, this company publishes several popular U.S. magazines, including *McCall's, Family Circle, YM* and *Parents*. Bertelsmann also is a major player in the recording industry.
3. Reader's Digest. The company's signature magazine, *Reader's Digest*, is distributed in the United States and around the world in 48 editions.
4. Meredith Corporation. With headquarters in Des Moines, Iowa, Meredith includes among its titles *Better Homes and Gardens, Ladies' Home Journal, Traditional Home, Midwest Living* and *MORE*.

Other major magazine publishers in the United States include Tribune, Conde Nast, the Walt Disney Company, and News Corporation.

Market Structure

The magazine industry represents a hybrid structure. The top tier has an oligopolistic structure, with four firms controlling the majority of the revenues in the industry. The remaining lower tier, however, resembles a monopolistic competitive market structure. Remember that in this type of structure, there are many sellers offering products that are similar but are not perfect substitutes for one another. Numerous publishing companies vie for a share at this end of the market.

The large number of individual publishers suggests that there will be several titles geared toward specific interests, yet each is somewhat unique in its presentation. Overall, the prices paid for magazines indicate more of a monopolistic competitive structure. If the entire magazine industry operated as an oligopoly, prices would be similar across the industry.

Market Concentration

To get an approximate measure of concentration in the magazine industry, the author calculated the top four (CR4) and top eight (CR8) concentration ratios using data from 1999 found in the *Communications Industry Forecast* published by Veronis, Suhler and Associates (2000a).

The CR4 ratio measured 77 percent, and the CR8 ratio was 91 percent. Recall that in Chapter 4, a market was considered concentrated if the CR4 ratio was equal to or larger than 50 percent and the CR8 was equal to or larger than 75 percent. Although this analysis is limited to a single year of data, the measures indicate that the magazine industry is concentrated.

Clearly, consolidation in the magazine industry has resulted in a more concentrated industry. There is room for further consolidation in the magazine publishing industry. As television becomes more and more fragmented, magazines will remain a viable option for reaching niche audiences. Magazine advertising is poised for healthy gains through 2004, with the industry advertising rate expected to grow at a rate of 7.4 percent (Veronis, Suhler and Associates 2000a).

The Impact of Regulatory Forces on the Magazine Industry

The magazine industry is not subject to any direct governmental regulation beyond that imposed on any other business operating in the United States (e.g., wages, taxes, employment and labor acts). No doubt one of the biggest regulatory concerns for magazine publishers is the rising cost of postage, which has a direct impact on magazine distribution. With so much of the magazine industry revenues dominated by subscriptions, any increases in postal costs directly affect the price and revenue structure of magazines. Ultimately, consumers absorb any increase in postage over time. Postal rate increases, coupled with a sluggish economy for advertising at the start of the 21st century, may affect industry performance (Rose 2001).

From a content standpoint, magazine publishers were dealt a serious blow by the U.S. Supreme Court in June 2001 when the court ruled 7–2 that free-lance writers can control whether articles they sold for print to a newspaper or magazine may be reproduced electronically, such as on a web page (Justices side with writers 2001). Free-lance writers produce a considerable amount of content for the magazine industry (Daly, Henry and Ryder 1997). Publishers must now negotiate separate fees for electronic works with free-lancers, which will no doubt increase their costs. The decision will have a direct impact on the way the magazine industry conducts its editorial business.

The Impact of Technological Forces on Magazines

Technology continues to change the magazine industry. Computer technology decreased the time needed for publishing and reduced the number of people needed to produce a magazine. Downsizing led to a loss of jobs in magazine publishing during the 1990s. The entire magazine industry employs approximately 130,000 people (Daly, Henry and Ryder 1997). According to Worthington (1994), a single graphic artist and one editor can produce a 100-page monthly magazine using free-lance writers.

Many publishers have created online editions of their magazines for consumer access via the Internet's World Wide Web. The Internet edition of a magazine is not of course a direct substitute for the physical printed magazine. Online magazines have distinct physical limitations, but they also offer ways to extend the brand of the magazine and draw new audiences. Further, online magazines represent a way to extend advertising revenues for publishing companies.

Online editions are often successful when combined with other media forms. For example, *Sports Illustrated* has found success with its annual swimsuit issue, which cross-promotes a television special and the sale of calendars. *ESPN The Magazine* is regularly cross-promoted with its signature TV program, SportsCenter, and its online website. Last but not least, Playboy uses its website to promote both domestic and international editions and its pay television service.

Magazine publishers will continue to experiment with various online models in hopes of developing both new audiences and revenue streams. To date, the magazine industry has been more successful than a number of other media industries in establishing an a strong online presence to complement existing printed publications.

The Economic Future of the Magazine Industry

Magazine publishers will continue to try to maintain advertisers and consumers while controlling costs and extending their products via the Internet. Publishers will continue to be challenged to meet the demands of both advertisers and readers amid growing competition from other publishers and the electronic media.

Magazines that specialize in key audiences will be attractive to advertisers in a competitive, fragmented media environment. Publishers will continue to hone and improve the quality of their editorial divisions to be certain they are providing readers with material that serves their needs.

International publishing opportunities continue to provide additional markets for U.S. magazines. The most lucrative international markets are Europe, Latin America, the Middle East, Asia and Africa. The numerous special-interest titles produced by American publishers have found favor in many countries where the economy tends to support broader-based, national magazines. American publishers also benefit from the fact that English is understood in most parts of the world, resulting in reduced language barriers for readers.

Consumer magazine advertising is expected to reach $16.4 billion by 2004, and circulation spending on magazines should reach $10 billion, for a consumer magazine total of $27.3 billion (Veronis, Suhler and Associates 2000a). Business magazines are expected to generate $17 billion in advertising and another $2.1 billion from circulation, for a total of $19.1 billion in 2004. Total consumer and business magazine revenues are expected to reach $46 billion in 2004 (Veronis, Suhler and Associates 2000a).

Summary

Magazines have played an important role in entertaining, educating and informing Americans since the early 1800s. Magazine publishing is accomplished through the combined efforts of two divisions. The business division handles all business aspects, while the editorial division handles the actual creation of the magazine. Over the years, the magazine industry has evolved into a specialized industry serving readers with a number of specific interests.

Magazines draw revenues from two sources: advertisers and circulation. Advertising accounts for approximately 55 percent of revenues, and circulation consists of subscriptions and single-copy sales. The magazine industry can be analyzed in terms of three markets: the consumer market, the advertising market and the market for the actual publications.

The magazine industry operates in a monopolistic competitive market structure. Four major firms (AOL Time Warner, Bertelsmann, Reader's Digest and Meredith Corporation) hold key positions in the magazine industry. These four firms tend to dominate industry revenues.

Postal increases present the greatest regulatory threat to magazines, as distribution is directly affected by rising postal rates. A Supreme Court decision in favor of free-lance writers will in all likelihood raise costs for magazine publishers, who will be forced to negotiate separate fees for electronic publication. In terms of technology, the magazine industry has fully embraced the Internet, publishing numerous online editions, although the success of attracting new audiences and revenue streams has been limited. Questions remain as to the demand by users for online magazines.

Magazine publishers will try to build on existing market share, control costs and seek expansion through international editions and online revenues. Domestic revenues for advertising and circulation are projected to grow at a rate of about 6 percent through 2004.

Discussion Questions

1. How has the magazine industry changed during its history? What sort of new changes is the magazine industry likely to encounter?
2. What are the revenue sources for magazines?
3. What types of market structure are found in the magazine industry? How concentrated is today's magazine industry?
4. What are the two major divisions in magazine publishing? What does each division do?
5. How do changes in postal rates affect magazines?

Exercises

1. Compare copies of magazines found in your household with respect to the following criteria: (a) types of editorial content, (b) types of advertisers, (c) audiences likely to read the magazine and (d) publisher.
2. Compare a printed copy of a magazine with its electronic version on the Internet. How are they different? How are they similar? Describe the contents of each magazine. Does the online version charge for any of its content?

3. At a drugstore, bookstore, newsstand or other retailer that carries a number of magazines, identify how many magazine titles exist for a particular hobby or interest (e.g., gardening, needlepoint, cooking, motorcycles, jazz, cats). Examine these magazines to try to determine how they are unique. Also compare the cost, number of pages and publisher of each title.
4. Arrange to have a graphic artist, free-lance writer or member of a magazine editorial staff visit your class as a guest speaker to gain his or her insight into magazine publishing.

References

Daly, C. P., P. Henry and E. Ryder. (1997). *The Magazine Publishing Industry*. Boston: Allyn and Bacon.

Greco, A. N. (1993). Publishing economics: Mergers and acquisitions in the U.S. publishing industry, 1980–1989. In *Media Economics: Theory and Practice*, edited by A. Alexander, J. Owers and R. Carveth. New York: Lawrence Erlbaum Associates, pp. 205–224.

Interconnect. (2001). E-mail list distributed by Arthur Andersen Company, 30 January.

Justices side with writers in dispute over electronic publication of articles. (2001). *Wall Street Journal* online edition, 25 June. Available via online subscription: http://interactive.wsj.com.

Magazine Publishers of America. (2000). Available online: http://www.magazine.org. Accessed 20 April 2001.

MPA Handbook. (2001). Available online: http://www.magazine.org/resources/downloads/MPA_Handbook_01.pdf. Accessed 23 April 2001.

Rose, M. (2001). Magazine revenue at newsstands falls in "worst year ever." *Wall Street Journal*, 15 May, B6.

Rose, M., and N. Deogun. (2001). Primedia to buy Emap's U.S. titles for $515 million in cash, warrants. *Wall Street Journal*, 2 July, B6.

Veronis, Suhler and Associates. (2000a). *Communications Industry Forecast*. New York: Veronis, Suhler and Associates.

———. (2000b). *Communications Industry Report*. New York: Veronis, Suhler and Associates.

Vivian, J. (1995). *The Media of Mass Communication*. 3d ed. Needham Heights, Mass.: Allyn and Bacon.

Worthington, R. (1994). Research review: Magazine management and economics. *Electronic Journal of Communication* 4, nos.2–4.

13

THE BOOK INDUSTRY

After reading this chapter, you should understand:

- The major players, market structure and economic characteristics of the book publishing industry.

- The various markets for books.

- How the demand for books is a combination of many macroeconomic and microeconomic factors.

- Regulatory concerns facing the book publishing industry.

- How technology is expanding the market for electronic books.

The book industry has the distinction of being the first true mass medium in history, made possible by the invention of movable type by Johannes Gutenberg, which historians believed happened around 1446 (Vivian 1995). The printing process that Gutenberg perfected quickly spread throughout Europe and other developing nations. The ability to mass-produce the printed word revolutionized communication and changed the world. It made information available to the common people that previously had been held only by the privileged few. The same basic processes used in printing books would later expand into the publishing of newspapers and magazines.

Today, the consumer book publishing industry remains an important industry, with total 1999 revenues exceeding $17 billion (Veronis, Suhler and Associates 2000b). Like other mass media industries, the book industry faces many challenges in the years ahead as it tries to maintain consumer interest and market share in competition with other forms of leisure activities and as it continues expansion into electronic publishing.

The book industry draws revenues primarily from the sale of books to various categories of buyers, including consumer, educational, business and institutional (library) purchasers. Individuals buy most consumer books through various types of bookstores and online vendors such as Amazon.com. Educational bodies such as colleges and universities, state education boards and local school districts buy educational books (textbooks). Businesses purchase books of particular interest to them, and institutions such as libraries buy books to serve the reading needs of the people who visit them. Unlike many sister media industries, the book industry is not dependent on advertising for revenues.

It is estimated that more than 50,000 new books are published each year in the United States, and the average American purchases at least one book per year. Retailing, marketing and promotion are critical functions of book publishers.

Book publishers range from large media conglomerates to small, specialty publishing houses. In recent years, larger companies have acquired many smaller publishers. For example, Blackwell, a company based in the United Kingdom, acquired the publisher of this book, Iowa State University Press, in 2000. International publishers have established a strong presence in the United States, and domestic-based publishers are also pursuing opportunities in marketing books to other countries in both traditional and electronic formats.

Demand for books is influenced by several microeconomic and macroeconomic factors. In the United States, the state of the economy, educational enrollments, household disposable income, professional employment and institutional and library funding are some of the key variables that affect the demand for books. In the international arena, the demand for books is related to many factors, including currency exchange rates, literacy rates, occupational status and English fluency.

While the book industry represents the oldest of the mass media industries covered in this text, it is by no means static and resistant to change. This chapter demonstrates how book publishing is evolving and adapting in order to remain competitive in a growing, media-saturated environment.

The Market for Books

The book industry can be broken into several markets for analysis. Most industry sources examine the book publishing industry in three broad categories: (1) consumer books, or *trade books* (books intended for general readership), (2) professional books and (3) educational books (textbooks). In analyzing the market for books, this chapter will follow a similar approach, reviewing the demand for consumer, professional and educational books, as well as the demand for book publishers.

Demand for Consumer Books

Consumer or trade book sales are further divided into the subcategories adult trade, juvenile trade, religious, book clubs, mail order, mass-market paperbacks, university press and subscription reference. Books published and total sales figures for consumer books are listed in Table 13.1. As the table illustrates, the total sales of consumer books have risen steadily every year, reaching an estimated $25.3 billion in 2000.

The adult trade subcategory remains the largest in the consumer book market, accounting for approximately 30 percent of total consumer book sales and about 18 percent of total book sales. Within the adult trade category, most of the sales represent adult fiction, advice and how-to books. Juvenile trade book sales have been more cyclical in recent years but surged after the introduction of the *Harry Potter* series by J. K. Rowling. Sales of adult and juvenile trade books reached $6.4 billion in sales in 2000 (Association of American Publishers 2001).

Note that in Table 13.1, most categories outside of adult and juvenile trade have experienced little growth. Mass-market paperbacks remain the third highest category of sales. Mass-market paperbacks are usually less expensive than trade paperbacks. Book clubs and religious books rank fourth and fifth, respectively, in sales. Sales of subscription reference, university press and mail-order books are lower because they have smaller target markets.

Book retailing and marketing experienced two major trends during the 1990s. The first trend was the continuing development of book superstores (e.g., Barnes and Noble, Borders), which feature inventories of 30,000 to 150,000 titles. The average mall bookstore, by comparison, carries only about 20,000 titles. Many of these book superstores feature a variety of amenities for

Table 13.1. Consumer book sales (millions of dollars)

Year	Adult Trade	Juvenile Trade	Religious	Book Clubs	Mail Order	Market Paperbacks	University Press	Sub-scription Reference	Total Sales[a]
1987	2077.7	635.1	638.8	678.7	657.6	913.7	170.9	437.6	12,190.3
1992	3484.2	1177.4	907.1	742.3	630.2	1263.8	280.1	572.3	16,918.5
1997	4395.3	1078.9	1132.7	1143.1	521.0	1433.8	367.8	736.5	21,641.9
1998	4659.8	1189.1	1178.0	1209.4	470.5	1514.1	391.8	767.4	23,033.3
1999	5083.9	1708.2	1216.9	1272.0	412.8	1551.0	411.7	788.9	24,480.6
2000[b]	4586.6	1954.2	1246.9	1291.6	431.8	1599.2	402.0	809.1	25,322.7

[a]Includes profession, educational and other book sales category.
[b]Preliminary estimates.
Source: Association of American Publishers (2001)

shoppers' comfort, such as couches and recliners for reading, a coffee bar or refreshment area and play areas for small children. Staff members at the superstores tend to be more knowledgeable and specialized in particular areas, increasing the level of service demanded by customers.

The second major trend of the 1990s involved buying books via the Internet, a process initiated by one of the pioneer dot-com companies, Amazon.com. Amazon captured the imagination of consumers around the world with its ability to deliver books to any place in the developed world in a manner of days. People who had never purchased a product on the Internet were attracted to Amazon, with its ease of purchasing and distribution. Amazon forced other competitors, primarily the major book superstores, to rush to the Internet and to lower prices. Amazon developed a new retail model to reach consumers, adding a new revenue stream to the publishing industry.

Demand for Professional Books

Professional book publishing includes the subcategories of business, law and medicine, as well as technical and scientific fields. The number of books published and total sales figures for professional books are listed in Table 13.2. As the table illustrates, the total sales of professional books were expected to reach an estimated $5.1 billion in 2000.

Books that contribute heavily to professional book sales are business, computer, software and medical publications. Growth in professional employment and an increase in the number of college-educated adults also stimulate demand for professional books.

Demand for Educational Books

The market for educational books or textbooks can be broken into three submarkets: (1) textbooks for students from elementary through high school (referred to as "elhi" in the book industry), (2) college textbooks and (3) standardized test books. Sales figures for all three categories are listed in Table

Table 13.2. Sales of professional books (millions of dollars)

Year	Business	Law	Medicine	Technical, Scientific	Total Sales
1987	388.8	780.0	406.6	632.0	2207.3
1992	409.3	1128.1	622.7	865.6	3106.7
1997	768.1	1502.7	856.5	1029.1	4156.4
1998	852.0	1591.1	919.0	1055.6	4418.7
1999	909.9	1726.9	982.8	1100.8	4720.4
2000	n/a	n/a	n/a	n/a	5129.5[a]

Source: Association of American Publishers (2001)
[a]Preliminary estimate. Breakdown by category not available.

Table 13.3. Sales of educational books (millions of dollars)

Year	Elhi (K–12)	College	Standardized Tests	Total Sales
1987	1695.6	1549.5	104.0	3349.1
1992	2080.9	2084.1	140.4	4275.4
1997	3005.4	2669.7	191.4	5866.5
1998	3315.0	2888.6	204.6	6408.2
1999	3415.9	3128.8	218.7	6763.4
2000[a]	3881.2	3237.1	234.1	7352.4

Source: Association of American Publishers (2001)
[a]Preliminary estimates.

13.3. In 2000, the combined sale of all categories of educational books was expected to reach $7.35 billion.

Demand for elhi books is driven by several factors. State adoption schedules vary for textbooks. Heavily populated states, such as California, Texas, Florida and New York are among the largest states ordering textbooks. Enrollment levels also have an impact on elhi sales. Figures from the National Center for Education Statistics indicate that enrollments will remain steady through the year 2005, averaging around 4 percent a year (Digest of education statistics 2000). School district budgets are also critical in assessing demand for elhi books. Local property tax revenues support local school budgets; tax revenues around the country have been erratic, with many challenges to local tax rates by constituents.

Demand for college textbooks is based almost entirely on enrollment. College publishing remains the most profitable form of all book publishing, with costs relatively low and prices relatively high. A few universities are experimenting with distributing books in electronic formats, primarily through CD-ROM. However, regular hardcover and softcover books remain the standard. Another influence on the sale of college texts is the growth in the number of nontraditional students attending college courses. Finally, whenever the economy declines, workers often return to school to improve education and retrain for new job skills. As the economy grows and creates more job opportunities, enrollment tends to drop, especially for part-time students.

Colleges and universities are heavily engaged with new technologies to supplement textbooks. Computers, the Internet, CD-ROM texts, e-books, electronic mail and computer conferences all provide alternative means of educating students. Tremendous investments have been made at many institutions in distance learning involving audio, video and interactive teleconferencing and in developing Web-based learning systems (Aikat 2000). Success varies across campuses. Distance learning is expected to become much more widespread as broadband diffusion continues (Goff 2000). Learning via the Web will likely become the standard for most students utilizing distance education because of the flexibility it offers users in terms of access.

Finally, the category of standardized tests simply refers to the number of publications devoted to test taking, including but not limited to the SAT, ACT, GRE, GMAT and LSAT examinations. As Table 13.3 illustrates, the sale of standardized test materials was estimated at $234 million in 2000, a small figure compared to the sale of elhi and college books.

Demand for Book Publishers

Mergers and acquisitions among book publishing firms have resulted in increasing consolidation across the book industry. Most of the acquisitions have involved larger publishers acquiring smaller publishers. Viacom's $10 billion acquisition of Paramount Communications in 1994 represents one of the largest single publishing-related transactions in history. Vivendi Universal's acquisition of Houghton Mifflin for $2.2 billion in 2001 is the largest book publishing transaction in the new century to date, allowing the French-based company to become a major player in the sale of educational books in the United States.

Other transactions in the book industry in recent years include Thomson Corporation's acquisition of the Macmillan Library Reference USA; the John Wiley and Sons (also owned by Thomson) purchase of Jossey-Bass; the HarperCollins (News Corporation) acquisition of both Avon Books and William Morrow and Company and the Penguin Putnam (Pearson) purchase of Avery Publishing.

Major Players in the Book Industry

There are hundreds of book publishers that make up the book industry, ranging from international media companies to small, specialty publishers. Among the parent companies that own major book publishers in the consumer market are Viacom (Simon and Schuster), Bertelsmann (Random House and Bantam Doubleday Dell), News Corporation (HarperCollins) and Vivendi Universal (Houghton Mifflin). Other major publishers include Pearson (Penguin Putnam), Readers Digest Association, Golden Books Family Entertainment, Thomson, Harlequin and Thomas Nelson.

In the area of business and professional books, there are five companies that control most of the revenues in this segment of the industry (Veronis, Suhler and Associates 2000b). These companies are Franklin Covey, Apollo Group, Berlitz International, DeVry and Sylvan Learning Systems. Most of these companies are involved in publishing a variety of adult educational materials and degree courses for distance learning.

Market Structure

The consumer book industry has evolved into an industry with an oligopoly structure, with the majority of the revenues dominated by only a few of the larger publishing companies, such as Viacom, Bertelsmann, Pearson and News Corporation. However, a number of smaller publishers vie for the remaining share of the market. In this sense, we have another industry with a two-tier structure: a traditional oligopoly on one tier and a second tier with multiple publishers with small, individual market shares.

The large number of publishing acquisitions during the 1980s indicated that the book industry was moving toward an oligopoly structure (Schiffrin 2000). As larger publishers dominate the industry, critics contend that it limits the diversity that once existed in the field of publishing (Bagdikian 2000; Schiffrin 2000), making it more difficult for books with limited economic potential (fewer than 1,000 copies sold) to find a publisher. At the same time, authors who have found success in capturing large consumer markets (e.g., John Grisham, Danielle Steel, Stephen King) have the best chance to get future works published.

Market Concentration

No systematic studies have been identified that examine concentration in the book industry, although the author has utilized concentration ratios to measure concentration in the consumer book industry. Using data from 1993 reported in the first edition of this book, the CR4 ratio measured 30 percent, whereas the CR8 ratio was calculated at 50 percent. These calculations fell below levels indicating a concentrated market at that time. However, in 1993, the top eight (publicly reporting) firms accounted for 50 percent of the revenues in the book industry out of more than 700 publishers, illustrating the existence of the two-tiered market structure discussed earlier.

Using data from 1999 (Veronis, Suhler and Associates, 2000b), concentration ratios were again calculated for the consumer book industry. The CR4 ratio had climbed to 77 percent in 1999, while the CR8 increased to 94 percent. In both cases, the data indicate a very concentrated market. One caveat should be noted—the 1993 data included both consumer books and business and professional publishing, which contributed to the lower ratios reported in the first edition of this text.

The Impact of Regulatory Forces on the Book Industry

Like the magazine industry, the book industry does not encounter any direct governmental regulation beyond that imposed on other types of business activity (e.g., taxation, employment). Perhaps the most important regulatory actions in the book industry since the 1970s have concerned copyright laws and intellectual property (Greco 1997).

U.S. copyright law was revised during the 1970s, with several key changes affecting international markets. During the 1990s, publishers took advantage of international copyright protection of their works. Exports of book shipments accounted for approximately 10 percent of industry revenues, whereas foreign payments to domestic publishers rose steadily during the 1990s. Still, copyright infringement and the resultant loss of revenues in the international arena is a major concern for publishers.

Electronic books, or "e-books," are seen as an area with good growth potential for the 21st century, but the outcome of a key court case could change how the industry approaches electronic publishing. The final outcome of a court case involving Random House and Rosetta Books LLC will be of great interest to the publishing industry. A lawsuit was initiated when Rosetta signed Random House authors Kurt Vonnegut, William Styron and Robert Parker to contracts to distribute electronic versions of eight previously published works (Rose 2001a). Random House claimed that Rosetta violated existing contracts and cannot publish the material in any form. Rosetta argued that only a paper, printed book constitutes a book and that an electronic version is not the same.

A federal court denied Random House's request for an injunction against Rosetta, citing that "existing contracts do not include e-books" (Rose 2001b). Random House was appealing that decision as this book went to press. No doubt the outcome of this case may set key precedents regarding who controls electronic rights in book publishing—the publishing company or the author. At the least, the case should clarify intellectual property issues for authors and their publishers.

The Impact of Technological Forces on the Book Industry

As in other media industries, technology is affecting the book industry in many different ways. One key change has been in the physical distribution of books via electronic commerce. Spending on books purchased over the Internet reached $1 billion in 1999 (Veronis, Suhler and Associates 2000b), a revenue stream that didn't exist for the publishing industry prior to the mid-1990s. The Internet will continue to be the fastest-growing distribution channel for the book publishing industry.

As discussed in the preceding section, the greatest change in publishing has been the expansion of books into various types of electronic formats, beginning with audio versions of popular works. Audio books have proven to be very successful since their introduction during the early 1980s. Audio books complement hardcover and paperback editions and tend to reach commuters, people who have less time for reading, and those with visual disabilities.

CD-ROM technology represents many exciting opportunities for the book industry, especially for educational books. Supplemental material can be provided on a CD-ROM (compact disc-read-only memory) to enhance traditional textbooks and improve teaching methods. For example, Wadsworth Publishing developed an interactive CD in conjunction with a television production course in which users learn various aspects of production. Allyn and Bacon offer a CD version of various news clips to supplement a popular textbook used in an introductory mass media course.

But the development of e-books has raised considerable excitement in the publishing industry as a way to market and sell books to consumers (Robinson 2001). Users can download e-books from the Internet to their computers or handheld devices. E-books are still in their infancy, and the revenue projections for e-books are expected to reach only $14 million by 2004 (Interconnect 2001). But publishers are optimistic that e-books will not only produce revenues but also cut down on distribution and marketing costs.

The Economic Future of the Book Industry

Overall, the consumer book industry is projected to show modest growth over the next several years, averaging around a 4 percent growth rate through 2004. By 2004, consumer book revenues are expected to reach $21.5 billion, up from $17 billion in 1999. Consolidation in the book industry and expansion via the Internet for distribution and marketing should help control expenses for the major book publishing companies in the immediate future (Veronis, Suhler and Associates 2000a).

Expanding markets through the development of electronic formats will create new revenue streams for publishers over the next several years. As mentioned in the previous section, audio books, CD-ROM and e-books represent alternative markets to traditional publishing.

Book publishers in the United States and around the world are facing challenges in the area of intellectual property protection that can impact economic performance. Book publishers face a number of issues, including securing copyrighted works against unauthorized use in both print and electronic formats in the domestic and international market as well as protecting the integrity of copyrighted works in the growing digital environment. The publishing industry must develop better tracking systems regarding the use of these works and initiate workable compensation agreements with authors in order for the industry to grow.

Summary

Book publishing has existed since the 15th century as a form of mass media, and it remains a viable industry today. Book publishers draw revenues through the sale of books in three major markets: consumer, professional and educational. Demand for books is influenced by several microeconomic and macroeconomic factors.

The consumer market is the largest market, accounting for nearly 75 percent of all publishing revenues. The consumer market consists of adult and juvenile fiction, paperbacks and other subcategories primarily sold through retail outlets and bookstores. Professional books include medical, legal and business publications. Educational books are divided into two submarkets, the elementary and high school, or elhi, market and the college textbook market.

There are numerous book publishers, although several large media companies capture most of the book industry revenues. Among the major domestic and international publishers are Viacom, Bertelsmann, News Corporation and Pearson. The book industry operates under an oligopoly market structure.

Regulatory concerns for the book publishing companies revolve around the issues of copyright and intellectual property. A key court case should determine whether electronic rights belong to authors or to publishers.

Publishers continue to develop nonprint formats as a means to build new revenue streams. Audio books, introduced during the 1980s, remain a popular format. Reference works are now available on CD-ROM, with other products in progress. The Internet will be an important source for the distribution of traditional books as well as e-books.

The consumer book industry is expected to grow at a rate of 4 percent through 2004, when total revenues are expected to reach nearly $21.5 billion.

Discussion Questions

1. How has the book industry changed during its history? What impact is technology having on today's book publishing industry?
2. What are the publishing markets within the book industry? Describe them.
3. How would you describe the book industry in terms of market structure?

4. How has book retailing changed over the years? What changes has the Internet brought to the marketing and distribution of consumer books?

Exercises

1. Compare best-seller lists found in several sources, such as the *New York Times* Sunday edition, the *Chronicle of Higher Education* and your local newspaper. Are the lists similar or different? Why?
2. Visit a local bookstore in a shopping mall or retail outlet. Find out how many titles are in stock. If possible, visit a book superstore if one is available in your area for comparison.
3. Find out what audio books are the most popular in your community. What types of audiences use audio books?
4. Locate a reference work available on CD-ROM, such as *World Book Encyclopedia, Grolier's Encyclopedia* or the *Encyclopaedia Britannica*. What does this format offer compared to the standard encyclopedia?
5. Using the Internet, locate a major book publisher on the Web and examine the material you discover online. Write a brief report on your findings. Compare prices for the book online at several sites versus what the book would cost from a local retailer. Why is the pricing different?

References

Aikat, D. (2000). Cyberspace of the people, by the people, for the people. In *Understanding the Web: Social, Political and Economic Dimensions of the Internet*, edited by A. B. Albarran and D. H. Goff. Ames: Iowa State University Press, pp. 23–48.

Association of American Publishers. (2001). Industry statistics. Available online: http://www.publishers.org/home/index.htm. Accessed 13 July 2001.

Bagdikian, B. H. (2000). *The Media Monopoly*. 6th ed. Boston: Beacon Press.

Digest of education statistics. (2000). Available online: http://nces.ed.gov/pubs2001 /digest/ch1.html#1. Accessed 17 April 2001.

Goff, D. H. (2000). Issues of Internet infrastructure. In *Understanding the Web: Social, Political and Economic Dimensions of the Internet*, edited by A. B. Albarran and D. H. Goff. Ames: Iowa State University Press, pp. 239–266.

Greco, A. N. (1997). *The Book Publishing Industry*. Needham Heights, Mass.: Allyn and Bacon.

Interconnect. (2001). E-mail list distributed by Arthur Andersen Company, 16 January.

Robinson, S. (2001). Forget e-books. *Interactive Week*, 2 April, 57–58.

Rose, M. (2001a). Definitions are key in publishers' dispute over electronic book rights. *Wall Street Journal*, 7 May, B1, B8.

———. (2001b). Publisher Random House suffers setback as judge denies injunction in e-book suit. *Wall Street Journal*, 12 July. Available online: http://wsj.com. Accessed 30 July.

Schiffrin, A. (2000). *The Business of Books*. New York: Verso.

Veronis, Suhler and Associates. (2000a). *Communications Industry Forecast*. New York: Veronis, Suhler and Associates.

———. (2000b). *Communications Industry Report*. New York: Veronis, Suhler and Associates.

Vivian, J. (1995). *The Media of Mass Communication*. 3d ed. Needham Heights, Mass.: Allyn and Bacon.

VI

Media Economics
Research

14

ISSUES IN MEDIA ECONOMICS RESEARCH

In this summary chapter, you will:

- Review how consolidation and conglomeration, technology, globalization and regulatory trends are affecting media markets and industries.

- Consider questions about the future of media economics research and areas for further study.

What does the future hold for the study of media economics? How will media economics research evolve in the 21st century? This summary chapter considers these questions by centering on some of the trends and patterns observed in the preceding chapters on individual media industries. The goal of this chapter is not to posit specific predictions but rather to offer a few educated assumptions about how the study of media economics will evolve, based on current developments in the field.

The industry chapters in this text illustrate the diverse range of economic activities taking place across the mass media. At the same time, several trends run across many media industries. Among the most important similarities are the increasing levels of consolidation, the impact of technology, the increasing globalization of the media industries and regulatory forces. We will take a closer examination of each of these trends.

Trends across Media Industries

Consolidation of Media Industries

Increasing levels of concentration were found across several media industries examined in this text. Mergers and acquisitions have reduced the number of companies in many media industries to a handful of powerful conglomerates. Ozanich and Wirth (1998) claim that media mergers and acquisitions have been driven by technological change, liberalization of regulatory policy and the availability of capital. Most media industries, including radio, cable television, motion pictures and the recording industry, were found to be heavily concentrated.

For example, companies such as AOL Time Warner, Viacom, Disney and News Corporation produce and distribute products across a range of different markets, involving print and electronic media (see Table 14.1). Horizontal expansion is just one strategy companies use to maximize economic potential, and vertical integration is another method found among several media companies. By increasing their size and market share within an industry, companies are able to lower economies of scale, develop different revenue streams for the same product and maximize shareholder value (Turow 1992).

At the same time, industry concentration raises issues and concerns regarding the presentation of diverse views, particularly in the dissemination of news and informational products (Bagdikian 2000). For the most part, regulators, especially in the United States, have shown greater tolerance with media consolidation than with other, more pressing domestic issues. While consolidation activity may have slowed from the torrid pace of the 1990s, by no indication is consolidation over. Further deregulatory actions, such as relaxation of the audience reach cap for television stations or the removal of cross-

Table 14.1. Examples of media conglomerate interests across industries[a]

Firm	Radio	TV	Cable/ Sat	Motion Pictures	Records	News- papers	Maga- zines	Books
AOL Time Warner		X	X	X	X		X	X
Bertelsmann A. G.		X			X			X
The Walt Disney Co.	X	X	X	X	X		X	X
Vivendi Universal		X	X	X	X		X	
Viacom	X	X	X	X	X			X
Sony		X	X	X	X			
News Corp		X	X	X	X	X	X	X

Source: Data for the table compiled from various sources by the author.
[a]Industry in which firm is involved marked with X.

ownership limitations between newspapers and broadcasting, could easily trigger another wave of consolidation.

All of the consolidation experienced to date suggests we are moving toward a world dominated by a powerful oligopoly of media conglomerates (Demers 1999). Companies such as AOL Time Warner, Disney, News Corporation, Viacom, Bertelsmann and Vivendi Universal are clearly emerging as global media superpowers. Media economics researchers have a unique opportunity to observe and analyze the impact and effect of industry consolidation on both the market level and the consumer level and provide recommendations for policy and regulatory action.

Technology

Perhaps the key driving force across the media industries is technology. All media industries are moving away from an analog base to a completely digital world, leading to massive changes in the development of both hardware and software as new innovations continue to create new markets for entertainment and information products. Companies, as well as consumers, struggle to keep up with the numerous changes brought about by technological growth and development.

The digital environment places great emphasis on the distribution of content, and considerable investment has taken place to develop broadband networks to move large files of data that will eventually be decoded in the form of video programming or even feature films (see Evans and Wurster 2000; Gilder 2000). But what type of broadband network will most users access? Early in the game, it appears that the cable television industry has the lead, but the satellite and telecommunications industries are eager to compete with cable. And the personal digital assistant and the cell phone have demonstrated capability of receiving wireless material via the Internet.

The Internet is transforming media companies, opening up new paths to promote, market and distribute media content. Virtually all media companies are interested in the power of the Internet to develop new revenue streams. Some models, such as the interactive version of the *Wall Street Journal*, have been extremely successful, while other sites, such as Time Warner's *Pathfinder* service, failed miserably. Where is the Internet headed? Will consumers continue to be attracted to the Internet at the expense of traditional media outlets? What business models will be the most successful? Clearly, many unanswered questions remain about the Internet and its economic potential for media companies and industries.

A big part of the impact of technology will ultimately be measured by consumer demand. Will consumers want the new technological services offered by media companies? Given the demise of the dot-coms in 1999 and

2000, how many of these new innovations will survive? More important, how much will consumers be willing to spend on new products and services delivered via the Internet? Media economics research will help identify the demand for digital services as well as new hardware and software products across the media industries.

Globalization

Globalization is another trend identified across many media industries in this text. Economic growth and expansion continue in many areas of the world, especially in Western and Eastern Europe, the Pacific Rim, and North and South America (Micklethwait and Wooldridge 2000). New markets for trade and commerce continue to emerge, especially in regard to media products and services. For example, Spanish-language programming for television is booming in Spain, Mexico, and many countries in South America. Rupert Murdoch's SKY TV services can be found throughout Asia and Europe.

The push for international marketing of information and entertainment products by U.S.-based companies is not necessarily new, but revenues from the global arenas are critical in many industries, including television programming, motion pictures and recorded music. Most domestic markets in the United States are saturated. For example, 99 percent of all households have a radio and television receiver, 95 percent of all households have a telephone, 87 percent have a VCR and 67 percent subscribe to cable TV services (Veronis, Suhler and Associates 2000). Europe, Asia (especially China), South America and the Pacific Rim offer excellent opportunities for business expansion and development.

The United States continues to be a major exporter of media content products, but its future as the world leader will be affected by the rise of powerful media companies from other countries such as Bertelsmann, Sony, News Corporation and Vivendi Universal. Hirsch (1992) explains that the globalization of media content, production and technology raises significant questions for further study, including issues related to media ownership, control and audience effects. The field of media economics can help provide answers to these important questions.

Regulatory Forces

The Telecommunications Act of 1996, discussed at various points throughout the text, produced significant changes among many U.S. media industries, especially among cable and satellite television and other electronic media. The 1996 act fueled tremendous consolidation in the radio, television and cable TV industries (see Bates 1999; Drushel 1998; Howard 1998; Tseng and Litman 1998). In the telecommunications industry, the number of competitors also declined in both the local exchange and long-distance markets. These mergers and acquisitions led to further consolidation in other industries, including motion pictures and the recording industry.

At an international level, the rise of what some scholars call transnational media corporations benefited from relaxation of regulatory policies, both in the United States and in Europe (see Gershon 1993, 2000). Clearly, several major corporations such as Viacom, AOL Time Warner, Disney, News Corporation, Bertelsmann, and Vivendi Universal will dominate the global media marketplace well into the 21st century.

Policy decisions, at both the domestic and global levels, need to be carefully studied to determine their effectiveness as well as their shortcomings. New models to analyze policy decisions are needed, and media economics researchers must be critical of regulatory actions and their impact on consumers (see, e.g., Hendricks 1995).

Questions for Further Study

The trends reviewed in the previous section of the chapter indicate that media economics research will continue to be an important field for future study but that changes may be necessary in how to approach future research. For example, consolidation, technology, globalization and regulation all have an impact on media product markets. It is becoming more and more difficult for media economic researchers to address the critical question of "What is the market?" The blurring of markets, along with the multiple revenue streams or windows for media content products, make differentiating the market a significant challenge for media economics research. Some researchers have offered new ideas on this subject, such as contributions by Ramstad (1997) and Wirth and Bloch (1995).

Coupled with the changes in studying individual markets are the likely changes in understanding and analyzing market structure. Will monopoly, oligopoly and monopolistic competition continue to be the best ways to classify and describe the structure of media markets, or are new models necessary?

For example, consider the newspaper industry, which primarily operates in a monopolistic environment. Do we continue to consider the newspaper a monopoly when it develops interactive and multimedia products for consumers in conjunction with the daily newspaper? Hardly. But how do we address these changes? Further, what impact will changes in market structure have on market conduct and performance? These questions raise issues regarding how we theorize market structure as well as how we can evaluate and measure media markets in the future.

Finally, how do we study the impact of all of these changes in economic structure on the individual firms involved in these evolving markets? And what sort of impact will these changes have on society, both domestically and from an international perspective? Which approaches and methodologies will best provide us with the data we need to answer these questions effectively? The impact on individual firms and society at large is another issue that must be considered in determining a course for further study.

Obviously, more questions than answers are raised by a discussion of how media economics research will change as a result of major trends affecting the media industries. Media economics research has many exciting challenges ahead as it attempts to sort out and analyze the complex and changing world in which the mass media industries operate.

Summary

The mass media industries continue to evolve and adapt due to the influence of several major trends occurring across markets and industries. Industry consolidation is one of the most significant trends, driven by an increase in mergers and acquisitions across the media industries. The result has been increasing concentration of control in many media industries, particularly in radio, cable television, motion pictures and the recording industry.

Technology is another trend shaping media markets. The development of the Internet and the shift from an analog to a digital environment is creating new markets for media firms.

Globalization of media products and services is the result of a saturated domestic U.S. market and opportunities for economic growth in other areas of the world, especially in Europe, Asia and South America. The United States continues to play an important role in serving as the major exporter of media products, but its overall position as the world leader has declined in recent years.

Regulatory reforms, including the Telecommunications Act of 1996, produced structural changes across several media industries that are continuing to manifest themselves in the 21st century.

These trends raise significant challenges to the future study of media economics. The blurring of market boundaries and changes in market structure, conduct and performance raise questions about traditional methods used to evaluate media markets, media firms and societal impact. Media economics research will be challenged to address these and other issues in the years ahead.

Discussion Questions

1. What are some of the reasons given for so many mergers and acquisitions across the media industries?
2. How is technology changing the makeup and structure of media markets?

3. Globalization is a growing trend across the media industries. Why is there so much interest in the international marketplace for media products and services?
4. What impact will the changing structure of media markets have on the study of media economics? How will it affect future research?

Exercises

1. Conduct an ownership study of the local media in the market in which you currently reside. Who owns the local newspaper, broadcast stations, cable systems, etc.? What other media properties do they own?
2. Select a domestic-based company involved in some area of the mass media, and conduct research to determine the degree of international ventures and expansion. Prepare a report on your findings.
3. Using the Internet, compare websites of different media companies and services. Report on the similarities and differences you observe.
4. Think about how industry structure may change in the future from the traditional models of monopoly, oligopoly and monopolistic competition. What other types of market structures are possible?
5. What do you envision as the major challenges facing media economics research in the future? What suggestions do you have for improving media economics research?

References

Bagdikian, B. (2000). *The Media Monopoly*. 6th ed. Boston: Beacon Press.
Bates, B. J. (1999). The economic basis of radio deregulation. *Journal of Media Economics* 12 (1): 19–34.
Demers, D. (1999). *Global Media: Menace or Messiah?* Cresskill, N.J.: Hampton Press.
Drushel, B. E. (1998). The Telecommunications Act of 1996 and radio market structure. *Journal of Media Economics* 11 (3): 3–20.
Evans, P., and T. S. Wurster. (2000). *Blown to Bits: How the New Economics of Information Transforms Strategy*. Boston: Harvard Business School.
Gershon, R. A. (1993). International deregulation and the rise of transnational media corporations. *Journal of Media Economics* 6 (2): 3–22.
———. (2000). The transnational media corporation: Environmental scanning and strategy formulation. *Journal of Media Economics* 13 (2): 81–101.
Gilder, G. (2000). *Telecosm*. New York: Free Press.
Hendricks, P. (1995). Communications policy and industrial dynamics in media markets: Toward a theoretical framework for analyzing media industry organization. *Journal of Media Economics* 8 (2): 61–76.
Hirsch, P. M. (1992). Globalization of mass media ownership. *Communication Research* 19 (6): 677–81.
Howard, H. H. (1998). The 1996 Telecommunications Act and TV station ownership: One year later. *Journal of Media Economics* 11 (3): 21–32.
Micklethwait, J., and A. Wooldridge. (2000). *A Future Perfect: The Challenge and Hidden Promise of Globalization*. New York: Crown Publishers.

Ozanich, G. W., and M. O. Wirth. (1998). Media mergers and acquisitions: An overview. In *Media Economics: Theory and Practice*, 2d ed., edited by A. Alexander, J. Owers and R. Carveth. Mahwah, N.J.: Lawrence Erlbaum Associates, pp. 115–133.

Ramstad, G. (1997). A model for structural analysis of the media market. *Journal of Media Economics* 10 (3): 45–50.

Tseng, K., and B. R. Litman. (1998). The impact of the Telecommunications Act of 1996 on the merger of RBOCs and MSOs; Case study: The merger of US West and Continental Cablevision. *Journal of Media Economics* 11 (3): 47–64.

Turow, J. (1992). The organizational underpinnings of contemporary media conglomerates. *Communication Research* 19 (6): 682–704.

Veronis, Suhler and Associates. (2000). *Communications Industry Report*. New York: Veronis, Suhler and Associates.

Wirth, M. O., and H. Bloch. (1995). Industrial organization theory and media industry analysis. *Journal of Media Economics* 8 (2): 21–34.

VII

Supplements

REFERENCE SOURCES FOR MEDIA ECONOMICS RESEARCH

Many of the following sources are available at university and public libraries. Call numbers are provided in brackets at the end of each entry for sources found at the University of North Texas Libraries.

Reference Sources on Corporations

National Directories

Directories may list corporate addresses, officers, annual sales, number of employees, and SIC* codes. Look at the preface of each volume to determine the extent and type of coverage.

America's Corporate Families and International Affiliates. Dun and Bradstreet, 1986–1987. International companion to *America's Corporate Families: Billion Dollar Directory,* same format as *Million Dollar Directory.* [HG4057.A146]

America's Corporate Families: Billion Dollar Directory. Dun and Bradstreet, 1984–1987. Continues *Billion Dollar Directory,* same format as *Million Dollar Directory.* [HG4075.A147]

D&B Business Rankings. Dun and Bradstreet, 1997–present. Continues *Dun's Business Rankings;* public and private businesses ranked within industry category and state by size, sales, employees; includes stock ticker symbol cross-reference. [HG4057.A238]

Directory of Corporate Affiliations. National Register Publishing Co., 1977–present. Continues *Who Owns Whom;* brief profile of parent companies, cross-reference index to subsidiaries, geographic, SIC, and "Who's Where" index, for public and some private companies. [HG4057.A219]

Million Dollar Directory. 5 vols. Dun and Bradstreet, 1990– present. Includes roster of parent companies, parent/subsidiary cross-references, brief profile of public and private companies (alphabetically), geographic and SIC* code indexes. [HF5035.M53]

Standard and Poor's Register of Corporations, Directors and Executives. 3 vols. Standard and Poor's Corporation, 1973–present. Includes public companies, corporate listings (Vol. 1), directors and executives (Vol. 2), and index (Vol. 3).[HG4057.A41]

Standard Industrial Classification: A list of SIC code numbers is on the introductory pages of the Dun and Bradstreet publications and of *F & S Index.* For more detail, see *Standard Industrial Classification Manual.* [HF1042.N67]

Ward's Business Directory of U.S. Private and Public Companies. 8 vols. Gale Research, 1996, 1998–1999. [HG4057.A575]

Company Overviews

Handbook of Common Stocks. New York: Mergent FIS, 1999—present. Continues *Moody's Handbook of Common Stocks.* Revised quarterly. Provides basic financial and business information on over 900 stocks with high investor interest. Information is arranged in one-page format, with chart showing stock performance since 1979 (where applicable). [HG4905.M816]

Hoover's Handbook of American Business. Austin, Tex.: Reference Press, 1996–present. Profiles of 500 American-based companies. Divided into four sections: (1) a review of basic business concepts, (2) lists of the largest companies overall and largest companies in various industries, (3) 500 company profiles arranged alphabetically and (4) indexes by industry and location. [HG4057.A28617]

Hoover's Masterlist of Major U.S. Companies. Austin, Tex.: Reference Press, 1997–present. Contains information on 4,812 publicly listed U.S. companies, the top 500 largest private companies, the 500 fastest-growing companies and the 200 most important foreign companies. Entries include address, phone and fax numbers, chief executive officer (CEO) and chief financial officer (CFO) names, number of employees, stock symbol and exchange (if public), ownership (if private) and industry name. [HF5035.H66]

Standard Corporation Descriptions. Standard and Poor's Corporation, 1941–1999. Regularly updated. Includes company history, financial information, subsidiaries. [HG4501.S76631]

Journal Indexes

Business Periodicals Index. New York: Wilson, 1958–1993. Indexes more than 275 periodical titles.

F&S Index United States Annual. The Company, 1993–present. Has two sections: Section 1 arranged by SIC number, Section 2 alphabetically by name of company. Continues *Predicasts F&S Index United States Annual Edition.*

Wall Street Journal Index. Wall Street Journal, 1958–present. First half of volume indexes by name of company, second half indexes general news. Back issues of the *Wall Street Journal* are on microfilm. Reference sources on industries.

General Reference Sources

CD-ROM 300 *U.S. Industry and Trade Outlook.* Washington, D.C.: U.S. Department of Commerce/International Trade Administration, 2000–present. Continues *U.S. Global Trade Outlook.* Information on recent trends and economic outlook for over 200 industries.

Dun and Bradstreet/Gale Industry Reference Handbooks. 5 vols. Gale, 1998. Provides overviews, ratios, statistics, and other key industry information. [HF5035.D78]

Standard and Poor's Industry Surveys. New York: Standard and Poor's Corporation, 1973–present. Published quarterly. Industry analyses and comparative financial statistics for major companies in each featured industry. [HC106.6.S74]

Value Line Investment Survey. New York: Value Line, 1936–present. Reports on many industry groups and analyzes approximately 1,500 stocks. [HG4501.V26]

Statistical Sources

American Statistics Index: A Comprehensive Guide and Index to the Statistical Publications of the U.S. Government. Washington, D.C.: Congressional Information Service, 1974–present. Provides citations to statistical sources. [Z7552.A4]

Irwin Business and Investment Almanac. Burr Ridge, Ill.: Irwin Professional Publications, 1994–1996. Continues *Business One Irwin Business and Investment Almanac* (1991–1993) and *Dow Jones Business and Investment Almanac* (1982–1990). Includes 1- to 3-page tables on trends and forecasts on 21 major industry groups; also stock market averages (charts) by industry group, along with many other statistical tables and charts. [HF5003.D683]

Predicasts Basebook. Cleveland, Ohio: Predicasts, 1974–present. Compiles forecasts on products, markets, industry and economic aggregates for United States and North America as reported in trade and business press. Arranged by SIC numbers.

Predicasts Forecasts. Cleveland, Ohio: Predicasts, 1974–present. Short- and long-range forecast statistics. Current journal citations accompany all data.

Sourcebook of Global Statistics. New York: Facts on File, 1985. Reviews and provides tables of contents and bibliographic data for 209 statistical publications. Subject index.

Statistical Reference Index Washington, D.C.: Congressional Information Service, 1980–present. Selective guide to American statistical publications from sources other than the U.S. government. [Z7554.U5S79]

Industry Financial or Operating Ratios

Industry Norms and Key Business Ratios. New York: Dun and Bradstreet Credit Services, 1982–present. Continues *Dun and Bradstreet's Key Business Ratios* (1979–1981). [HF5681.R25I5]

RMA Annual Statement Studies. Philadelphia: Robert Morris Associates, 1977–present. Continues *Robert Morris Associates Annual Statement Studies.* [HG1507.R6]

Indexes to Journal Articles

Almanac of Business and Industrial Financial Ratios. Englewood Cliffs, N.J.: Prentice-Hall, 1999–present. [HF5681.R25A4]

Business Periodicals Index. New York: H. W. Wilson, 1958–1993. Indexes more than 275 business periodical titles.

F&S Index United States Annual. Foster City, Calif.: Information Access Co., 1993–present. Continues *Predicasts F&S Index United States Annual Edition.*Indexes 750 financial and business publications which contain company, product and industry information.

Public Affairs Information Service (PAIS). New York: Bulletin, 1968–1990. A selective subject listing in the areas of economic and social conditions, public administration and international relations. Includes books, government documents and journals. [Z7163.P91]

Additional Industry Sources

Business Information Sources. 3d ed. Berkeley, Calif.: University of California Press, 1993. Selected annotated list of business books and reference sources, including online databases and CD-ROMs. [Z7164.C81D16]

Encyclopedia of Business Information Sources. 14th ed. Detroit, Mich.: Gale Research, 1994. Comprehensive bibliography of specialized publications on many industries. [Z7164.C81E93]

General Media Sources

Yearbooks and Directories

Broadcast Communications Dictionary. 3d ed., rev. New York: Greenwood Press, 1989. While somewhat outdated, still a decent reference source. [PN1990.4.D5]

Broadcasting and Cable Yearbook. R. R. Bowker, 1993–present. Continues *Broadcasting and Cable Market Place.* Current industry information. Includes programming information, some federal rules; describes major markets; lists producers, distributors and production services; directory of radio, television and cable stations. [HE8689.B775]

Editor and Publisher International Yearbook. New York: Editor and Publisher, 1966–present. List of U.S. dailies and weeklies and Canadian and foreign weeklies with management and production information including circulation, rates, editors, etc. [PN4709.E3]

Gale Directory of Publications and Broadcast Media. Detroit, Mich: Gale Research, 1990–present. [Z6951.A972]

Television and Cable Factbook. Washington, D.C.: Television Digest, 1982–present. [TK6540.T4531]

Webster's New World Dictionary of Media and Communications. New York: Macmillan, 1996. A good general dictionary with information on media industries. [P87.5.W45]

Working Press of the Nation. Chicago: National Research Bureau, 1988–present. Directory covering newspapers, magazines, radio and television, feature writers, photographers and internal publications. [Z6951.W6]

Indexes and Abstracts

Communication Abstracts. Beverly Hills, Calif.: Sage, 1978–present.

Dissertation Abstracts International. Ann Arbor, Mich: University Microfilms, 1861–present. Available in print and CD-ROM formats.

Humanities Index. New York: H. W. Wilson, 1974–1984. Available on CD-ROM from SilverPlatter as *Humanities Abstract.*

Index to Journals in Communication Studies. Falls Church, Va.: Speech Communication Association, 1995.

Journalism and Mass Communications Abstracts. Columbia, S.C.: Association for Education in Journalism and Mass Communication, 1994–1999. Continues *Journalism Abstracts* (1963–1993).

News Index and Abstracts: A Guide to the Videotape Collection of the Network Evening News Programs. Nashville, Tenn.: Vanderbilt Television News Archives. Website: http://tvnews.vanderbilt.edu.

New York Times Index. New York: New York Times, 1851–present.

Public Affairs Information Service (PAIS). New York: Bulletin, 1968–1990.

Times Index. London: Times Pub. Co., 1973–present. Continues *Index to the Times* (1958–1972).

Wall Street Journal Index. New York: Dow Jones, 1958–present.

Electronic Reference Sources

Your individual library may not obtain rights to all of these electronic databases. Some databases may be restricted to library use; others may be available for online access. When in doubt, check with one of the reference librarians at your college or university. Be sure to check different libraries in your area, including public libraries and libraries housed at community colleges.

ABI INFORM: Updated monthly, this database covers five years for about 800 business and management periodicals worldwide; 300 core titles are covered fully. Subject areas include accounting, banking, data processing (DP), economics, finance, human resources, insurance, general management, law and tax, organizational behavior and administration (OBA) and management science, marketing, advertising, sales, real estate, public administration, new product development and telecommunications. There are full citations and abstracts of about 200 words.

ACADEMIC UNIVERSE: This full-text database from Lexis-Nexis offers complete company news and financial information.

BUSINESS ABSTRACTS: This SilverPlatter database cites articles from 345 business-related periodicals.

BUSINESS AND COMPANY RESOURCE CENTER: This Gale Group database offers company profiles, company brand information, rankings, investment reports, company histories, chronologies and periodicals.

BUSINESS DATELINE: This product, updated monthly, provides access to hard-to-find, regional business information. It covers most of the same materials as ABI INFORM from 200 local, state and regional business publications. These articles are the full text of the publication. Press releases from Business Wire provide a corporate perspective on events and people.

BUSINESS SOURCE PREMIER: This online database from EBSCOhost offers full text for 2,260 scholarly business journals covering management, economics, finance, accounting, international business and more.

BUSINESS WIRE NEWS: This full-text newswire database from EBSCOhost incorporates business wires worldwide.

COMPACT DISCLOSURE: This product consists of business and financial information extracted from 10K reports that public companies file with the Securities and Exchange Commission. It includes all financial statements (three to seven years for comparison purposes), subsidiaries, description of the business, officers and directors, stock information, president's letter and management discussion for more than 11,000 public companies. Financial data can be converted to files that can be imported as numbers directly into spreadsheets.

DUN'S MILLION DOLLAR DIRECTORY: This database provides comprehensive business information on 161,000 U.S. public and private companies. Listings are limited to companies with $25 million or more in sales, or 250+ employees, or a net worth of $500,000 or more. File records can be searched by geographical area, primary and secondary SIC codes, annual sales, or number of employees. This is a useful tool for job searching.

FIRST SEARCH: This online service offers access to a number of databases useful to business researchers: Articles1st, Contents1st, ERIC, the GPO Monthly Catalog, and WorldCat, an electronic card catalog of 24 million bibliographic records representing the holdings of 13,000 libraries worldwide. Check to see if this service is available at your library.

INFOTRAC BUSINESS INDEX: Updated monthly, this database contains bibliographic references to and abstracts of articles from more than 800 business, management and trade publications, including the *Wall Street Journal, New York Times, Asian Wall Street Journal,* and *Financial Times* of Canada; contains back files to 1982.

MORNINGSTAR MUTUAL FUNDS ONDISC: This product provides such items as description and analysis, basic operating facts and several years of statistics for total return, income, capital gains, and performance/risk factors.

WALL STREET JOURNAL: Updated monthly, this full-text product contains every *Wall Street Journal* article, including daily stock market reports, finance, investment, and business-oriented news. Its coverage runs from 1989 to the present.

Industry Websites

The following websites, some of which are referenced in individual chapters in the text, are also useful in finding current industry statistics and other contemporary information. These websites are listed by industry in the order in which the industries were presented by chapter.

RADIO INDUSTRY

Duncan's American Radio	www.duncanradio.com
National Association of Broadcasters	www.nab.org
Radio Advertising Bureau	www.rab.com

BROADCAST TELEVISION INDUSTRY

Don Fitpatrick Associates	www.tvspy.com
National Association of Television Program Exec.	www.natpe.com
Television Advertising Bureau	www.tvb.com

CABLE AND SATELLITE TELEVISION INDUSTRIES

Cable Advertising Bureau	www.cabletvadbureau.com
National Cable Television Association	www.ncta.com

INTERNET INDUSTRY

Forrester Research	www.forrester.com
Interactive Advertising Bureau	www.iab.com
Internet World	www.internetworld.com

MOTION PICTURE INDUSTRY

Motion Picture Association of America	www.mpaa.org
Movie Web	www.movieweb.com

RECORDING INDUSTRY

Music Publishers Association	www.mpa.org
Recording Industry Association of America	www.riaa.org

NEWSPAPER INDUSTRY

Editor and Publisher Online	www.editorandpublisher.com
Newspaper Association of America	www.naa.org

MAGAZINE INDUSTRY

Dr. Samir Husni	www.mrmagazine.com
Magazine Publishers of America	www.mpa.org

BOOK INDUSTRY

Book Industry Study Group	www.bsig.org
Book Wire	www.bookwire.com

COMMONLY USED FINANCIAL RATIOS

Financial ratios are useful in media economics. Ratios can be calculated using the information found in company financial statements. Many research sources list financial ratios for both companies and industries. The following are some of the most common ratios used in financial and performance analysis.

Liquidity Ratios

$$\text{Current Ratio} = \frac{\text{Current Assets}}{\text{Current Liabilities}}$$

$$\text{Acid Test Ratio} = \frac{\text{Liquid Assets}}{\text{Current Liabilities}}$$

Debt Ratios

$$\text{Leverage Ratio} = \frac{\text{Total Liabilities}}{\text{Total Assets}}$$

$$\text{Debt-to-Equity Ratio} = \frac{\text{Total Liabilities}}{\text{Total Equity}}$$

Capitalization Ratios

$$\frac{\text{Total Shares of Preferred Stock}}{\text{Total Shares of Common Stock}}$$

$$\frac{\text{Long-term Liabilities}}{\text{Total Shares of Common Stock}}$$

Common Growth Measures

$$\text{Growth of Revenue} = \frac{\text{Current Period (month, quarter) Revenue}}{\text{Previous Time Revenue}}$$

$$\text{Growth of Operating Income} = \frac{\text{Current Operating Income}}{\text{Previous Operating Income}}$$

$$\begin{aligned}\text{Growth of Net Worth} \\ \text{(Owner's Equity)}\end{aligned} = \frac{\text{Current Period (month, quarter) Net Worth}}{\text{Previous Time Net Worth}}$$

$$\text{Growth of Assets} = \frac{\text{Current Period (month, quarter) Assets}}{\text{Previous Time Assets}}$$

Profitability Measures

$$\text{Return on Sales} = \frac{\text{Operating Income}}{\text{Total Revenues}}$$

$$\text{Return on Assets} = \frac{\text{Operating Income}}{\text{Total Assets}}$$

$$\text{Return on Equity} = \frac{\text{Operating Income}}{\text{Owner's Equity}}$$

$$\text{Price-Earnings (PE) Ratio} = \frac{\text{Market Price of a Share of Common Stock}}{\text{Earnings Per Share}}$$

Profit Margins

$$\text{Cash-Flow Margin} = \frac{\text{Cash Flow \small (After-tax net profit plus interest, depreciation, amortization)}}{\text{Net Revenue \small (Revenues minus operating expenses)}}$$

$$\text{Net Profit Margin} = \frac{\text{Net Profit \small (Revenues, expenses and taxes)}}{\text{Total Revenues (Sales)}}$$

GLOSSARY OF KEY TERMS

addressable technology—equipment used in the cable and satellite industry to decipher scrambled signals; necessary on some systems to receive pay-per-view programming.

allocative efficiency—occurs when an individual market functions at optimal capacity, spreading its benefits among both producers and consumers.

AM—amplitude modulation, a radio wavelength.

analog—traditional form of recording; creates an analogous similar copy of sound or video using electrical impulses.

banner—type of advertising found on many web pages.

barriers to entry—obstacles new sellers must overcome before entering a particular market.

broadband—a high-capacity, high-speed distribution system using cable, fiber optics or satellite transmission.

browser—a piece of software used to access websites on the World Wide Web.

cable modem—a device offered by cable television operators; the modem allows users high-speed Internet access.

capitalization ratios—mathematical formulas used to analyze the capital represented by both preferred and common stock.

chain—in the newspaper industry, a collection of newspapers owned by a corporation or group.

click-through—term used to describe what happens when an Internet user "clicks" on (selects) a button or banner and is taken to another web page.

clustering—the merging of smaller cable television systems into larger multiple system operators in specific regions.

command economy—type of economy in which the government makes all decisions regarding production and distribution. The government also establishes wages and prices and plans the rate of economic growth.

complement—a product or service that enhances another similar product or service.

concentration—the number of producers or sellers in a given market; a characteristic of market structure.

concentration ratios—mathematical computations used to measure the degree of concentration in an industry; compares the ratio of total revenues of the major players to the revenues of the entire industry, using the top four firms (CR4) or the top eight firms (CR8).

consumption—the utilization of goods and resources to satisfy different wants and needs of consumers.

consumer—a buyer of goods and services.

cost structures—the costs for production in a particular market.

cross-elasticity of demand—occurs in the media industries when a number of competitors produce similar media content and consumers sample and substitute other media products.

DARS—digital audio radio services; satellite-delivered radio services offering several channels of digital music for a monthly fee. Designed primarily to reach commuters, DARS began operation in 2001.

DBS—direct broadcast satellite(s).

debt—the amount of money owed by a company.

debt ratios—measures of the debt of a firm or industry. Common debt ratios include the leverage ratio and the debt-to-equity ratio.

debt-to-equity ratio—a measure of debt calculated by dividing total debt by total equity.

demand—the measure of the quantity of a particular product or service that consumers will purchase at a given price.

demand curve—a graphical illustration of the quantities of a good or service that will be purchased at each of various possible prices at a given time.

digital audio radio services—*See* DARS.

digital cable—optional service offered by cable television operators, offering a wider variety of channels that are also digitally encoded to produce a higher-quality picture.

digital compression—technology that allows multiple television channels to be squeezed into the existing space of a standard 6-megahertz analog channel.

digital technology—a distribution system that converts analog recordings into a binary code of 1s and 0s and has excellent reproduction quality.

diversification—the extent to which a company draws revenues across different markets or business segments.

dot-com—an Internet-based business, so named because of the commercial suffix on its Web address.

DSL—digital subscriber line; type of high-speed Internet access sold through telephone companies.

DTV—digital television.

dual must carry—a cable television system's offering of both analog and digital channels for local TV broadcasters.

dual product market—a market situation unique to the media, in which a media company produces one product but participates in two separate good and service markets, one aimed at consumers and the other at advertisers.

duopoly—Duopoly rules were modified during the 1990s, allowing for multiple ownership of radio and TV stations within the same geographical market.

DVD—digital videodisc; rapidly replacing VHS videocassettes as the preferred way to view movies at home. DVD technology offers many advanced features as well as digital-quality sound and pictures.

economic problem—the process of deciding issues of production and consumption according to societal needs or wants.

economics—the study of how societies use scarce resources to produce valuable commodities and distribute them among various groups.

economies of scale—the decline in average cost that occurs as additional units of a product are created.

efficiency—the ability of a firm to maximize its wealth.

elasticity of demand—occurs when a change in price results in a change in the quantity demanded by consumers.

electronic commerce or e-commerce—buying and selling through the Internet, involving business-to-business (B2B), business-to-consumer (B2C) and consumer-to-consumer (C2C) transactions.

equilibrium—the economic balance point at which supply and demand are equal.

event television—another term for pay-per-view; audience members select among various content choices in the form of movies, sporting events and specials.

FCC—Federal Communications Commission, the national government's regulatory body for the media industry.

fixed cost—cost that remains constant; the cost to produce a single unit of a product, regardless of the total number produced. Examples of fixed costs are land, buildings and equipment.

FM—frequency modulation, a radio wavelength.

franchise—in the cable television industry, the awarding of a geographical area to a cable TV operator by a local government for the purpose of providing exclusive cable television service.

geographic region—a way of defining a market according to physical location and area. Geographic regions may be generally described as local, regional or national.

growth measures or growth ratios—mathematical formulas that calculate the growth of revenue and assets over time and also document historical trends.

HDTV—high-definition television; touted as television of the future. HDTV employs digital technology and offers a higher resolution capacity.

HTML—hypertext markup language; the programming language most commonly used on the World Wide Web.

Herfindahl-Hirschman Index (HHI)—a method for precisely measuring concentration of market share within an industry, calculated by summing the squared market shares of all firms in a given market.

industrial organization model—a theoretical model that shows the relationships among market structure, conduct and performance.

industry—the sellers in a particular market.

insertion advertising—occurs when national cable networks such as ESPN, MTV and USA offer advertising availabilities to local systems for their local commercials.

interactive TV—highly touted television of the future enabling the user to utilize many consumer services (e.g., banking, shopping, playing games) through a television receiver.

interconnect—exists when two or more cable television operators join together to distribute advertising simultaneously over their respective systems.

Internet—meaning *interconnected network of networks*, a vast network of computers connecting many of the world's businesses, institutions and individuals.

invisible hand doctrine—theorized by Adam Smith, this doctrine suggests that the economy is directed by an unseen force to the benefit of all producers and consumers.

ISP—Internet service provider; a company that offers online access to users, either free or for a fee.

joint operating agreements (JOAs)—arrangement in the newspaper industry under which editorial operations remain separate but all other operations (printing, advertising, distribution, etc.) are combined.

labor—the workers needed to produce a good or service; typically the most expensive cost of an organization.

Laissez-faire—term derived from the French for "let do," meaning an economic system that allows people to do as they choose, without government interference.

leverage ratio—a measure of debt calculated by dividing total debt by total assets.

liquidity—a firm's ability to convert assets into cash.

liquidity ratios—measures of a firm's ability to convert assets into cash; they include the quick ratio, the current ratio and the acid test ratio.

local marketing agreement (LMA)—used in the broadcast industry; an arrangement that allows one station to take over marketing and programming of another station without releasing control of ownership.

Lorenz Curve—a method of measuring industry concentration by illustrating inequality of market share among various firms.

LPFM—low powered FM; a new class of stations approved by the FCC with maximum operating power of 100 watts. All LPFM stations are noncommercial.

macroeconomics—examines the whole economic system, primarily studied at a national level. Macroeconomics includes topics such as economic growth indexes, political economy and national production and consumption.

major-distributed independent label—a recording industry company that signs artists to contracts with major or mini-major labels and is responsible for everything except the actual recording.

major label—one of the five large companies that dominate the recording industry; it handles its own administration, contracting, production, manufacturing and distribution.

market—where buyers and sellers interact with one another to determine the price and quantity of the goods produced. A market consists of a number of sellers that provide a similar product or service to the same group of buyers.

market conduct—the policies and behaviors exhibited by sellers and buyers in a market.

market economy—a complex system of buyers, sellers, prices, profits and losses that determines the answers to questions regarding production and distribution, with no government intervention.

market performance—analysis of the ability of individual firms in a market to achieve goals based on such performance criteria as efficiency, equity and progress.

market structure—the characteristics of a market. Among the many criteria that have an impact on market structure are concentration of buyers and sellers, differentiation among products and services offered, barriers to entry for new competitors, cost structures and the degree of vertical integration.

microeconomics—centers on the activities of specific components of the economic system, such as individual markets, firms or consumers.

mixed capitalist society—an economic system in which both public and private institutions produce and distribute goods and services, with some government regulation. The United States is an example of a mixed capitalist society.

mixed economy—a combination of the market and command economies.

media economics—the study of how media industries use scarce resources to produce content that is distributed among consumers in a society to satisfy various wants and needs.

monopolistic competition—type of market structure that exists when there are many sellers offering products that are similar, but not perfect, substitutes for one another.

monopoly—type of market structure in which only a single seller of a product exists and thus dominates the market.

MP3 or MPEG-3—Motion Pictures Experts Group format 3, an audio and video storage and retrieval system that allows users the opportunity to create and share digital music recorded from CDs.

multiple ownership rules—in the broadcast industry, the limits imposed by the Federal Communications Commission on the number of stations in which an individual or group may hold ownership interests.

multiple system operators (MSOs)—large cable system operators such as AT&T and AOL Time Warner.

multipoint multichannel distribution services (MMDS)—also referred to as *wireless cable*, offer programming packages via microwave transmission.

music video—a short film based on a popular song, showing the musicians playing the song and sometimes including other images to create a mood or tell a story; typically shown on cable TV.

must carry—regulations that require cable operators to offer all local broadcast stations.

needs—basic items required by individuals and society for survival.

network—term used in the broadcast industry to describe a service that provides programming to affiliates.

oligopoly—type of market structure that features more than one seller of a product. Products offered by the sellers may be either homogeneous (alike) or heterogeneous (differentiated).

overbuilds—areas served by more than one cable television system.

owned and operated stations (O&Os)—network-owned stations in the television industry.

perfect competition—a market structure characterized by many sellers in which the product is the same and no single firm or group of firms dominates the market.

performance ratios or profitability measures—mathematical formulas used to measure the financial strength of a company or industry.

personal digital assistant (PDA)—handheld electronic device that offers such applications as calendar, e-mail, expense reports and to-do lists.

portal—the website entry point for an Internet user.

price elasticity of demand—*See* elasticity of demand.

price maker or price setter—a producer under conditions of monopoly.

price taker—an individual firm operating under conditions of perfect competition.

private companies or private sector—companies that are privately owned by individuals; cannot purchase stock or other ownership in private companies.

product differentiation—the subtle differences (either real or imagined) perceived by buyers to exist among products produced by sellers.

production—the actual creation of goods for consumption.

product placement—payments made by companies to motion picture studios to have their merchandise appear in films.

progress—the ability of firms in a market to increase output over time.

public companies—companies that are publicly owned by individual and institutional stockholders who invest in a firm in hopes of obtaining profits through stock appreciation and corporate dividends.

public sector—government companies and entities.

reach cap—limitation by the FCC on the number of television stations that may be owned by a single group or individual.

resources—items used to produce goods and services.

retail trading zone (RTZ)—in the newspaper industry, a geographic area of circulation.

retransmission consent—outcome of the 1992 Cable Television Consumer Protection and Competition Act, which allows broadcast stations to negotiate with cable TV operators for the right to carry their signals in lieu of regulations that required cable operators to carry all local broadcast stations.

revenue stream—a source of income.

satellite master antenna television (SMATV)—a form of private cable that is restricted to specific areas such as apartment and condominium complexes, motels and hotels.

scatter market—unsold network television advertising time that is retained by the network and offered during the television season.

search engine—a computer program that allows an Internet user to locate information by typing in key words or phrases; the search engine then pulls up addresses of websites that most closely match the request.

STV—standard television.

supply—the amount of a product that producers will offer at a given price.

technical efficiency—use of a firm's resources in the most effective way to maximize output.

tiers—cable industry term used to distinguish between different classes of service.

toll broadcasting—old term for the sale of radio advertising.

trade book—a book intended for general readership; may be hardcover or softcover (paperback).

true independent label—a recording industry company that has no affiliation or connection with major or mini-major labels and markets its products through independent distributors.

UHF—ultra high frequency, a television wavelength.

unique visitors—different individuals accessing a website, as opposed to multiple accesses by the same people.

upfront market—network television advertising time purchased during the early summer months for the upcoming fall season.

utility—what consumers perceive in the way of satisfaction from a good or service.

value—the worth of a product or service; measured by an exchange in dollars or other monetary measure. Value changes over time.

variable cost—cost that changes in direct relation to the quantity of a product produced. Examples of variable costs are labor, utilities and raw materials.

vertical integration—occurs when a firm controls different aspects of production, distribution and exhibition of its products.

VHF—very high frequency, a television wavelength.

video compression—technology that allows compression, or squeezing, of existing television signals to allow greater capacity for channels; employs digital technology to compress signals.

wants—items that individuals desire to improve the quality of life but are not really necessary for survival.

website—a collection of information at a specific address on the World Wide Web.

windows—in the motion picture industry, revenue streams beyond the box office, including home video, pay-per-view, premium cable, syndication sales and international distribution.

wireless cable—another term for multipoint multichannel distribution services (MMDS).

World Wide Web (WWW)—a part of the Internet that uses text, graphics, and audio and video files to present information.

INDEX